To Dan
Happy Birthday!

**BLACK AND GOLD**

# BLACK AND GOLD
## FOUR DECADES OF THE BOSTON BRUINS IN PHOTOGRAPHS

**Rob Simpson**

Photography by
**Steve Babineau**

**WILEY**

John Wiley & Sons Canada, Ltd.

*Library and Archives Canada Cataloguing in Publication Data*

Simpson, Rob, 1964–

Black and gold : four decades of Boston Bruin photographs / written by Rob Simpson ; photographs by Steve Babineau/NHLI.

Includes index.

ISBN 978-0-470-15473-1

   1. Boston Bruins (Hockey team)—History.   2. Boston Bruins (Hockey team)—History—Pictorial works.   I. Babineau, Steve   II. Title.

GV848.B68S54 2008       796.962'640974461       C2008-902160-6

**Production Credits**
Cover and Interior text design: Adrian So
Cover concept: Brian Babineau
Typesetting: Adrian So
Printer: Quebecor Taunton

John Wiley & Sons Canada, Ltd.
6045 Freemont Blvd.
Mississauga, Ontario
L5R 4J3

Printed in the United States

1 2 3 4 5 QW 12 11 10 09 08

To Dan,
All the Best.
My Life - my team.!
"⌣"
Babs

To Ian Simpson, my favorite hockey fan—RSS

To my wife Anita and our kids Christopher, Brian, Keith, and Jamie—SPB

# CONTENTS

# FOREWORD

*above:*

*Don relaxing at home in his basement with his dog, Blue, the original.*

*left:*

*Don Cherry in his prime as coach of the Bruins.*

Fran Rosa, a writer for the *Boston Globe*, described our Boston Bruins team of the '70s as the "Lunch Pail Gang," meaning that we punched in the time clock at 7:30 and never stopped working. Fran was right. Sometimes teams would outscore us (not often) but never, never would they outwork us, and that is why the Lunch Pail Gang was so popular with the Boston Bruins fans (especially the Gallery Gods).

Fortunately for us, Steve Babineau was there to catch the excitement. I remember the first time I met Steve. I was the Boston Bruins coach and I noticed this young kid always taking pictures at our practices, almost every day. One day he introduced himself and showed me some of his pictures. I was blown away, how he had captured the image and flow of hockey and our club. I knew he would go far.

Steve has taken wonderful pictures and I know you will agree with me when you see them. Steve has the touch, and I must admit that I get a little misty and sweet memories flow back when I see Steve's pictures of the "Lunch Pail Gang." They were a great bunch.

Don

Brian Babineau

Brian Babineau

*above:*

*Babs with Nikon film camera.*

*left:*

*Babs taking the 2006–2007 Boston Bruins team photo.*

The illustrious Bruins' names jump off the pages: Orr, Esposito, Cherry, Bourque, Neely, Babineau…Babineau!?

Photographer Steve Babineau, covering the NHL in Boston since 1973, probably wouldn't describe his career as illustrious, although he should. In almost four decades shooting hockey in Boston, he's taken *the* photos, and had them appear in countless magazines, newspapers, hockey collections, and websites the world over.

*Black and Gold* recounts the careers of the aforementioned players and other Bruins legends through vintage photographs, many of them never before seen. The coaches, the players, the famous and infamous moments, and the original Boston Garden—are all preserved in written and illustrated detail for real hockey fans and historians to enjoy.

Aside from recollections from the players, *Black and Gold* also takes fans behind the scenes, when the shutter wasn't clicking, when the flash wasn't going off, for Steve Babineau's perspective behind the camera. "Babs" has scanned through hundreds of thousands of photographs to select the few hundred found inside these pages. Six chapters are dedicated to specific Bruins legends, whom Babineau captured in action on Garden ice. All others who donned the Spoked-B, are categorized by position, or by their ability to fight, grind or score. Who belongs where? Let the arguments begin.

Originally, the "Basic Babs" opening chapter was entitled "Babs's Best," until we realized it was next to impossible to really qualify a select two dozen or so as the "best." Basic Babs sums it up better. The photos tell Babineau's story, while highlighting a cross-section of his most compelling photographs for various reasons: lighting, action, angles, history, timing, and subject matter. From there, it gets pretty clear-cut. The ensuing chapters reveal the last 35 years of Bruins hockey, through the eyes of one of the greatest photographers in all of professional sports. The volume concludes with the "Scrapbook." This is Babineau's personal collection—moments when the photographer and his family became the subject. True, behind-the-scenes images of a hockey club and the man documenting its existence.

ShellyCastellano.com

As much as anything, this book honors the life lesson of perseverance. Steve Babineau was a late blooming, shaky-legged high school hockey player who enjoyed a simple love for the game. He combined that with his overwhelming interest in sports photography. Through dedication, luck, timing, and creativity, Babineau literally turned a career dream into reality. The tangible realization of living that dream is laid out across these pages for all hockey fans, especially those who bleed black and gold, to enjoy.

Rob Simpson

*above:*

*Babs on the visitors' bench during the pre-game skate.*

# ACKNOWLEDGMENTS

Thank you to Nora for making it possible for me to write. Thank you to our friends and cohorts at Wiley for their guidance and professionalism, the illustrious Karen Milner, Liz McCurdy and Michelle Bullard for making me appear smarter than I am, and Adrian So for the lay-out of lay-outs. To Mick Colageo and Kevin Vautour for their input on our player categories and backgrounds; you've started many an argument. To Kate Stanley for her assistance compiling backgrounds and statistics. To Amy Latimer, Dan Zimmer, and Kerry Collins with the Bruins, and to the multiple others associated with the organization who contributed reflections. Special thanks to the many Bruins alumni for making themselves available, lending a helping hand, and with rare exception, always being supportive of my many multi-media efforts. You're good friends and a great bunch. All the best.

Rob

Thank you to my rock and soul mate Anita, for giving me the freedom to live out a dream the past 35 years. To the Bruins: the Jacobs family, Harry Sinden, Nate Greenberg, Paul Mooney, Heidi Holland, Peter Chiarelli, and Sue Byrne. To Joyce Papaamoroso, the electricians, the security team, and all the guys in the bull gang. To the many photographers/assistants: Armen James, Brian Babineau, Robert Rooks, Lee Calkins, Shelly Castellano, Glen James, Andre Ringuette, Graig and Dave Abel, Jim Turner, Dave Lyons, Chris Relke, Paul Whalen, Keith Babineau, Richard Lewis, Rick Marshall, Leo Echavarria, Steve Malloy, Jamie Babineau, Renata Greene, and Chris Babineau. Thank you to the players and coaches for making my job special by treating me as more than just a photographer.

Babs

CHAPTER

# 1

---

# BASIC BABS

---

Brian Babineau

*above:*

*Steve Babineau, in his new "studio," the Fleet Center [now the TD Banknorth Garden].*

*left:*

*Arguably the two greatest defensemen of all time, and they both spent the great bulk of their careers in Boston. Ray Bourque and Bobby Orr.*

Steve Babineau is a rink rat: a rink rat with a camera, who happens to be the team photographer for one of the most storied franchises in hockey history. What the Bruins lack in Stanley Cup victories over the course of their proud history, they make up for in grit, toughness, and personality. The number of characters and legendary moments captured by Babineau in just the past 35 years are more than most organizations could hope for if they stayed in business for a century. Maybe it's the attitude. Maybe it's hardy New Englanders and their love for a game played on ice, by generation after generation: by grandpa on a pond, by grandson in the Sunday morning squirt house league. Whatever draws the locals to love the finesse, the skill, the sound, the banter, and, most importantly, the physicality of the game, is what attracted Cambridge, Massachusetts, native Steve Babineau.

"My Uncle Lenny always took me to Celtics games," Babineau remembers. "I was wiry and tall, and he wanted me to be a basketball player. His buddy was a writer for the old *Record American* and we got great seats."

To Babineau, naturally ordained "Babs" via the hockey world, the hoops just didn't seem to fit. Fortunately for him, an intervention occurred.

"My next-door neighbor Paul Harrigan in 1964 took me to a B's game. I'll never forget it. It was Original Six hockey. The B's were the doormats but it just didn't matter," Babs recalls. "Jerry Toppazzini, Murray Oliver, John Bucyk, Orland

Kurtenbach, and Eddie Johnston in net. I loved watching these guys and the uniforms were classic."

The game stirred quite a bit of passion in a kid who didn't even skate.

"I was born in 1952. When I was eight, I remember watching the 1960 U.S. Olympic team win the gold medal in Squaw Valley. It was on *Wide World of Sports* or something," Babineau ponders. "From that point forward I was out in the street playing hockey, or banging it around somewhere playing floor hockey. I was the best street hockey player on the planet; even the kids who played ice hockey wanted me on their street team."

Living in North Cambridge, Babs used to walk to a ballpark in West Cambridge to play baseball, with the same kids who were already skating. Lack of family funds for equipment and transportation to the rink, and living in a different part of the city, hindered his opportunity to play the frozen variety of hockey early on. Finally, in eighth grade, with encouragement from the other kids and families, he took up the game on ice.

"I picked up the skills of passing and shooting pretty quickly. I just couldn't put it together with my feet," he says.

Ah, but of course, therein lies the basic challenge to the greatest game on the planet.

*above:*

*Early ticket stubs and photos from Babineau attending the Boston Braves and Bruins games in the early 70s.*

*Bottom*

*The lanky photographer can skate, sort of. Since his high school team lost 44 straight, he's improved dramatically.*

Armen James

Nevertheless, despite lacking skill, a demographic shift of sorts opened up an opportunity for the poor skater. With an influx of African-American kids into the neighborhood, the more popular sports at the time became basketball and track. Very few of the new kids, if any, played hockey at the time. The hockey and baseball teams at Rindge Technical High School suffered for a lack of talent and numbers. Babineau tried out and made the freshman hockey team.

> I would cut physics class and lunch to hustle down and watch about 30 minutes of practice.

(By the way, the athletic swing continued. Where hockey and baseball were popular and very successful at Rindge in the 1950s, by the mid-1960s the emphasis was on football, track, and basketball. Georgetown and NBA great Patrick Ewing came out of Rindge, as did many exemplary track athletes.)

"Playing our games at the old Boston Arena, where the Bruins started," Babineau recalls, "I'd go in and skate and practice and sit on the bench and say, 'Gee, I wonder if Eddie Shore sat here, or Dit Clapper.'"

Meanwhile, with Babineau's father being a union laborer, a carpenter, and a painter, it seemed safe to assume that young Steve might follow in his footsteps in some way or another. The idea at Rindge Technical was to load up the grades for college, or in most cases, line oneself up with a vocational opportunity.

*below:*

*Phil Esposito of Boston just misses against his younger brother, Chicago netminder Tony, after leaving Blackhawks defenseman Keith Magnuson in his wake.*

*left:*

*"Turk" and "Pie," Derek Sanderson and John McKenzie, walking to practice at Harvard's Watson Rink.*

In Babineau's mind, his vocational opportunity, official or not, within the scholastic curriculum or not, was photography.

"I had an attraction to the Bruins," Babs recalls. "They used to practice at Harvard's Watson Rink, about two miles from my high school. I would cut physics class and lunch to hustle down and watch about 30 minutes of practice and then return to school. I'd go on my own with a little Instamatic camera. I have a picture of Johnny McKenzie and Derek Sanderson walking across Harvard Yard carrying their skates. Then my friend Rick Marshall and I would jump on the bus and the trolley to go on Saturday mornings to watch the Bruins practice at the Garden."

It remained to be seen whether Steve Babineau's photography career showed early promise. His hockey career, despite plenty of opportunity, did not.

"Coach Dick Kelly, a former Boston University star, used to call me 'Alice,' because when I was in high school I was 6-foot-2, and dripping wet I was lucky to weigh 115 or 120 pounds. 'Hey Alice, get out there.'

"I remember one game he benched me after my first shift. I made a bad pass, so he benched me. We only had 12 skaters. We're losing the game 10-nothing to Waltham, and with 35 seconds left in the game, he put me back in to take a face-off. I won the draw. Ned Yetton was in goal for Waltham. Our point guy took a slap shot, the rebound came right out to me, and I put it top shelf. The game ended two seconds later."

Not bad for 35 seconds, eh coach?

*below:*

*Ray Bourque as a rookie. Babineau documented Bourque's entire career in Boston.*

"We had so few players, anybody who made freshman was eligible to play junior varsity. I was playing both," Babs says with astonishment. "I played about 30 games that year. We went at it six days a week; practice Monday, JV game on Tuesday, practice on Wednesday, and so on. As a sophomore I made varsity, and if you weren't captain of varsity, you could also play JV. I was getting a ton of ice time."

But the team was awful. In fact, Babineau played for one of the most infamous teams in the Commonwealth's hockey history. They weren't cheap or dirty or delinquent; they were just bad.

"We set the high school league record for most consecutive losses," Babineau points out. "The streak started when I was a freshman, and it went until my first game as a senior. We lost every single game, 44 straight. We beat Brockton the first game of my senior year 1-0, and you'd think we'd won the Stanley Cup. It was in all the papers."

Babineau scored three goals his entire senior year.

*below:*

*Don Cherry coaches the Rochester Americans at the Garden against the Braves. That's Brave's defenseman, part-time Bruin, Nick Beverley along the boards.*

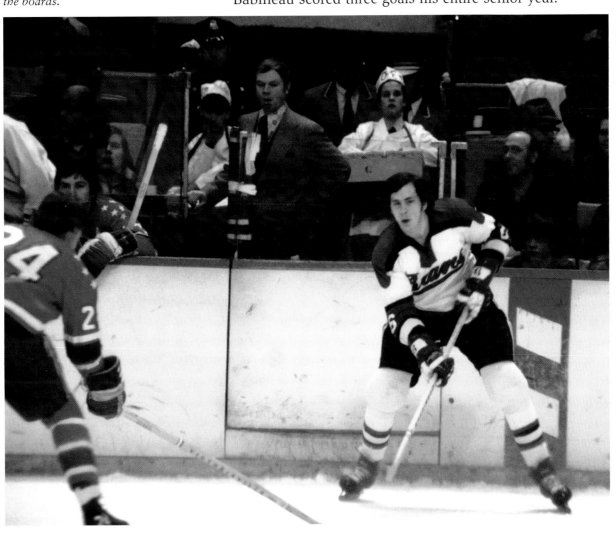

"A typical game: we'd play Arlington," Babineau says. "There would be three hundred fans for Arlington, three fans for us. I remember we were tied nothing-nothing after one period, and the Arlington fans gave us a standing ovation. Between periods we said to each other, 'Let's just try to keep it under five goals this period; let's hold 'em to five.' We were gassed. We went down 9-nothing after two."

Despite his less-than-stellar experience on the ice, Babineau's love affair with hockey was raging. About the time Babs was playing high school hockey, some guy named Orr was on the top of his game.

*below:*

*Shots of the great Bobby Orr when Babineau was still an amateur photographer, taken from his seat in the Garden. Left, Orr's lone game as a Boston Brave [against the Bruins] played as a charity exhibition, and right, Orr as a Bruin.*

"I remember when I was a bit younger...the talk of the 'second coming.' I saw Bobby play an exhibition game at the Garden when he was still a defenseman with Oshawa. It was the Oshawa Generals with Orr against Niagara Falls featuring star forward Derek Sanderson. Orr had the shaved head. Sanderson was gritty. I remember Orr and Sanderson fought at center ice," Babs says with a smile. "It was unreal."

By 1969, Orr established himself as the best overall player in the League, while Babineau's interest in photography had taken off. Hockey and photography dominated his young life.

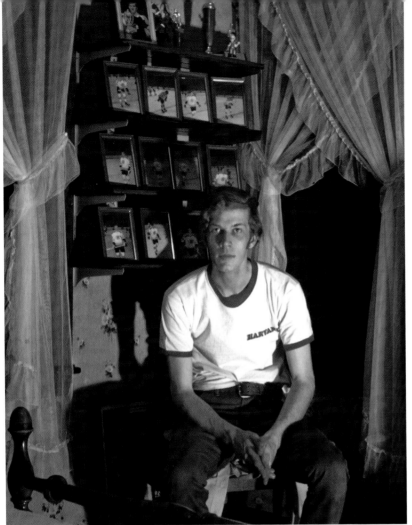

*above:*

*Self-portrait of teenager Steve Babineau at home in Cambridge in front of his framed hockey collection. At the time Babs worked as a rink attendant at Harvard.*

"I lived in Porter Square, North Cambridge, and I worked at the rink at Harvard making ice. I have a picture of me when I was 17, 18 years old, sitting in a chair in my house, with all of these framed pictures I had taken behind me.

"I also remember trying to get Bobby Orr's autograph," Babs continues. "At the old Garden, North Station, there were double doors that were used as the main entrance, and one of the doors was open. Rick and I used to get there early and sneak up to the level where the players came in through security. I remember Orr and Gilles Marotte walked in."

When Babineau asked for an autograph and Orr obliged, Babineau froze. Orr tried to hand Babineau his coffee to hold while he signed and Steve's hand didn't open. Orr spilled coffee on both their hands.

"I was young, not much younger than him," Babs states the obvious, "but I was nervous then."

Within the same decade, those nerves would turn to pure adrenaline and emotion for Babineau. After being a fan and seeing Orr lead the organization to two Cup wins, Babineau would have the opportunity to shoot a brief stint of Orr's career before it ended, and then be on hand for the ultimate night: Bobby's jersey retirement on January 9, 1979.

"Needless to say he was an unbelievable player and to have a chance to overlap with his time here just a little bit is special to me," points out Babineau. "He was one of a kind and I still get emotional when I watch clips of the night they hoisted number 4. A great night for probably the greatest player."

Because of Orr and others, Babineau gradually learned to keep his composure around superstar players. He also recalls another valuable job-related lesson from watching those blessed with the ultimate in talent: always have your camera ready.

"We got in to see a Red Wings practice: Howe, Delvecchio, Gadsby. After practice Gordie Howe was standing in front of the crease like a baseball batter, Roger Crozier [the goalie] was crouched behind him in front of the net like a catcher, and Andy Bathgate was sending slappers in from near center ice. Pow. Pow. Pow. Gordie is swinging his stick like a baseball bat and hitting pucks upstairs. He got a piece of everything. I don't know how he did it. I kept yelling at him to give me his stick. He kept hitting the pucks into the balcony, and finally the stick shattered into a million pieces. I remember him looking at me with the end of the broken stick and wondering if I still wanted it. I passed, but he gave me an autograph instead."

From that point forward Babs always carried his camera along, his nerves settled, the comfort level from the experience of being around the NHLers started to kick in, and Babineau started to get a feel for the building.

I went out and bought season tickets to the Boston Braves.

As is often the case, getting something one wants badly enough also means making small sacrifices. He gave up a crack at the best hockey tickets to the best games, just to improve his opportunity to work on his craft.

*above left:*

*Normand Leveille, whose career ended suddenly during a game in Vancouver in October 1982 when he suffered a cerebral hemorrhage, returns to the Garden for the first time. Bruin Barry Pederson (#10) is clapping to the left, immediately next to retired Bruin Jean Ratelle in a plaid jacket. Media man Nate Greenberg is next to security guard clapping.*

*above right:*

*Leveille with "Mr. Hockey" Gordie Howe at the Fleet Center, during festivities for the 1996 NHL All-Star game.*

"I just needed to get into the building to take pictures at hockey games, which I could do before the game by walking down to the glass," Babineau recalls. "The glass was short, I was 6-foot-2, and I could walk down and shoot right over it. Plus, I could shoot from my seat. It may have been the year the WHA [World Hockey Association] started [1972]. I went down to buy Bruins tickets on a wicked cold night. The mayor didn't want the fans waiting outside, so they funneled us inside and into two lines: Original Six or expansion tickets. I thought, well, everyone's going to want to see the Canadiens and Red Wings, so I'll get in the expansion line. I really wanted to see the better teams but I knew it would be next to impossible. Rick and I were third in line for expansion games. We get to the front, looking to buy seats for the Blues and Flyers and such, and they hand us obstructed view. The season ticket holders had already bought all of the rest of the seats before they opened it up to us.

"How can this be? This sucks. I went out and bought season tickets to the Boston Braves."

The Bruins American League affiliate, the Braves, also played at the Garden. Even with six extra teams at the NHL level in those days, the talent wasn't that watered down, and the hockey at both levels was outstanding.

Babs bought season tickets to the Boston Braves, plus a ticket package for the first seven games of the season of the New England Whalers of the World Hockey Association (WHA).

*below:*

*What Babineau calls a "onetimer" shot, a posed effort outside the norm. Here, goalie Andy Moog, Ray Bourque and Cam Neely don three different Bruins sweaters; black, white and NHL 75th-anniversary "throw back," worn by the Original Six teams.*

"I saw guys when they were young play against and for the Braves like [Larry] Robinson and [Terry] O'Reilly. I have pictures of Terry O'Reilly playing for the Braves. We used to keep track of how many times O'Reilly would fall down during a game. He made himself into an unbelievable player. Not a great skater then, but he turned himself into a solid skater and a great player. First on, last off. By the end of his career, in his heyday, you couldn't knock him off his skates. He might fall after running through you, but you're not knocking him down. He was best ever at controlling the puck in the corner with his skates. Pass it or keep it, he'd protect the puck with his body."

O'Reilly is one of only two non-Hall-of-Fame players [Lionel Hitchman is the other] with his name and number in the Garden rafters. He's the mold of a true Bruin.

"I was dating my soon-to-be-wife, Anita, at that time. I used to take her to games," Babs recalls. "I remember us watching O'Reilly chasing Dave Schultz down the runway. Schultz butt-ended me once when I leaned over and called him a p———. O'Reilly chased him down the rink. O'Reilly probably doesn't remember that and obviously he'd have no idea that was me. Pretty cool actually when you think about it."

Babineau's season tickets were in the third row. His simple plan: he'd take photos leaning over the glass before the game, and from his seat during.

The next big step in the young photographer's development: ironic luck.

*above left:*

*Terry O'Reilly "bided his time" playing the game rough and tough as he gradually improved his skating, a weakness when he came up with the AHL Boston Braves.*

*above right:*

*Two men fit in the mold "ultimate Bruin." Grinders, scorers, fighters, and relentless leaders, Terry O'Reilly and Cam Neely truly epitomize the Bruin ideology.*

A burglar broke into the Babineaus' house one spring afternoon while Steve was down the street playing baseball. When he and his father came home, the crook was still in the house. The front chain was still hooked; the man had come in and was about to go out a back window.

"He heard us, jumped back out, and ran across a field and crossed the railroad tracks," Babs recalls.

The burglar had swiped a strongbox out of Steve's uncle's room, and he had also taken Steve's camera.

"I had a simple SLR [single lens reflex]. One fixed lens. I was able to go out with the insurance money and get a camera with lenses. I started shooting my second year of the Braves with a good camera," Babs says thoughtfully.

Babineau got married in 1973, two days before he turned 21.

"Getting married set my life in motion," Babineau says. "I had to get a job."

He sold his first photo to *The Hockey News* that same year.

"I was an avid reader of *The Hockey News*. My neighbor Paul Harrigan got it, and then I started getting it when I could afford it," Babs recalls. "After three or four issues, I worked up the nerve to call them."

"The middle of *The Hockey News* had three pages dedicated to the new league [WHA] but no photos, so I called Charlie Halpin, the editor in Montreal," remembers Babs.

Babineau explained that he was an avid reader of the weekly, and wondered why photos of the WHA never showed up inside. He added a little passion behind his argument, by pointing out the fact that he had turned his bathroom into a darkroom, and had a number of great photos of the WHA's burgeoning stars. He then sent in some black-and-white photos of Tim Sheehy playing for the Whalers and Bobby Sheehan playing for the New York Golden Blades.

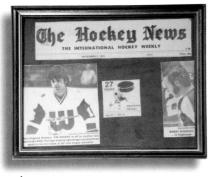

*above:*

*The first Steve Babineau efforts to make* The Hockey News. *He was paid three dollars a piece for these WHA images of Tim Sheehy and Bobby Sheehan. Printed in Montreal at the time, this was the November 2nd, 1973, issue of the weekly.*

*below:*

*New England Whalers of the WHA, Boston Bruins of the NHL, and Boston Braves of the AHL. As an amateur, Babineau was shooting all three during the same season.*

Halpin not only bought some shots, he offered to get Babineau a season pass to cover the Whalers games.

"I got six bucks, three dollars each, for my first two published photos," Babs says with a smile. "And I got a season credential. The Whalers went on to win the championship that year. I came across the great Gordie Howe again that year. He was playing for Houston."

The second year, the team split its games between the Garden and the Boston Arena.

"I'd come full circle," Babs adds. "I was back in the same rink where I played high school hockey, photographing professional hockey."

Events were working out well for the young, up-and-coming photographer. The next logical step was the "big show."

When the WHA moved to Springfield and then Hartford, Babineau convinced *The Hockey News* to get him a press credential to shoot the Bruins. The timing was fortuitous. The Boston Braves of the American Hockey League (AHL) disbanded, and their PR guy, named Nate Greenberg, moved over and replaced Bruins PR guy Herb Ralby. Greenberg gave Babineau his first NHL credential in 1975. On top of *The Hockey News*, Babs started taking photos for four or five other different hockey publications. What came next seemed inevitable.

*above:*

*An image from the first Bruins game Babineau attended on a press credential. Left to right: Phil Esposito, former Bruin turned Atlanta Flames defenseman Doug Mohns, goalie Phil Myre, Flames d-man Noel Price, with Bruins Wayne Cashman and Bobby Orr swarming.*

"The Bruins had two photographers during the Cup years," Babineau explains. "Al Ruelle took the black-and-white shots, while Jerry Buckley did color. Jerry left and went to work for the Red Sox, and the guy who took over was Dick Raphael. After a couple years, he and the Bruins apparently had a falling out at one point. He left, but I don't think it was a big deal for Dick because he was also shooting for the Celtics, the Sox, and the Patriots, as more of a freelance guy. Meanwhile, I had taken a few NHL photos along the way for *The Hockey News* and for *Hockey Illustrated*, beginning in 1974, which would open the door when Raphael left. The media guy Nate Greenberg came up and said, 'We need your photos for the

Boards and Blades Club. I thought he was proposing photos for the press room, but it turned out to be for the 'B and B' season ticket holders' room, which was literally underneath the ice."

Babineau received a call about a meeting. He met and showed photos to former coach and assistant general manager Tom Johnson, general manager Harry Sinden, Greenberg, and Garden president Paul Mooney, who ran the building. They ordered about forty 16-by-20 framed prints and also wanted to use some photos in the Bruins yearbook. Soon after, they offered Babineau the job as full-time Bruins color photographer. It was 1977.

"You're the team color photo- grapher until I tell you otherwise."

"You're the team color photographer until I tell you other-wise," Greenberg told Babineau.

"When Babineau came along, he gradually brought along a bit more technology," Greenberg remembers. "It worked out well for all of us because at that time we were adding more promotions and more color publications. The press guide went to color. I started doing the yearbook with a lot more color photos, so we needed a lot more than we had before."

13

*below:*

*Babineau captures the action: Bruins defenseman Kyle McLaren hammers Detroit's Anders Eriksson as Boston center Mike Sullivan looks on.*

Over the course of the next three-and-a-half decades, Babineau snapped hundreds of thousands of photos, including almost every one of those found in this collection. His son Brian took the remaining few. The Babineau business became a family affair in the early '90s. They called it Sports Action Photography, and it became one of the biggest suppliers of NHL images to licensees of the League. Clients in the hockey card industry included Topps, Upper Deck, Score, and Pro Set. One of Babs's claims to fame was taking the photos for the Wayne Gretzky and Mario Lemieux rookie cards for Topps. Poster and calendar companies, video game companies like EA SPORTS, and equipment manufacturers like Bauer, Easton, Mission, ITECH, and Louisville Slugger soon came calling. Steve and Brian stayed very busy.

"Never in a million years when he was 15 years old and I let him shoot at ice level at a game against the New Jersey Devils did I think he'd be so into it and be so good at it," Babineau says proudly of Brian. "He had played the game and had a real understanding of how to capture it. I knew he had it figured out soon after he started. We were still using primitive equipment then, so to speak, but he could really capture the angles and the images. When I was young I used to go up to [highway] 128 to shoot cars zipping by to work on my timing. Brian just seemed to inherit it. He had the timing and the movement of the skaters figured out right off the bat."

Greenberg's "until I tell you otherwise" expired when, after 34 years with the team, Greenberg departed in 2007. But

*above:*

*Prominent Bruins through the years pose together for a "onetimer." Joe Thornton, Gerry Cheevers, John Bucyk, Phil Esposito, Cam Neely, Ray Bourque and Bobby Orr.*

Bob Morello

*above:*

*Steve and Brian (standing) Babineau with a Bruins Zamboni on the Zakim Bridge outside the big rink, fooling around during a commercial/print ad shoot.*

*below:*

*The past, present, and future of Sports Action Photography, dad Steve Babineau and son Brian.*

Babineau didn't outlast him by much. With the NHL wrapping its arms around the licensing of hockey photographs, including Babineau's massive collection, 2008 became time for Babs to wind it down. The league purchased his entire collection in December of 2007.

"I felt that my work would be protected for all time by being part of the NHL image collection and would always remain intact," Babineau explains. "I'm grateful to the League for seeing the value of my work. Many other photographers I have known, their work has disappeared or been sold off into public hands, and I didn't want that to happen. My dad always told me to leave something behind.

"At the same time, moving and selling the archive is like losing a child," Babs points out, "but it makes sense, since I wouldn't really be in touch with the clients like I always was before, with the licensing, and sales, and distribution in the hands of the NHL. So I wouldn't really have direct contact with the clients anymore anyway."

Babs's son Brian will take over day-to-day photography responsibilities with the Bruins and with the Celtics as well.

"This is my last hurrah," Babineau says, "a few hundred thousand hockey photos down the road. The path is now set for Brian to keep our name imbedded in Bruins history."

Bruins history, at least for the past three-and-a-half-decades, is unceremoniously synonymous with the name Steve Babineau. This collection culminates his efforts. A for-the-most-part anonymous existence producing images for the masses now becomes more tangible: priceless moments and memories released by the man who captured them.

Matthew West

# CHAPTER

# THE GARDEN

*above:*

*The Boston Garden, 1928-1995.*

*left:*

*The interior of the old Boston Garden from the northeast corner above the Zamboni entrance.*

The original Garden was built in 1928 with boxing in mind, but during its 70-year existence it saw a whole lot of everything—legendary fights, basketball games, political rallies, speeches, concerts, circuses, and shows. For hockey, the building was unlike any other, with its own peculiarities not found in any of the other Original Six buildings. The attendance often ballooned beyond the often uttered original hockey capacity of 13,909. Standard NHL rinks are 200 feet long by 85 feet wide, while the old Garden was nine feet shorter and two feet narrower. The small rink with its tight corners gave the Bruins a distinct home-ice advantage: intimidation on and above the ice gave the home team a feeling of dominance and comfort that literally could transfer to the scoreboard.

"The building itself when coming in to play [gave] maybe a goal-and-a-half, two-goal advantage or lead right off the bat, which was nice; the fans were right on top of the players with the balconies. It was close and just a fun place to play," sums up Don Marcotte, a Bruin for 13-plus seasons.

The Garden could best be described as a bandbox. The fans seemed to hang from the balconies right out over the playing surface. The crowd noise was deafening, inspiring, and sometimes simply hard to believe.

In 70 years it saw Stanley Cups lifted in celebration, it saw Bobby Orr revolutionize the game, and it saw legendary names hoisted to its rafters.

Kevin Paul Dupont, 30 years a Bruins observer for the *Boston Globe,* describes the feeling.

"You were just perched right over. You felt like you could reach right out and touch it, and almost like you were overlooking a slot-hockey game. You felt like you could control it," reflects Dupont. "Beyond that, you not only watched it, you were just immersed in it. The game was so much more emotional then anyway because of the fighting and hitting. You were just absorbed by it, so that was wonderful."

Hall of Fame left winger John Bucyk, 21 years a Bruin, says the atmosphere was unforgettable.

"It was fun because the fans were right above you in the overhang," "the Chief" recalls. "You could hear the fans cheering for you or yelling at you one way or the other and they enjoyed it too because they could hear what we were saying on the ice. It was just so much fun because the building was a little bit smaller, so you really enjoyed it."

For some fans, sitting in the stadium seats beneath the balconies meant watching just half a game. Wide pillars, support beams for the balcony, each easily a foot wide and spaced out almost evenly around the building, blocked the view of some of the fans in the last four rows of the lower section. Meanwhile, spectators in the last three rows of the upper balcony on the side couldn't see the near boards unless they

*above:*

*Shot from the catwalk above center ice, Jacques Lemaire of the Canadiens just won back an opening face-off against Jean Ratelle of Boston.*

stood up, and those on the end couldn't see the goalie's net closest to them. At times, simply for the purpose of being able to see, fans got to know each other a little bit, through all of the leaning, standing, and coercing.

"Certainly it was cozy," states Nate Greenberg, who spent the last 23 years of the old Garden's existence handling media for the Bruins, and then as assistant to the team president.

"The rink was unlike any other; today the rinks are all uniform. Boston Garden was the best. The people were right on top of the game. The entertainment value every night was off the charts, and I enjoyed every single night like you wouldn't believe. The team had a lot to do with it, but so did the building. The atmosphere was unbelievable."

*below:*

*Just what it was like to sit "obstructed view" in the lower balcony (behind a support beam which held up the 2nd balcony) at the Garden. Babineau's partial view of the Blackhawks and Bruins in January 1971.*

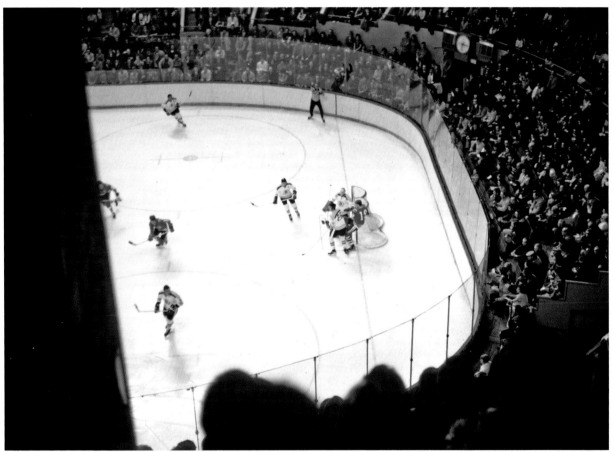

The Bruins played their first playoff game at the Garden on March 19, 1929, beating the Montreal Canadiens 1-0. Cooney Weiland scored the lone goal at 7:20 of the first period and Cecil "Tiny" Thompson made 29 saves for the shutout. The Bruins swept the three-game semi-final and beat the New York Rangers in a best-of-three sweep of the final for Boston's first-ever Stanley Cup. Bill Carson scored the Cup-clinching goal on March 29.

Ten years later, the Garden saw the Bruins win their second Cup. The semi-final series format had expanded to seven games, and the Bruins/Rangers series went the distance. The Bruins won Game 7 in overtime, with a goal by Mel "Sudden Death" Hill. He earned the nickname by establishing a record that still stands today. Hill tallied three overtime winners in the series. The Bruins whipped the Maple Leafs four games to one to win the final and the organization's second Cup.

That 1939 Bruins roster featured notable names: Frank "Mr. Zero" Brimsek in goal, Eddie Shore on the blue line, and Milt Schmidt, Bobby Bauer, and Woody Dumart on the young Kraut Line up front. Shore, Dit Clapper, and Weiland had won in 1929 as well, with Weiland retiring after the '39 Cup win.

Two years later, in March of 1941, the Garden added its first four-sided clock over the playing surface, at a cost of $25,000. A month later the Bruins won their third Cup, with a seven-game semi-final win over Toronto, and a four-game sweep of the Red Wings. Bobby Bauer scored the Cup winner at 8:43 of the second period on April 12, in a 3-1 win.

For the next three decades little changed at the Garden. The improvements to the building were minimal, the team gradually fell into a playoff drought, and the curse of the Canadiens began. The last time the Bruins beat the Habs in a playoff series prior to 1988 was in 1943, when Boston won a semi-final series four games to one. The win in Game 1 of the series featured a 5-4 sudden death victory for Boston, after the team had fallen behind 3-0 in the second period. The Bruins then lost the Stanley Cup final to Detroit in a sweep.

The 1941 Cup win two seasons earlier would be the club's last until 1970.

*above:*

*One of the Garden's great charms and advantages for the home team: the intimate proximity of the fans to the action. Here, the Boston faithful celebrate a playoff victory against Montreal.*

The small rink with its tight corners gave the Bruins a distinct home-ice advantage.

By the time the core of the future Cup champions began appearing on the scene, little had changed in terms of player accoutrements. John Bucyk and Marcotte and the 20-man rosters of the 1960s, were using the same dressing room that Bill Cowley and 16 teammates had used in the 1930s and '40s.

"The first time I was in the old Garden was 1964," remembers Marcotte. "I was playing for a junior team and we walked in and couldn't believe what bad shape the dressing room was in; wood floor with cracks all over the place, filthy, dirty, one little tiny shower in the corner. I came from a junior team which was minor but our room was good there and the junior building was nice. I came back in 1968–'69 and the room was redone. It was very nice, more like a professional team. They had done a real nice job."

*below:*

*The bandbox packed to capacity.*

"First of all, when I first came in the League, the dressing room was a dump," confirms Ken Hodge. "Both locker rooms at the old Garden were dumps, but after I got traded here in '67, they made a concerted effort to make sure everyone was going to feel a lot more comfortable in the new locker room. Dan Canney [head trainer] and the Bruins staff went through a major renovation of the new locker room and made it very comfortable to live in and play in."

"The first time I went in that building, all I can remember is seeing the clock and the Original Six banners hanging

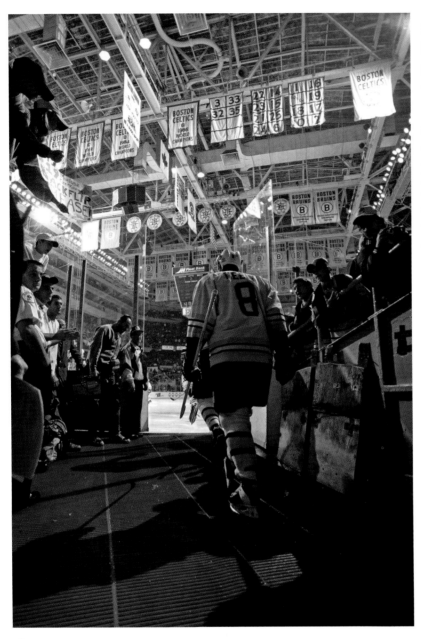

from the catwalk," remembers Steve Babineau. "The ceiling seemed so far away when I was a kid.

"I had been in there for the circus and by the basketball court, but it was different for hockey," adds Babineau. "The hanging clock, the ice surface, it was amazing to me. Over time of course, I got to know the building with all of its nuances."

"All of the little nooks and crannies," remembers veteran PR woman and Bruins publicist Heidi Holland. "One thing comes to mind...there was a circular staircase that if you weighed over 120 pounds—I don't know how some of the players got down it—that went from the dressing room down to the players' lounge downstairs. That was just very bizarre."

"The hallways were small and all of the floors around the concourse were sloped," adds Babineau. "At the Zamboni end, it seemed like the floor dropped away; I wonder if they did it for drainage in case the ice melted and they had a flood. And speaking of the Zamboni, it would literally leave the ice, cross the concourse where people were walking to their seats, up through an overhead door that they'd open, out through a weird little alley between the Garden and 150 Causeway, and dump the snow."

Outside in the arena area, aside from the chicken wire above the boards changing to glass, little changed. Intimate meant intimidation: the bigger, taller, faster bodies of the expansion era on the same small ice surface equaled less time and space.

"To play in that building with the people right on top of you, things happened so quick in that building and you either

*above:*

*Cam Neely walks to the ice surface one last time. This shot is from May 14, 1995, the last official Bruins game in the old building, a 3-to-2 playoff loss in the first round to New Jersey. The Devils wrapped up the series that night four games to one.*

*left:*

*The Bruins, including Ray Bourque, Randy Burridge (#12), and Bob Sweeney (#20), celebrate a goal. The crowd noise in the old Garden could get "beyond deafening."*

hit, or got hit," reminisces Andy Brickley, a former Boston forward turned TV commentator. "It's what hockey's supposed to be. It's supposed to be about scoring chances, it's supposed to be about being physical, it's supposed to be about fights, and in that building it happened every game."

The key factor in the noise adding to the aura, and to the influence the fans had on driving the home team, came from the vertical nature of the spectator area. While the Garden and the other Original Six buildings were built "up," almost all modern arenas erected since are built "out," tapering away from the rink. The bandboxes placed fans on top of the action.

"That was the best," Brickley continues. "When you think of the Garden you think of places like Chicago, Buffalo, where the people were right on top of you. The building had a pulse, and that's the thing you appreciated most about the Garden. Obviously, the great players that played there, the sweater, putting that on, and playing in front of fans that had an unconditional love for the team…"

"The proximity of our crowd to the action, that was probably an advantage. They were right on top of the play," affirms longtime Bruins coach, GM, and executive Harry Sinden. "The other thing about the old Garden was that the players, as they entered the building and left the building, they did it right through the middle of the crowd, and that kind of touchy-feely atmosphere between the players and fans was great."

Onetime Bruins captain and current off-ice official Ed Sandford remembers the adrenaline rush from "the walk" across the concourse—the home players as heroes, the road team as villains.

"Ted Lindsay of Detroit, I remember he used to jab his stick at the fans as he went by," Sandford says. "They'd get into it. It was a unique time. The players would walk right along and the crowd

below:

*Another perspective on the fans' proximity to the ice and the action, especially in the tight corners. Left to right during a playoff game on May 7, 1995: Bruin Dave Shaw (#34), Devil Neal Broten against Adam Oates on the draw, Blaine Lacher in net, and Ray Bourque.*

*above:*

*In 1988-89, Bruin Andy Brickley crashes the net against Sabres goalie Jacques Cloutier and backchecker Pierre Turgeon.*

To Dan,
Best Wishes
From all
the
Bruins!

would be yelling for us on one side and against them. It was different."

That same area of the concourse took on a different feel on non-game days and during morning skates.

"One thing I really liked was on weekend game days, guys would come in for the skate, and a lot of times they'd bring their kids and they'd bring their dogs," remembers Holland. "And the kids would be out on the concourses playing hockey with balls of tape, what have you, and because there were—no rats in the Garden—very large mice, the way the stands were set up, the dogs would just be having a field day, running all over the place chasing the mice. It was a neat atmosphere. Nobody was around, and it was unique to that building. In traveling around I never saw that at morning skates anywhere else except for the Garden."

Mice?! Rats?!

"There were a few animals running around, four legged, with long tails," adds Ken Hodge. "They'd come across— you'd listen to them at night—they'd come running across the [locker room] ceiling and you'd hear them. A couple times, animals fell out of people's pockets or fell into their hockey pants and stuff like that, but that's what it was all about, the old Garden."

As for the canine camaraderie, that tradition came to a screeching halt.

"I remember one guy had a cute Labrador puppy...it may have been Jay Miller, I can't remember for sure...but one day the dog hopped the boards and started running around the ice during practice," reflects Holland. "The coach, I think Taz, absolutely lost it. The guys were skating around trying to get ahold of it, while the coach was yelling, 'Get that bleeping dog out of here.' That was the end of dogs in the building."

Photographer Steve Babineau remembers the Garden for a special reason of a completely different sort: it's where he broke into the full-time sports photography business.

"Being a new kid on the block, there were a lot of old-timers, and any time a 'foreign' photographer came in it was like, 'What the heck are you doing here?' There was a breaking-in period," Babs remembers. "When I finally got *The Hockey News* credential, in the mid-'70s, I was accepted somewhat, but I was still low guy on the totem pole in terms of shooting positions in the building. In those days, everybody wanted the side holes, along the face-off circles. The problem was,

*above:*

*Ted Irvine of the Rangers against Bruins goalie Gilles Gilbert. A fan back left gets a clutch photo of his own.*

*above:*

*The Bruins score on the Flyers during the 1992-93 season. From left to right, Steve Leach, Flyer and former Bruin Gord Hynes, Dave Poulin, Flyer Brent Fedyk, netminder Stephane Beauregard, Flyer Dmitri Yushkevich, and Ray Bourque.*

you couldn't turn all the way and shoot down the ice in either direction. Guys wanted the Bruins' attacking zone twice, and they were happy shooting the action there. I was fortunate enough to get a hole on the curvature of the boards, so I could shoot one goal, and all the way down the ice. Those are the preferred holes still today, because you can shoot more of the ice surface. I was in a spot ahead of its time by accident."

As for handling the photographers and the rest of the media, that job belonged to Greenberg.

I was fortunate enough to get a hole on the curvature of the boards, so I could shoot one goal, and all the way down the ice.

"When I first started, the press box was in the first balcony, and the things that happened to us there, you wouldn't believe," Greenberg professes. "We had problems with the power. We used to put out these little black-and-white televisions because we televised all of our games in the '70s, and we'd have these little TVs we'd put out across the press box, and sometimes those wouldn't work. If it wasn't the TVs it was the phones. The stuff was put in place in the '20s, and very little had been done, of course. Nothing ever seemed to work right. It probably took about 10 years off my life, that building. But I enjoyed it immensely. It was unique and it was wonderful."

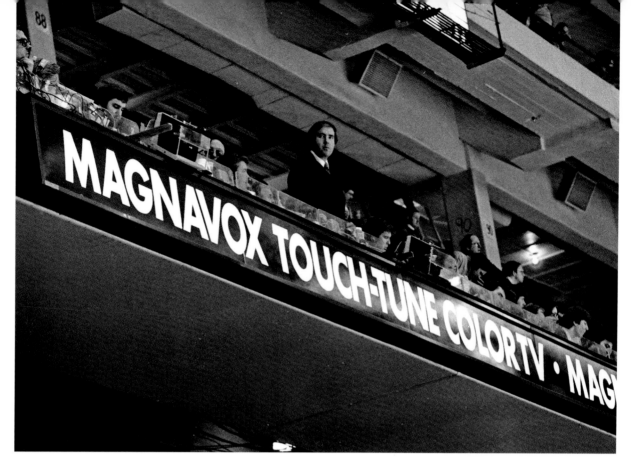

*above:*

*Long time Bruins PR man and executive Nate Greenberg overlooks the proceedings from his perch in the Garden balcony.*

From his start in 1973 until 1984, when he hired Holland as an assistant, Greenberg worked alone. Most of the NHL teams worked with just one PR person.

"At one point we moved the press box to the second level, probably in the mid-80s, and that was like moving to a new building for us," Greenberg remembers. "To go up to the second balcony, there was a lot more room, but you were still hanging off a balcony. I wouldn't go as far as to say it was plush, but it certainly was better than the first balcony. The one issue was to get up, there was this little fire escape. You had to duck down and kind of sneak your way through. If you tended to be on the portly side, it could be a challenge."

"When [the press box] moved up, it wasn't all that bad; in fact, by today's standards it was excellent," chips in Dupont. "Your angle was vastly different then, especially that first balcony. You were almost even with the boards, that near board; that's how pitched the angles were in the old buildings."

"It was very steep. You had to watch yourself coming down and often times things would fall over into the seats," Greenberg adds. "In the original balcony we had people sitting right behind us where the balcony went up, and occasionally we'd have someone from the road team come in and we'd have some issues. We knew everyone. We'd have NHL officials come in, or supervisors, visiting GMs or visiting scouts, former players, and there was some interesting give and take there over the years. The visiting GMs, because there were no boxes, they'd be sitting right out in the press box and they'd be mad at a call or something, and they were close enough where the players and officials could actually hear them from the press box. They'd be that close and they'd be givin' it to 'em. It was unique; I'll tell you that."

Longtime *Boston Globe* reporter Fran Rosa describes it another way.

"At one time, the press box at the old Garden was in section 60, part of the balcony at center ice. There was just one row on top of the other, about six or eight rows, like a desk top," Rosa describes. "Officials used to come in with other teams, general managers, and people like that—they would sit up there, too. One guy, King Clancy from Toronto, who was kind of a legend, and a very charming guy—when he used to come in the Garden, he'd always come in through the east lobby, and I think all the women who were hockey fans would stand there and wait to talk to the King, because he was a very charming guy…. Anyway, he'd go up in that press box, that old press box, and overhead, in the second balcony, is where the Gallery Gods were."

The Gallery Gods, led by Revere's Roger Naples, were vocal season ticket holders who occupied the first couple of rows of the second balcony. They've been attending Bruins games in both Gardens, old and new, for the last half-century.

"They had a section chief who got all the tickets," Rosa continues. "One guy up there, I think he came from Medford, I'm not sure, he was known as "Foghorn" because he was always yelling, nothing dirty, just always yelling. So Clancy would come up to the press box and Foghorn would yell down to him, 'Clancy, we named a town after you!' Clancy would look up at him, and Foghorn would yell,

*below:*

*The penalty box at the old Garden, a home-away-from home for many a Big Bad Bruin and for those in the Lunch Pail Gang. The near bench now resides in photographer Steve Babineau's home in Florida (if anyone's wondering what happened to it).*

'Marblehead!' So you know what Clancy did? He'd go buy a strong case of beer, get the ushers and Gallery Gods to send down a piece of rope; [then] he'd tie the case to it and send it up."

Often, more so by accident, that same beer or two might find its way back down the stairs and into the press area. Coats hanging in the back would change flavors, depending on what came trickling down the steps. Getting your clothes occasionally doused by beer wasn't supposed to be part of the allure of covering the team.

Later, the Bruins let me in the penalty box and I was right in the game.

"God forbid you had to go to the bathroom," Greenberg adds. "You had to fight your way over to the corner where it was loaded with smoke, that beer smell…it was unbelievable. The press had to stand in line with the masses to get to the facilities."

Being a photographer downstairs much of the time, Babineau didn't have to deal with similar confinement and traffic. In fact, his opportunity to discover new spaces and places around the building actually grew with time.

"Gradually, as ushers and other people always saw me around, I was recognized, and at the same time, I started adding more advanced equipment," Babineau declares. "As the Bruins became more popular, and more photographers started to show up, they added spots. I started to have access to everything. I wasn't under a deadline like a newspaper guy, so I would hang out in cool spots and patiently wait for the best shots. Eventually I ended up in the balcony and the catwalks.

*below:*

*The Bruins line up for the 1990 Stanley Cup final. From left to right: Reggie Lemelin, Cam Neely, Bobby Carpenter, Randy Burridge, Bobby Gould, Dave Poulin, Bob Sweeney, Craig Janney, Glen Wesley, Dave Christian, Garry Galley, Jim Wiemer, John Carter, Don Sweeney, Lyndon Byers, Andy Moog, Brian Propp, Greg Hawgood, Al Pedersen, and Ray Bourque. The two lights in the ceiling are Babineau's strobe flashes going off as he takes the photo.*

*left:*

*A successful Boston net crash shot from the catwalk. That's Wayne Cashman at top, having run into Habs goalie Ken Dryden. Bruin Rick Smith is also in the crease. Beaten Montreal defenseman Bill Nyrop (#2) and Guy Lapointe are on their knees. Celebrating are Brad Park (#22), Peter McNab and Terry O'Reilly.*

"By the time everybody knew me," Babs continues, "I added strobes in the ceiling. [A building-wide system of high-powered flash units, which are wired together in a sequence, and tied to a line that ran down to where the strobe could be triggered remotely by Babineau's camera. Early on, a single wire ran all the way down to where Babs would plug in. Today, the system is wireless, and essentially triggered electronically by remote control.] Later, the Bruins let me in the penalty box and I was right in the game. The game was two inches away; I could feel the breeze as guys went by; I could feel the game."

On September 28, 1995, the final Garden party was held: the Last Hurrah. Following a preseason game against the Montreal Canadiens, the Bruins brought back every legend possible for one final skate in front of a packed house.

Milt Schmidt, Bobby Orr, Johnny Bucyk, Terry O'Reilly, other legends, other members of the Big Bad Bruins and the Lunch Pail Gang all took laps around the ice for one last time. To cap off the emotion, Normand Leveille, a talented young Bruins winger whose 75-game career ended when he suffered a cerebral hemorrhage during a game in Vancouver in 1982, skated out onto the ice with the help of Bruins Superstar defenseman Ray Bourque.

"It was incredibly emotional," Bourque recalls. "It was a special moment I'll never forget and an incredible evening."

Literally inches behind the old Garden, the new TD Banknorth Garden, originally ordained the Fleet Center, had been built. It offered restaurants, luxury suites, and a seating capacity of 19,600. One night after the Last Hurrah, a gala event opened the new building.

With the increase in luxury, came the inevitable decrease in personality. The original Boston Garden had a distinct feel and persona likely never to be seen or felt again. The venerable old barn, unable to be razed by dynamite due to its proximity to the new building, came down in chunks—back-hoe and power-shovel-sized mouthfuls over the ensuing months. Hockey lost a shrine, while Bostonians lost their home away from home.

EDWARD W. SHORE
2
1926-1940

AUBREY V. CLAPPER
5
1927-1947

LIONEL HITCHMAN
3
1925-1934

Dan Canney and Frosty Forristal

Bob Wilson and Mike Milbury

Babs and Al Ruelle

36

Milt Schmidt

Fred Cusick and Ray Bourque

Bobby Orr and Tom Johnson

Tom McVie, Zibby Puleio Jr. and Ray Bourque

Bull gang: Frank Mastrorilli, Armando Maderios and Paul Chambers

Bruins Execs

Joe Curnane, Nate Greenberg and Harry Sinden

Ed Sanford

37

Tony Nota and Pat Considine

Paul Mooney

Rene Rancourt

Anthony Velente – garden pizza

Doc Fleger

Locker room crew

Babs and Andy Carroll

CHAPTER

# BRUINS LEGEND:
# JOHN BUCYK

*above:*

*The most recent "Chief Night" on February 13th, 2007, celebrated Bucyk's 50th year in the Bruins organization.*

*left:*

*John "Chief" Bucyk was inducted into the Hockey Hall of Fame as a player in 1981.*

Hundreds of Bruins players and employees have come and gone during John Bucyk's tenure with the organization. He's presently past the 50-year mark and counting with the hockey club. He's known by everyone as "Chief," a moniker first applied to him in the 1950s by teammate Bronco Horvath.

"Bronco said I took care of business. I'd do all of the running around, arranging things," Bucyk remembers. "I also scored goals, so he called me the Chief. 'Hey, you get everything done; you're the Chief,' he said."

Many associate the name with an assumed Native North American background. However, one shouldn't let Chief's appearance fool them; his complexion and native look and his nickname are purely coincidental. John Bucyk is of Ukrainian descent.

Chief is *still* getting everything done as he continues in his sixth decade with the Bruins. After retiring as a player in 1978, Bucyk jumped on the radio broadcasts as color commentator at the invitation of play-by-play man Bob Wilson.

"It was great fun, and I appreciate Bob asking me to do it," Chief says. "It was a great second career. Heck, I was on there for years."

During his two-plus decades on the air, Chief gradually added other job responsibilities. He handled public relations, media relations, and travel secretary chores along the way. Today, he's still the full-time road services coordinator.

"Chief could do it all, on and off the ice," says Bruins legend Milt Schmidt. "He had a great hip check. He was a solid defender. He reminded me of my teammate Woody Dumart in that area, and he's still a Bruin today—just the way it should be."

"He'd set up the postgame socializing, get everyone out to eat and whatever," recalls former Bruins goalkeeper Gerry Cheevers. "He'd get you a starting time at your local golf club. If you needed a submarine, he'd get it for you."

"When you think of the Bruins, you think of John Bucyk," says former Bruins captain Wayne Cashman. "He was a great leader, a leader on our winning clubs, and he's a great guy on and off the ice. To this day, he helps Bruins players and ex-players."

If a man wore the Spoked B, there's a good chance Bucyk helped him with something along the way, and there's equally as good a chance he'd still help that man today.

"I enjoy it," says Chief. "Nowadays, traveling with the team, I like helping the kids, teasing them a bit, and it's fun. They joke around with me and all in all we have a good time."

*above:*

*Chief on the rush. Bucyk still holds the record for most career assists by an NHL left wing, with 813. He's being chased by New York Islander Lorne Henning (#10) and watched by former Bruin Ed Westfall.*

The best of times for Boston in terms of on-ice success came with Bucyk in his elongated prime. During the three-season span in which the Bruins won two Stanley Cups, from 1969–72, Bucyk tallied 114 goals and 154 assists in the regular season, and added an impressive 22 goals and 24 assists in 36 playoff games. He barely missed being a point-a-game man over the course of his entire playoff career.

*above:*

*Bucyk battling in the final months of his final season 1977-78, against LA Kings defenseman Steve Short.*

Of course, as was the case for all of the Bruins over the years, the Chief's main playoff nemesis was the Montreal Canadiens. Bucyk's Bruins never beat them head-to-head in a series, although he did earn their respect.

"They had very good players. It was scary every time we played them," Canadiens Hall of Famer Guy Lafleur recalls. "Bucyk was late in his career when I played against him but he was strong, a scorer, and a real gentleman on the ice. He was very good with the younger guys. He'd help out the younger players a lot, I remember."

Twice Bucyk earned the NHL's Lady Byng Memorial Trophy, awarded each season to the player who exhibits the best type of sportsmanship and gentlemanly conduct combined with a high standard of playing ability.

"He was very sneaky," adds Pierre Bouchard. "You wouldn't chase him up and down the wing or anything; he'd just know where the puck was going to be."

Bucyk found the puck in the right spot enough times to pot 545 goals as a Bruin, still the club record and one unlikely to be broken for a very long time. Ray Bourque passed Bucyk in the games played, assists, and overall points categories. Bucyk took over the career points mark in 1967 and held it for thirty years, until Bourque passed him with his 1,440th point on February 1, 1997. Both men played 21 seasons, with Bourque catching Chief in actual number of games played during Ray's next-to-last season in Boston.

"I've always said that records were made to be broken," Bucyk says. "I'm happy for the guys. I remember when Ray passed me for points. I mean that's fine. It was good for him, and the team, and it's going to happen. The younger

*above:*

*Chief's NHL career lasted 23 seasons, almost four times longer than the Colorado Rockies franchise, which lasted six (1976-82), before moving to New Jersey and becoming the Devils. Bucyk leaves behind teammate Al Sims (#23) and Colorado's Wilf Paiement (#9).*

generation is going to come along and it's time to move on, and the records get broken. I still have a few."

In 1970–71, Bucyk scored 51 goals, his career high for a single season and the only time he eclipsed the 50-goal mark. He's still the oldest player ever to do it in the NHL, turning the trick at age 35.

Bucyk still holds the NHL career record for assists by a left wing, with 813, 19 of those coming in his first two seasons in Detroit.

43

Bucyk found the puck in the right spot enough times to pot 545 goals as a Bruin, still the club record.

"It was those years in Detroit I learned the ropes," Chief says. "Gordie Howe was my idol, still is, and he and Ted Lindsay, the captain back then, took the young guys under their wings and showed them around. They really took care of all of the players, and that's where I learned it."

The 20-year-old from Edmonton played just 38 games his first season with the Red Wings, and scored only one goal.

"It was tough. You'd sit on the bench for 45 minutes and then he'd [the coach] tell you to go out," Bucyk explains. "You'd be stiff. It was tough to do your job properly. But they had some great players and I was a rookie and I had to wait my turn."

The following year the youngster played 66 games, and reached double-digit figures in goals with 10—maybe not enough to be a top-liner just yet, but apparently enough to catch the eye of the Boston Bruins. On June 10, 1957, the Red Wings sent Bucyk and some cash to the east coast, in exchange for goaltender Terry Sawchuk. Number 9 has been here ever since. Bucyk would have plenty of opportunities to burn his former team, given the nature of playing in a league with only six teams.

"The kids nowadays don't know the type of hockey we used to play," Chief explains. "I mean we had full-scale bench-clearing brawls. It was different. It was tough. There were only six teams at that

*below:*

*Chief battles the Flames, another team that changed locations, from Atlanta to Calgary. Known for his hip checks and lower body strength, Bucyk holds off Atlanta's Dave Shand (#8) while Ken Houston looks on.*

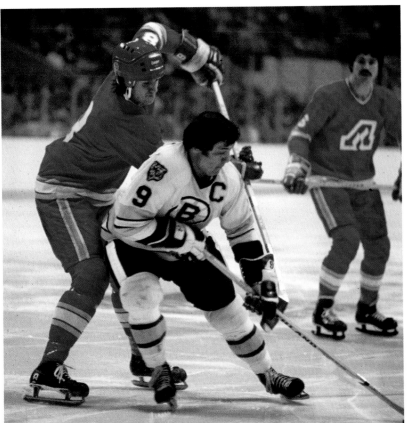

time and you'd see the same players night in and night out. We'd play in Montreal on a Saturday, jump on the train and play in Boston on the Sunday. And we'd ride down on the same train, us in one private car and the Canadiens in another."

Even with frequency and familiarity, the fights and battles would soon be forgotten.

"We'd never let it carry over much, maybe every once in a while. But we'd usually just play, forget about it, and move on. I do remember Rocket Richard separated my shoulder once. Nothing malicious, just a hit along the boards, but he separated my shoulder. I remember that, and I remember playing against him."

It was late in the Rocket's career. One legendary time span winding down, the other one practically just gearing up, and the Chief was paying attention.

"He was a competitor, I'll tell you that," Chief says of the Rocket. "He was fierce; he'd play every game hard. It was neat to play against a guy like that and of course knowing who he was."

During an eight-year span in the '60s, the Bruins failed to make the playoffs, but the team, and the hardy fans in Boston, still managed to have a good time.

"We got beat up sometimes," Chief recalls, "on the scoreboard. But we would fight. I mean, we might lose a game 6- or 7-1, but if we had one big fight, and we won that, the fans would go home happy."

For the most part, rather than fists, Bucyk preferred to leave a physical impression with his hips. He had a devastating old-fashioned hip check.

"Great hip check," proclaims Milt Schmidt. "One of the best. Chief would give hip checks and score goals."

Bucyk continued to produce through his penultimate season, with 43 points in 49 games in 1976–77. The next season, the Chief wound down with just 18 points.

It was during this time period, during the latter stages of the sturdy left winger's career, that photographer Steve Babineau appeared on the scene.

"He was more old-school in my mind," Babs remembers. "I was a little more intimidated by him when I first showed up. He was part of the old regime and I'm pretty sure he was friends with the previous photographer. It took a little while for him to warm up to the new kid, I think."

It was clear to Babineau at the time: the Chief was the man.

"Whenever players were doing promos or anything, or had to be somewhere for an event, it seemed like everything filtered through Chief. As a player and then obviously since then, he was the guy you went through to get things done."

*above:*

*Bucyk bowls through Brian Glennie (#24) of the Maple Leafs. That's Toronto's Rod Seiling on one knee.*

"His longevity makes him as important as anyone, any of the legends I've photographed retiring, and that's what makes it special for me. Growing up in Cambridge, when I was a kid, 8, 10, 12 years old, I used to listen to the games at night on the transistor radio and Chief was *the* star. Before Orr came along and Esposito, Bucyk was the star and he was on the BOW line [Bucyk, Oliver, Williams] with Murray Oliver at center and Tommy Williams streaking down the other wing. They didn't win much, but that was the line, and Chief was the main guy."

Bucyk wore the C for two separate stints as a Bruin, and even during a time when they didn't have a formal captain, Chief was the unnamed, de facto captain.

"He was the captain when I first got there," Babs remembers, "and even when he wasn't wearing the C, he was the guy the players looked up to."

After the 1977–78 season, Bucyk hung up his NHL skates for good. Two seasons later, on March 13, 1980, the Bruins retired his jersey, and hoisted number 9 to the rafters.

"That's when I really started to get to know Chief," Babineau recalls. "I took the shot of the ceremony—him watching his number go up—and we decided to make and sell a limited edition print of the occasion. It was sold in the pro shop for a couple of years. Chief was like 'sure, let's do it.'"

Twenty-eight years later, in early 2007, the Bruins had Chief Night number two, to honor Bucyk's 50 years with the organization.

*below:*

*Boston greats honor Chief in his 50th season. Ray Bourque, Bronco Horvath, Tom Johnson, John McKenzie, Doug Mohns, Don Marcotte (face in back), Chief, Cam Neely, Terry O'Reilly, Billy O'Dwyer, Derek Sanderson, and Ed Sandford.*

"That's really cool," states Babineau. "Again, as a kid, I'm listening to him play hockey; he's the star. Then I'm shooting pictures of him still as a player and I'm a young adult, don't know anything, and then here he is, all this time later, still with the club and I'm still taking his picture. I mean, with Orr, I caught him towards the end, but then he just went on his way. Chief is *still* going; he embodies my whole existence with the team."

At one point along the way, Babineau knew he had been accepted into the fold, old school, and otherwise.

"Chief was already an old-timer, and he and Gary Doak, and Pie McKenzie and Don Marcotte were playing in an alumni game against the Medford Youth Hockey coaches. I was one of the coaches. They left the other guys alone but every chance they got, they gave me an extra elbow, or a playful hook, or a whack, or would run me into the boards when they could. It was fun. They could get away with it with me, but they weren't going to do that with guys they didn't know."

Through the course of Babineau's career, Bucyk provided countless opportunities to add to the scrapbook. The awards and recognition he has received are as diverse as anyone's in hockey.

*above:*

*Chief receiving congratulations from Bruins Executive Vice President Charlie Jacobs, a member of the ownership family. Bucyk has worked for three different owners: the Adams, a local TV conglomerate, and the Jacobs.*

While still a player, during his final season in fact, Bucyk earned the Lester Patrick Award for service to hockey in the United States. Four years later, and in his first season of eligibility, he earned induction into the Hockey Hall of Fame.

Bucyk also holds the unofficial record for vehicles obtained from one team.

"You're gonna say that's a record," Chief laughs. "Yeah, I got one in 1965 when they thought I was going to retire because of a bad back. They gave me a '65 Mustang convertible. That was the fans' gift. They had a night for me."

Chief is *still* going; he embodies my whole existence with the team.

For John Bucyk Night number one after his retirement, he received a hefty stipend from the team toward a motor home, and then for John Bucyk Night number two almost three decades later, he picked up a Volvo SUV.

In 2008, Bucyk and his wife, Anne, celebrated their 50th wedding anniversary, while Bucyk's been married to the Bruins for 52 years...and counting.

"I can't believe it's been that long," Chief says of his relationship with the Bruins. "It goes by quick. I enjoy it. I've had fun every year."

*right:*

On the first "official" Chief night, March 13, 1980, former teammate Stan Jonathan presents Bucyk his head dress. Jonathan is native American, Bucyk is Ukrainian, but often mistaken for indigenous, especially given his nickname.

*below:*

Former teammate and Bruins captain Wayne Cashman presents Bucyk his # 9 Bruins sweater.

*right:*

Chief watches his banner go up. That's Harry Sinden to his immediate right.

**JOHN BUCYK** (LW) Edmonton, AB | #9 | 50-plus years in organization

| BRUINS REGULAR SEASON STATISTICS | GP | G | A | Pts | PIM |
|---|---|---|---|---|---|
| 1957–1978 | 1,436 | 545 | 794 | 1,339 | 436 |
| Bruins Postseason Statistics | 124 | 41 | 62 | 103 | 42 |

CHAPTER

# Bruins Legend: Bobby Orr

*above:*

*Orr stood alone as a hockey player. Knee injuries shortened a career that would have been the greatest in history, for a player who may have been the greatest in history anyway.*

*left:*

*Bobby Orr, working on his stick, which normally featured a single width of tape wrapped once around the blade.*

In Boston, "Bobby" is all one needs to say to instantly bring to mind the man who revolutionized the game of hockey from the blueline—the man many argue became the greatest player of all time. Robert Gordon Orr hailed from Parry Sound, Ontario, along the shores of Lake Huron's Georgian Bay, but it's Boston where his image will forever be immortalized.

To say his arrival in New England was anticipated would be an understatement, as the Bruins would have to wait until Bobby was 18 years old to play in the NHL. It became obvious well before that that Orr had extra special qualities and the potential to be a star. Signed by Bruins agent and Oshawa coach Wren Blair at age 13, Orr began playing in junior-A (then the Ontario Hockey Association, precursor to the OHL) at age 14. Despite playing with teenagers four and five years older, the Oshawa Generals' defenseman dominated.

*Boston Globe* sports writer Fran Rosa covered the Bruins occasionally starting in the early 1950s, and began covering them on a regular basis early in Orr's professional career.

"He was gonna be the savior. For so many years they [the Bruins] had finished last or next to last. It was between them and the Rangers as to who was going to finish last, back with only six teams," Rosa relates. "So the hockey experts and the Bruins people all said this kid was going to lead them out of the wilderness, and he did. He lived up to the expectations.

"You also have to remember that the Bruins made a big trade. I believe it was Milt Schmidt, the General Manager at the time," Rosa recalls. "They got Phil Esposito from the Blackhawks."

The deal is still referred to as "The Trade" by many from the time period. It occurred on May 15, 1967, and along with Espo, the Bruins received Ken Hodge and Fred Stanfield, in exchange for Pit Martin, Gilles Marotte, and goalie Jack Norris.

"That deal filled out what they needed," Rosa adds, "and with Orr along, they had something special."

After averaging two points a game his final year of junior, Orr led his team to the OHA championship and was named Most Valuable Player. The next season, his first in the NHL, he won the Calder Trophy, the award given to the Rookie of the Year. Despite only playing in 46 games the following season, 1967–68, Orr earned himself the first of an astounding eight consecutive Norris trophies, awarded to the League's best defenseman.

"The greatest player who ever played, and to be on the ice with him was just great," states Bruins netminding legend Gerry Cheevers. "Every game, every shift, you just marveled at what he could do. I'm sitting here right now watching Tiger Woods on TV, and I'm watching Tiger do things that no one else can do. I'm watching him do new things all the time, and that's exactly like Orr in his time. You loved watching him do it, and he would amaze you with the next thing you didn't know he could do. He was incredible and a tremendous team player to boot."

"Obviously he stood alone," recalls former Bruins coach and executive Harry Sinden. "He was the guy around whom we focused and how we operated."

He would amaze you with the next thing you didn't know he could do.

*below:*

*Orr in a battle for the puck with Vic Hadfield of the Penguins as Terry O'Reilly follows.*

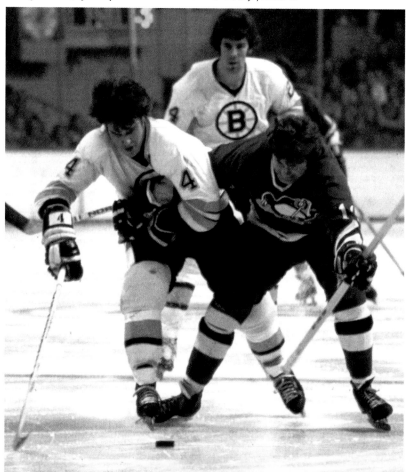

One can find Orr's list of awards and accomplishments anywhere. What's most impressive and enduring to New Englanders is the impact he had on hockey and its growth in the region.

"I work for the Department of Conservation and Recreation, what used to be the MDC," explains Cup-winning Bruins defenseman Gary Doak. "They did have 20 rinks in the area, and then about 20 more went up outside of Boston basically because of us winning the Stanley Cup in 1969–70. That's the era of Bobby and when hockey exploded in New England."

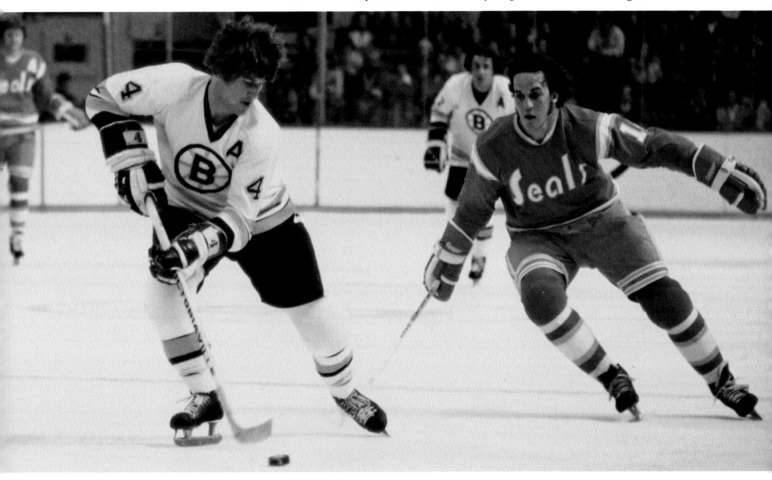

*above:*

*Orr under the watchful eye of California Seals forward Dave Hrechkosy. Phil Esposito expects a pass in the distance. Seals alternate captain and former Bruin Bob Stewart watches the play.*

Doak lived with Orr for a couple of seasons, and as a fellow Bruins D-man from 1965 to '70 (and later '72 to '81) he watched Orr's ascension firsthand.

"He's still the best player I've seen," Doak continues. "I've seen a lot of players, the players now and then. The things that he could do on the ice, he had like four or five different speeds, he played power play, he killed penalties, he did it all, and individually. I've never seen a player do all that he could do. You'd just sit on the bench and be amazed at what he could do."

Steve Babineau never worked directly with the legendary defenseman. He received his first full-time NHL press credential during Orr's last full season in Boston, and became team photographer after Orr had left. Prior to that, like all the other kids, moms, dads, staffers, and players for that matter, Babineau was simply an awestruck fan.

"When Orr hit, I was a youngster of six or seven years old, and my parents immediately gravitated to the Bruins and they used to watch all of the games on channel 38, or whatever channel they were on at that time," former Bruins' defenseman and Melrose native Frank Simonetti remembers. "You couldn't help but get sucked into the Orr era. Whatever team you played for, everybody wanted number 4, regardless of the team, growing up in the late '60s and early '70s. He changed the game of hockey, but he kind of put defensemen on the map too, where it became a position kids actually strived to play, instead of the glory positions of center or wing with scoring all the goals. Bobby made it cool to be a defenseman."

It's easy to look up to a guy who in the 1969–70 season won his first of two Art Ross trophies as the League's leading scorer with 120 points —the only defenseman ever to do it—the Hart Trophy as League MVP, the Norris, and the Conn Smythe Trophy as the playoffs' Most Valuable Player. He also scored the Stanley Cup winning goal against St. Louis, on a feed from Derek Sanderson, while being upended by Blues defenseman Noel Picard. The image of Orr flying through the air while beginning the celebration is the most famous hockey photograph of all time. Although there were almost a dozen different photos of the goal sequence from different angles, the definitive shot was taken by the late Ray Lussier, a New Hampshire resident, working for the *Boston Record American*.

*above:*

*From a shaved head as a teenager in the sixties to long flowing locks in the mid-seventies, Orr was the most popular figure around Boston. During that span he won an unprecedented eight consecutive Norris Trophies as the NHL's best defenseman.*

*above:*

*Before injuries shortened his final season in Boston and free agency took him to Chicago in 1976, Orr played a grand total of ten games with Brad Park, who came to the B's in a controversial multi-player deal for Phil Esposito in November of 1975. That's Bruin Hank Nowak (#18) in the background.*

"That was the first image everyone saw," Steve Babineau points out. "As the story goes, he was a guy who showed up unexpectedly. He was able to get the shot and get out of the building quickly. I watched the game on TV and they kept replaying that moment over and over and over. The fact that he was able to snap that moment was incredible, especially for a guy who wasn't normally a sports shooter. He found a crevice between the fans that was a prime spot most people didn't know about. It was a position I used years later."

Rumor has it another photographer had vacated the position to get a drink, go to the restroom, or to change ends. Lussier stepped in.

"The picture has been bootlegged a thousand times. It's everywhere," Babs continues. "The guys you'd expect to get it, didn't get it. Regular beat photographers, they could go to a thousand games and never get a shot like that, where Lussier showed up and gets this unbelievable shot. That's just the way it works sometimes.

"In fact, Frank O'Brien from the *Globe*, a photographer I idolized, took a sequence from up where the TV guys were, and he had all the shots, but from Orr's back and above. It was from the TV-38 overhang, from a perch above the blueline.

Not to say it was a bad shot or sequence; it was cool. It just didn't include *the* shot. I did notice that O'Brien had a motor drive camera, which shot a sequence of two or three frames a second. I was thinking the next day, 'I'd love to get one of those.'"

Babineau would later experience an incredible and opportunistic moment involving Orr's famous goal.

"Years later, when I was the team photographer, I was sitting in my office in Medford Square, and this little, old guy walks in," Babineau recalls. "His name is Ernie Cormier, and he knows who I am, and he introduces himself as a former season ticket holder and Gallery God member. From an envelope he pulls out some slides, and being busy at that moment, I was wondering if I even wanted to go through them. Well, I literally trembled when I pulled the first image out of the envelope. It was a 35mm slide transparency, on 'available light' film, from the first row of the Gallery Gods, reverse angle

*below:*

*Orr pursued by Los Angeles King Butch Goring, who would later play the last 39 games of his NHL career for Boston, and then would coach the Bruins for just more than a season. Chasing Orr was a full time endeavor for opponents, as was watching Orr for teammates and opponents alike. From left to right on bench, Bruin Dallas Smith, while on the ice it's King Bob Nevin, Gregg Sheppard, and King Bob Murdoch*

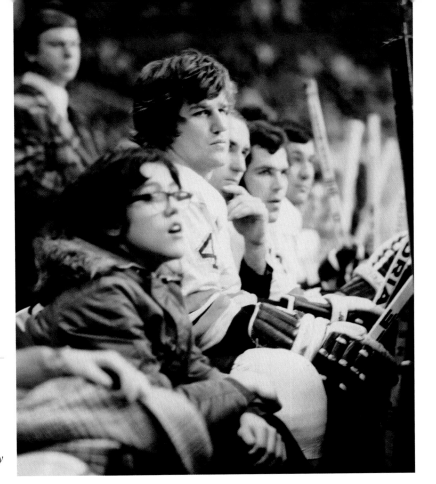

*right:*

*Orr on the end of the bench as his injury plagued career winds down in Boston. That's head coach Don Cherry in the background, and next to Orr: Dallas Smith, Don Marcotte, and John Bucyk. Question is: who's the kid? How's that for fan proximity to players.*

of the goal. He had the whole offensive zone, from about the blue line on the opposite side. You could see Lussier in the photograph. You can see every player on the ice in the picture except for [goalie Gerry] Cheevers, who's at the other end of the ice."

"Can you do anything with this?" Ernie said at the time.

"Holy moly!" reacted Babs, trembling.

"The photo standing alone needed something, so we added a shot of Orr holding the Stanley Cup, over the expanse of the white ice in the foreground," Babineau explains. "We struck a deal, made posters and prints of the two images together, and we shared a percentage of the sale when we sold the photos. It was later available on Bobby Orr's website. Might still be."

At the time of the actual goal, Babineau remained just a fanatic. He had watched the Cup win from home, and his official credential days were still a few years away. Meanwhile, Orr led the Bruins to the Cup finals in 1971, only to be upset by the Canadiens, and then back again for triumph in the 1972 final against the New York Rangers. Orr continued his Norris Trophy string, of course, and after the second Cup win, he once again earned the Conn Smythe MVP.

*left:*

*Known for his skating skill and his offensive prowess, Orr would combine all of his talents to also guard his own net, here working with Carol Vadnais against the St. Louis Blues.*

"I met him when we were both kids, with his shaved head, and then I watched him become this flying defenseman with the long hair," Babineau remembers, "and it was amazing to watch his transformation take place. He was literally toying with guys. On the penalty kill, he'd be chased around the ice. He'd skate back into his zone, pass it up, get it back, and keep going. He was so far ahead of his time, such a great skater, it seemed like the other guys were skating in sand.

"That was the pace of the game then, and then you threw this body out there; he almost seemed out of place," Babs continues. "It was like everyone was using triple-A batteries and Orr was using a car battery. No one else really did it. Coffey did it 10 years later, in terms of going end to end, but Orr did it consistently. Orr also used to set up behind the other net, something Gretzky made famous two decades later. Even when he had the knee problems, his vision of the ice surface was just unbelievable. Unfortunately for Orr, the deking and weaving left him vulnerable to being clipped in the knees and legs, and unfortunately for me, my first couple of seasons around the team were his last."

He was so far ahead of his time, such a great skater, it seemed like the other guys were skating in sand.

The aforementioned three-season period from 1969–72 may feature the most impressive sustained performance by any player in history. Orr won the League regular season MVP award all three seasons on top of the playoff accolades, and he set records for a defenseman that still stand almost four full decades later. In 1971, he finished with 102 assists and 139 points.

*above:*

*Orr and Phil Esposito in pre-game warm-ups. In their ultimate season as a defenseman/forward scoring machine in 1970-71, the two combined for 291 points (Orr 139). Orr's 102 assists that season remains the NHL's single season record for a defenseman.*

With the personal accomplishments came fame, obviously, but for Orr it may have also brought about a certain awkwardness, a shyness, an aversion for the ridiculous amount of attention and exposure, reserved in a more modern day and age for divas, rock stars, and heads of state. In the hockey world at the time, the media demands were simply overwhelming.

"I always used to say, one of my toughest jobs in the day was trying to get Orr to come out of the trainer's room to talk to the press," remembers longtime Bruins PR man Nate

Greenberg. "The reason he wouldn't or didn't all the time was that he really wanted his teammates to get proper accolades, while everybody, all the time, wanted him. Especially on the road. I remember one time we were in the Olympia in Detroit, and he was holed up in the trainer's room—in this old, old building, the room which was the size of a closet—and I used to have to go in and plead with him to come out. I knew what was going on: every night, every guy wanted to ask him the same old stuff, and he really felt like his teammates were being slighted at times. He would try to withstand it by staying in the trainer's room. He'd try to get his teammates some publicity."

To present, Orr still has never "authorized" a biography, and his desire to avoid the center of attention remains. He is active with the Bobby Orr Museum in his hometown in Ontario, an entity that inducted longtime friend, former Bruins coach, and Canadian icon Don Cherry in the summer of 2008.

Occasionally on his *Hockey Night in Canada* "Coach's Corner" segment, Cherry will still order up highlights of Orr skating around as a Bruin. "Look at him; isn't he something?" Cherry will say in awe. His on-air co-host Ron McLean oohs and aahs and reacts with "unreals" and "something elses" right along. The video and the response bring chills of sentimentality.

*above:*

*Orr about to take the puck away from Atlanta Flame Bryan Hextall. That's Bruin Don Marcotte back left, and Flame Fred "Buster" Harvey (#8) looking on.*

*above:*

*Constantly hounded by the media game to game, Orr attempted to deflect some of the attention to his teammates. Well spoken but shy, Orr would often delay post-game interviews as long as possible.*

"It seemed to me, and I don't know if anyone else felt it," adds Rosa, "that the better he played, the more difficult it was to find him in the dressing room after the game. He didn't want to take credit; he wanted the other players to get credit for the game. If you could afford to be patient, with your deadline and everything, he'd eventually come out and he'd be very gracious. You had to wait for it."

"I'm not sure what the reasons were but I do know that he was a very private, very shy guy," reflects teammate Terry O'Reilly, "who just happened to be the best hockey player in the world. And so, something had to give and he did what he had to do. I can tell you when he was asked to do something for a good cause for a charity he was there. I remember tapping him to be man of the year for the Liver Foundation one year, and you know, he didn't want to do it, but he wouldn't say no because it was a friend and a teammate asking him, and that's just the way he was. He couldn't say no."

"Bobby Orr off the ice was a great person," states 15-year Bruin and two-time Cup winner Don Marcotte. "He was one guy I was amazed with. He'd maybe meet a person one time, and then the same person five years later and he'd know the guy's name. Unbelievable. A great guy who never thought himself a superstar, always thought of the team; he wasn't the only guy on the ice; it was teamwork. When someone was called up, they were part of the family and equal to what he was, and he treated them that way."

O'Reilly possessed a unique and well-rounded perspective on Orr, having grown up a fan of the young star defenseman.

"Well, I was a lucky kid to be growing up in Oshawa and watching Bobby," remembers O'Reilly. "He was the phenom

*below:*

*Hard to say whether he's being pursued behind his own net or behind the opponent's. Orr would use the entire rink surface to his advantage, including the area behind the net in the offensive zone, long before it was claimed by another NHL great and nicknamed Gretzky's office.*

and then, as I came up through the Oshawa organized hockey rinks, I got an opportunity to play for the junior-B team. And our dressing room was just down the hallway from the junior-A dressing room, which belonged to the Generals. So I was with the junior-B and Bobby was with the Generals and I would look out the dressing room door down the hallway and see Bobby; he'd be scraping the stick and adjusting the blade and the stick. Then a couple years later I got drafted by the Bruins, got assigned to their farm team, the Boston Braves, and it was in the Boston Garden, the old Boston Garden, down the hall from the Bruins dressing

room. It was like déjà vu—I came walking out of the Braves dressing room and I look down the hall and there's Bobby Orr working on a hockey stick getting ready for practice. It was kind of neat. Then, the following year, I had an opportunity to join the Bruins and be his teammate, so it was kind of neat chasing him at practice for a few years."

"I was drafted by the Rangers, and I really only have one recollection of Orr because it was late in his career and maybe Bobby was hurt when we played them," recalls then soon-to-be Boston forward Rick Middleton, "but I remember one time in Boston Garden on the power play, Boston was killing the penalty and Orr had the puck and he wouldn't give it to us. I remember chasing him around the net. You know, the scene from many highlights, where he skates around and nobody can get him, nobody could get the puck off of him. I remember doing that, chasing him."

It's often said a good goaltender is a team's best penalty killer. In Orr's case, goaltender Cheevers disagrees.

"I think in his case the goaltender just had the best seat in the house."

In 1975, in his last "full" season in the NHL, Orr played in all 80 games, and despite being in the latter stages of his

*above:*

*Orr retired from hockey on November 8, 1978. He was inducted into the Hockey Hall of Fame less than a year later on September 12, 1979, at age 31. He remains the youngest inductee ever. Orr invited Steve Babineau to the induction in Toronto, where Babs took this never-before-published photo.*

career and being somewhat hobbled, he won the regular season scoring title for his second Art Ross Trophy. He finished with 46 goals, still the second-most ever by a defenseman in a single season, and tallied 135 points.

"I do believe he's the greatest Bruin of them all," declares Greenberg.

"Bobby is responsible for practically every American-born hockey player out here, because when he got here, all the rinks started springing up," says Middleton passionately, "and now New England is the hockey hotbed of the United States I believe, and I think every one of these American players should thank him for putting them on the map."

*below:*

*The Bruins held Bobby Orr night and retired his jersey on January 9th, 1979. Orr, alongside bull gang worker Zibby Puleio Sr., who helped unveil it, watches his banner go up.*

*above:*

*Donning # 4, Orr, arguably the greatest hockey player of all-time, addresses the Bruins faithful.*

*right:*

*Orr and former teammate John Bucyk display # 4, a sweater number many hockey fans felt should have been retired League-wide.*

**BOBBY ORR** (D) Parry Sound, ON | #4 | Some say #4 deserved League-wide retirement

| BRUINS REGULAR SEASON STATISTICS | GP | G | A | Pts | PIM |
|---|---|---|---|---|---|
| 1966–1976 | 631 | 264 | 624 | 888 | 924 |
| Bruins Playoff Statistics | 74 | 26 | 66 | 92 | 92 |

# BRUINS LEGEND:
# PHIL ESPOSITO

*above:*

*Outspoken, Espo never feared expressing his feelings as a player, a coach, or as a hockey executive. His 2003 book ruffled more than a few feathers of ex-teammates.*

*left:*

*Phil Esposito scored 1,012 points in 625 regular season games with the Bruins, and added 102 playoff points in 72 games while helping Boston win two Stanley Cups along the way.*

Of all the Bruins legends, Phil Esposito remains the most outspoken: about the game, about his time in and out of Boston, and about his life. In fact, he wrote a book about it.

"I didn't give away anyone that's still married to the same woman," states Espo, in regards to his book, *Thunder and Lightning: A No B.S. Hockey Memoir.* "If you're divorced you were free game, because I cut the hell out of myself because I'm divorced."

"I gave it to Alan Eagleson a little bit, absolutely," clarifies Espo. "I gave it to Harry [Sinden] a little bit too. Quite frankly, I didn't ever want to leave Boston. I wanted to end up my career in Boston, and that's what I wanted, and that's why I didn't go to the WHA. I thought I would end up my career in Boston, but things happen. I understand it though, because Harry had to make some tough decisions because he knew Bobby Orr was going to leave. Bobby didn't know he was going to leave at that time, but Eagleson [Orr's agent, and then the head of the NHL Players' Association] knew it, and they made the deal."

"Espo always had something to say," states former Bruins PR man Nate Greenberg. "He was outspoken. The one thing about Phil, he always wore his heart on his sleeve. No one could ever accuse him of being a phony; he was honest and outspoken."

Eight years after being acquired in "The Trade" from Chicago, Espo, along with Carol Vadnais, was sent packing to New York, for Brad Park, Jean Ratelle, and Joe Zanussi on November 7, 1975. It was a decent deal for both clubs, but one that still has Esposito a bit bitter today.

"He [GM Harry Sinden] said I would never leave Boston, or I would be there as long as he would be there," Espo states. "I shook hands with him, and I don't believe in no-trade contracts. I don't believe in them to this day. Then he traded me and I was bitter for a lot of years. I'm probably still a little upset about it—isn't that unbelievable. I was very, very sad. I didn't want to leave Boston. I could have gone to the WHA and made a million-dollar signing bonus, but I decided to stay in Boston, and give up that money, just because I loved it so much. Three weeks later I was traded, and that hurt. That hurt. That's what bothered me. Other guys like Derek Sanderson went, Johnny McKenzie went, Gerry Cheevers went....

*above:*

*Espo tries to fire a backhander past defenseman Ron Greschner with New York captain Brad Park (#2) also heading back.*

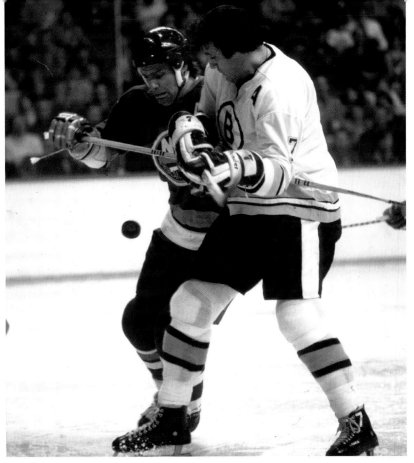

*above:*

*A battle for the bouncing puck in front between Bert Marshall of the Islanders and Esposito, who was well known for scoring "garbage goals," an arguable term, from the slot and around the crease area.*

They went, came back and he [Sinden] accepted them fine. Me, I stayed, as a loyal guy. No, that's not right."

Espo wasn't the only one upset by the deal. The fans had lost a prolific scorer, a favorite adopted son, and a two-time Cup winner.

"The guy had been a scoring machine," points out Greenberg, who was in the middle of the media maelstrom following the deal. "It was a really ballsy move by Harry Sinden, the ballsiest, and it worked out—a great deal. But at the time it created as much buzz as a Stanley Cup final. Harry had death threats. You talk about a buzz. I mean Brad Park was a good player but he was hated; he was the enemy. We traded a beloved player for a guy we hated. A lot of media was against it. Len Berman, who worked in Boston then, he was upset. He basically said any great player should spend his entire career with the same team. Now they'd laugh in his face, but back then, with Howe and others, they felt that way. D. Leo Monahan of the *Record American* took a level-headed approach. I'll never forget. He wrote, 'My heart said it was a bad deal; my head said let's wait and see.'"

One could understand the initial reaction. Before Gretzky, in terms of ridiculous offensive numbers, there was Esposito. In the 1970–71 season he tallied an unheard of 76 goals and 76 assists, a record at the time many believed would last a lifetime.

"Phil was a great centerman," states John Bucyk. "I spent a lot of time with him on the ice, particularly on the power play, and he could put the puck in the net."

"He was just one of the players you loved to play with because he hated to lose," adds linemate Ken Hodge. "You saw that in the Team Canada series [Summit 1972, when Canada beat the USSR in the eight-game series], you'd see it every day when he came to the rink. We just melded together—Cash,

He was just one of the players you loved to play with because he hated to lose.

him, and I—Cash on the one wing and me on the other and we just blended. We were just a very unselfish line and Esposito started to click, started to score goals at a rapid pace, and it didn't hurt matters that we had number 4 on defense, either. That was a big thing right there. Took a lot of pressure off."

Esposito was the leading scorer in the Summit Series and in 1972 was named Canadian athlete of the year.

Similar to the overlap with Bobby Orr, Steve Babineau's experience with Phil Esposito came early in the young photographer's career. He covered number-7 as a free-lancer, and Espo's existence in Boston came to an end prior to Babineau joining the B's staff. Of the two "overlap" legends, Babineau seems to lean the way of the defenseman.

"Esposito was successful in Boston because he played with Bobby Orr," argues Babineau. "Sure, he was on a line with Cashman and Hodge, but bottom line, the puck was coming into the net because of Bobby Orr. How many goals did Espo have that Orr assisted on?"

Orr finished with 37 goals and 102 assists that season. Ken Hodge had 43 and 62, while Wayne Cashman finished with 21 goals and 58 helpers.

"Hodgy was the guy who could just force himself in front of the net, probably the strongest guy on our team," says Esposito. "People had no idea how strong Kenny Hodge was, and how good he was in front of the net. He was in front of the net, I was 10 or 15 feet out, and Cash was the best corner man in the game, without a doubt."

Esposito drools at the possibilities that would have existed for him and his power play mates then, had the current no-hook, no-hack, no-grab rules existed.

*above:*

*At 6-foot-one, 205 pounds Espo used size and a scoring touch to remain a constant threat in the offensive zone. He was the first player in history to break the 100-point single-season scoring barrier, shattering it in 1968-69 with 126 points.*

"Our power play, we would have torn this League apart, and they never would have been able to stop Bobby," urges Espo. "Never! Never would they have been able to stop Orr, because Bobby was the greatest give-and-go guy in the history of the game. There's no way you could stop this guy unless you hooked him or interfered with him all the time, and as far as I'm concerned, in front of the net, by the hash marks and all that, man, if they just touched me and I fell down, I'd draw a penalty on the other guy, and we'd get *another* power play. These rules were made for us guys in the '70s."

"Regardless of rules, it was just a phenomenal era to be a part of Bruins hockey at the Boston Garden," adds Hodge.

Of course, the main reason was Cups—1970 and 1972—the last that Bruins fans have celebrated.

The 1970 trip to the championship ended a 12-year streak without visiting the final and a 29-year drought without the Cup. The tightest battle in the postseason came in the quarter-finals, with the Rangers pushing the Bruins to six games. The Bruins won Games 5 and 6 to close out that series, then swept Chicago and St. Louis in the semis and final, respectively, for a postseason-concluding 10-game winning streak.

Esposito set an NHL record for postseason scoring, with 13 goals and 27 points. The numbers included two hat tricks, one coming against his younger brother, Tony, in Game 1 of the Chicago series.

In 1972, after splitting the first two games of the opening series at home versus Toronto, the Bruins reeled off a nine-game winning streak. The run finished off the Maple Leafs, swept the Blues, and included the first two games of the final at home against New York. Espo had three assists in Game 1 against the Rangers and finished the postseason with 24 points, tied with teammate Orr. After the 3-0 win in Game 6 to wrap up their second Cup in three years and their fifth overall, Orr once again received the nod over Esposito for the Conn Smythe Trophy as postseason MVP.

It was 1972 and Espo and the boys were living large.

"Those teams then, to sum it up, one thing they had was a hell of a lot of fun!" says Greenberg.

Among the list of adjectives to describe Esposito—scorer, entertainer, pot-stirrer—one could also add snowbird. He's gradually moved south, to where he still resides today, in the Sunshine State.

"I lived mostly in Sault Ste. Marie [Ontario, his hometown], but New York was second. I lived there [New York] for 17 years," Espo points out. "I've been living in Florida now for about 15 years. I think Florida will be the place, but Sault Ste. Marie is still close to the heart; I lived there the longest. But the greatest time of my life was in Boston, without a doubt. I mean, I was on top of my game, we were winning, we had a great team, and a great bunch of guys. The fans were fantastic. It was just the greatest time of my life."

His production while in New York, although not as prolific as when he was in Boston, remained consistent. Esposito averaged better than a point a game during his first five years in Manhattan.

While a player for the Rangers, Esposito kicked off a sequence of events one night in Manhattan that will remain etched in hockey fans' memories forever. Two days before Christmas

*above:*

*Bobby Orr and Esposito celebrate yet another tally. Espo will be the first to admit, his huge point totals came with a great deal of help from defenseman number 4.*

in 1979, in the waning moments of a game against his former club, Espo had a chance to beat Gerry Cheevers on a breakaway to tie a game with the Bruins. (Terry O'Reilly's perspective follows in Chapter 6.) As he skated in, a fan threw a tennis ball at him, and although it didn't hit Espo, it distracted him enough to screw up the play. After failing to score, Espo smashed his stick on the ice in disgust with a two-armed tomahawk chop, skated to the bench, and headed to the dressing room. After he (and Cheevers) had departed, a melee began in one corner between the remaining Bruins and the Rangers. Then some Rangers fans became involved. One threw a punch at Stan Jonathan and stole his stick, and the Boston players ended up in the stands wrestling with the spectators. Espo had nothing to do with it.

*below:*

*Orr and Esposito discussing strategy or developments. John Bucyk is over Orr's shoulder. The patch on Orr and Bucyk's shoulder commemorates the 50th anniversary of the Bruins.*

"It [the tennis ball] went just over Cheesie's head, and it bounced right in front of me and I took my eye off it [the puck], and I looked away, and by the time I looked back up, Gerry was charging, and I didn't have anything to do with the puck, and it ticked me off, to tell you the truth," recalls Phil. "And I remember after the game, him and I were in the

*left:*

*Looking for a tip or rebound against Atlanta Flames goalie Dan Bouchard.*

*above:*

*Always the conversationalist, Esposito as a New York Ranger chats with former teammate, Bruins goalie Gerry Cheevers during a game at the Garden.*

hallway in Madison Square Garden, and Gerry comes out of his dressing room with a beer, and I come out of our dressing room with a beer, and we look and I said, "What's going on?" and he said, "I don't know," and somebody said there was a fight in the stands. Cheesie looked at me and I looked at him and he goes, 'Ahhh, the hell with it.'"

In his sixth season in New York, then in his late 30s, Espo hung up the skates midway through the 1980–81 season after tallying 20 points in 41 games. He would become assistant coach, have two stints as head coach, and later be named general manager for the Rangers.

> The greatest thing I've ever done in the game of hockey was getting the franchise to Tampa.

Soon enough, there'd be good reason for Espo's continued migration. After three years as GM in New York, where he earned the nickname "Trader Phil" for his proclivity to make deals, Esposito headed much further south to spearhead the effort to bring Tampa Bay an NHL expansion franchise. Despite intense competition from Peter Karmanos and Compuware (who eventually bought and moved the Hartford Whalers to Carolina), Esposito and his group prevailed.

"The greatest thing I've ever done in the game of hockey was getting the franchise to Tampa," insists Esposito. "I was completely out of my element. No one gave me one bit of a chance, and I like that, because when people underestimate me is when I'm at my best. I just did whatever I had to do to get the franchise. Sometimes in life you do that. Did I ever think that I would ever leave this place [Tampa front office]?... No. I never thought I would stay general manager. Eight years was a long time. I never wanted to do it for eight years. I just wanted to get the team set, but we had problems in the '95–'96 season when we built the building. We just didn't have enough money to pay some of the players. So, obviously we did some things we didn't want to do: trading players and getting rid of guys that were making too much money. That put us back two to three years. I'm convinced we could have won the Stanley Cup in 10 years, and that was the game plan going in. I get a big kick out of people who said Esposito had no plan when he came here. Well, I can tell you, I plan everything."

*below:*

*Esposito attacks the net of the Bruins arch-nemesis, goalie Ken Dryden and the Montreal Canadiens. That's defenseman, ex-Bruin Don Awrey behind Espo.*

ESPOSITO

*above:*

*Among his superstitions, Espo kept lucky charms hanging from the top of his stall in the Bruins dressing room at the Garden.*

Esposito lists his other greatest thrill as having his jersey retired and hung at Boston Garden. A dozen years after he was dealt, the man who earned five NHL scoring titles, two Hart Trophies as MVP, and two player-balloted Lester B. Pearson MVP awards while in Boston would get his due.

The celebration took place on December 3, 1987, three years after he was inducted into the Hockey Hall of Fame, and included an unforgettable turn of events. Ray Bourque, who wore Espo's number 7, had already played eight seasons in the NHL, had become a prolific scorer and was one of the League's best defensemen, decided to give Esposito a big surprise. Bourque had agreed to switch numbers to 77, to allow Espo to retain exclusive retirement rights to his number. Bourque skated out to Esposito wearing number 7, stopped, turned around, and peeled off the sweater to reveal "Bourque 77." He then handed Espo his number saying, "This is yours." Bourque and others joke it's the only time they've ever seen Esposito speechless.

"I watched him taking it off, and if you've ever seen replays you see me looking at him, and I said, 'What the hell are you doing?'" Phil recalls. "And he said, 'This is yours, big guy; it's not mine. It never should have been mine; this is yours.' I'm looking at him, like, is someone trying to play a joke on me here or what? We had talked about it that yeah, we'd put the number up, with my name on it, and when Raymond retired, they'd put his name on it. I had no problem with that and Bourqee had no problem with that, but when he did that, man, that really...I'll never forget that as long as I live."

On December 3rd, 1987, on Espo's jersey retirement night, Ray Bourque shocked everyone, especially Esposito, by taking sweater number 7 off his own back, presenting it to Phil for his exclusive retirement, and then switching to number 77 for the rest of his career. Espo is stunned, he addresses the crowd with great appreciation, while Bourque is praised by the Bruins alumni.

| **Phil Esposito** (C) Sault Ste. Marie, ON \| #7 \| First NHLer with a 100+ point season | | | | | |
|---|---|---|---|---|---|
| **BRUINS REGULAR SEASON STATISTICS** | **GP** | **G** | **A** | **Pts** | **PIM** |
| 1967–1976 | 625 | 459 | 553 | 1,012 | 512 |
| Bruins Postseason Statistics | 71 | 46 | 56 | 102 | 81 |

CHAPTER

# BRUINS LEGEND:
# TERRY O'REILLY

*above:*

*O'Reilly was the emotional leader of the Bruins as a player, and later as head coach. Despite his intensity and his success on the ice, his humility was one of his greatest attributes.*

*left:*

*Terry O'Reilly with his eyes on the prize. Whoever stood between Taz and the puck, he went through him or them to get it. The name "Taz" came from his ferocious style and tenacity, after the Tasmanian Devil on the Bugs Bunny cartoons.*

Every Boston Bruins name hanging in the rafters of the TD Banknorth Garden also resides in the Hockey Hall of Fame, except for two. One of those two, Terrence O'Reilly, hangs in the rafters simply because number 24 utterly and completely embodied what it meant to be a Boston Bruin. And although O'Reilly could be recognized in hockey's ultimate shrine for what should be the same criteria, he isn't; and maybe it doesn't matter.

He is the underrated talent, the fighter, the blue-collar worker, the emotional powder keg, the inspirational leader that belongs exclusively to Boston.

"There's nobody like the guy that I ever played with or against," states former Bruins roommate Mike Milbury. "Completely totally focused and relentless, to the point where we'd come back after a game on the road to the hotel room, and some of the guys would go out for a beer, for something to eat, but he'd come back to the room and do push-ups and sit-ups. I mean, it was really kind of sick when you think about it, but once the puck was dropped there was nobody you'd want more on your side than Terry: a physical player and a heady player, who was completely committed to winning the game."

"He played on a line with Peter McNab and John Wensink and they were a terror in the League for many, many years," points out former teammate Rick Middleton. "Most teams didn't want to come into Boston Garden and face that line, trust me. There was the unwritten O'Reilly rule [among opponents] that you might as well let him win the first one [fight], because he's just gonna keep coming back until he beats you. A lot of guys would just let him win the first one so they wouldn't have to fight him again."

The same intangible that helped him will his team to wins on so many nights is the same intangible that allowed the awkward forward to will his way into the League in the first place.

"I always said that I fell into the business," O'Reilly laughs. "You know my skating style was so rustic that I spent more time literally on the ice; before Phil Esposito nicknamed me Taz after the Tasmanian Devil, my nickname was Zamboni. And it was because I cleaned the ice with [my body]."

"He could barely skate the first couple years he was in the League," affirms Milbury, "and I'm one that's living in that glass house who shouldn't be throwing stones, but he made himself a player; he willed himself to be a player. He scored more than 90 points one season, which is a remarkable feat. He spent countless hours before practices; he'd play with anybody that was on the ice. He would go one-on-one, just work drills, and he developed himself into a world-class player, and certainly a player that is unforgettable in Bruins fans' memories."

> He made himself a player; he willed himself to be a player.

*below:*

*O'Reilly fights his way to the net against Buffalo Sabres Jerry Korab (left) and Andre Savard.*

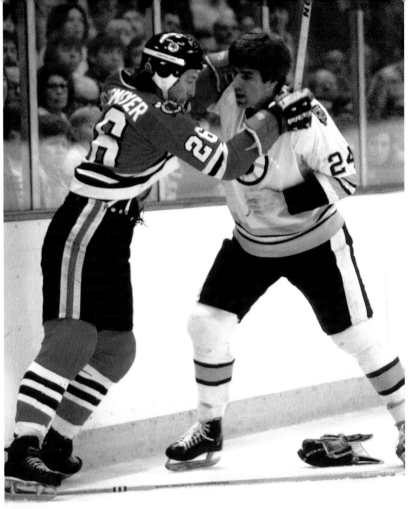

*above:*

*Bob Hoffmeyer of the Black Hawks doesn't look too excited, or ready, for an O'Reilly left.*

*below:*

*Terry O'Reilly as a Bruins rookie, after playing junior in Oshawa and 60 games with the AHL Boston Braves.*

Much of a player's success can be attributed to his mental makeup, reflected in his desire, his competitiveness, his selflessness, his ability and desire to lead, and his mental toughness. In O'Reilly's case, his drive overcame his physical limitations.

"Terry was a real team player, a hard worker, did everything he had to," says Hall of Fame teammate John Bucyk. "He was a real plus to any team. I'll tell you what, a big leader for the Bruins."

"People should look at what hard work does for you," states Hall of Fame ex-Bruin and current team Vice President Cam Neely. "We've all played with guys who had more talent, but the work ethic might not have been there and they didn't last very long. And then you have a guy like Terry who didn't have the best skating ability, and came in and worked extremely hard and obviously was a very physical, tough player, and ended up being a huge asset to the Bruins organization."

O'Reilly's performance and attitude three decades ago actually remains a benchmark for the Bruins. As Neely suggests, O'Reilly can still be an example for current players, regardless of whether or not the rules or style of play have been altered. He set an example for others that transcends any era.

"No doubt, I don't think you're going to find much tougher than Terry O'Reilly," says Bruins Head Coach Claude Julien. "He's one of those guys, you knew what you would get every night, and no doubt you'd want him on your team more than you'd want him against you. He was a pretty intimidating individual, and I don't think I ever saw him back down, and I don't think you'll ever see him back down even to this day. So he brought to the Bruins what the Bruins have always wanted, and that's an identity. In Boston, they like their teams to be tough, and when you look at Terry O'Reilly, that's exactly what he brought."

"Well, we'd like players like him, certainly," adds General Manager Peter Chiarelli. "You're not gonna get a player just like him, but you can certainly get a lot of the characteristics that he has—his fortitude, his forecheck, you know he liked to drop them, he went to the net; and he got a lot of goals in dirty areas. There are a lot of parts to how he played that I'd like to have in players, and we look to get."

Current Bruins Assistant Coach Craig Ramsay remembers the experience of playing O'Reilly firsthand, as a defenseman for the division rival Buffalo Sabres for 14 years.

"It was a long night, I can certainly say that. But one of the great things about Terry, and everyone knows how tough he was, was that he was one of those real honest tough guys. He hit you hard, but he didn't mind if you hit him back. You could play a physical game against him; you just couldn't do anything cheap, and he was always there to defend his teammates if there were cheap shots going on. In our day, there was a lot of it. Terry would jump right back in there," Ramsay states. "I always enjoyed my nights against Terry. I knew I was going to get hit, and I knew I would kind of get pounded around, but it was a fair, honest night. I always thought body contact was a great part of the game, even as a smaller player. I always thought those confrontations on the puck were what made our game very special. Against Terry, it was a long night but a very good night against a good hockey player."

*above:*

*A bear hug was one technique used to stop Taz, utilized here by Maple Leafs defenseman Bob McGill. That's Toronto goalie Allan Bester holding the post.*

"I loved hockey," O'Reilly says, explaining his basic motivation, "and at the time, that was hockey to me. I mean, that was hockey to everybody. A good, balanced, winning team, if you look at every team that won the Stanley Cup back in that era, had such a balance of skill and toughness. You know,

*above:*

*A 1975-76 shot of Guy Lapointe (#5) and Pierre Bouchard of the Canadiens versus O'Reilly at the Montreal Forum.*

the Montreal Canadiens, probably one of the best teams in the history of the game, won six Cups back in the '70s, and if you look at the tough part of their team they had, it was very well sustained. The Bruins, when they won their two Cups in '70 and '72, had a very tough contingent to their team. The Philadelphia Flyers won two Cups and they were a very physical team, and the Islanders didn't become a championship team until they added some toughness with Gord Lane and a few guys like that. Gillies, Nystrom, Howatt—that part of the game has to be addressed."

Young hockey fans now, witnessing clips of '70s-style "physical hockey," would likely be in for a big surprise. Hockey in those days featured line melees and bench-clearing brawls.

"Those were crazy," remembers O'Reilly, a man often found in the middle of the action. "You didn't know what was going to happen. We had one in Philadelphia that bled over onto the off-ice and into the runways and into the hallway behind...that connected the dressing rooms. I think [Paul] Holmgren and Wayne Cashman went at each other in the hallway, so both teams got in there and got onto the cement, more so our team than the Flyers.

"We were announced to start the next period," Taz continues. "We were trickling out because we were having our skates addressed with the sharpener. Well, the Flyers had more players on the ice, and it re-ignited on the ice, but we were vastly outnumbered. So I remember coming down the runway, after getting my skates touched up, to be met by three Philadelphia players. As soon as I came through the gate, I had a Flyer grab my left arm, my right arm, and they threw me down on my back, pinned my knees behind me, and the third guy got on my chest!" O'Reilly laughs. "I had three guys, and I couldn't even move my arms off the ice, so...I didn't do well in that one!"

Fortunately for O'Reilly, his reputation, and his on-ice way with words, defused the situation.

"Oh, it seemed like a lifetime [until our reinforcements showed up]," O'Reilly recalls. "I had to talk my way out of it. I said something like, 'OK, you got me, do what you have to do, but I've got all three of your numbers and I'll talk to you later.' That's all I said. Well, either they didn't want to hit me or someone else came to my rescue because I ended up getting out of it without getting badly hurt. I have to say, more to their credit, they just decided it wasn't the thing to do, but they did have me neutralized!"

*above:*

*O'Reilly was a Bruin for one game in 1971-72 and then for 13 straight seasons through 1984-85.*

*above:*

*Taz with the fat lip/cut lip combo, talking with interim head coach Harry Sinden.*

Not an easy task.

"Taz had both sides of the word *fear* covered. He was fearless, and you feared him," states former Boston forward and current NESN TV commentator Andy Brickley. "In the day, that was a big part of the National Hockey League, where intimidation was a big factor."

"Oh, there were a lot of guys in the League that I scrapped with that I didn't look forward to playing because I," O'Reilly thinks for a moment, "chances are, I was going to have a scrap with them. We had that one series against the Islanders [in 1980] where every time I looked up, Clark Gillies was on the ice against me. He was—I'm not sure how much younger he is than me, a few years younger [3]—but he was bigger, stronger, longer reach; other than that, I owned him." O'Reilly laughs. "But it was a tough match-up for me. All I could do was just try to get a good hold on him and hang on until the ride was over. I fully respected what he was doing for his team, and he was a great hockey player. I mean, that was...the New York Islanders having a guy like Clark Gillies, that combination of skill and toughness, was one of the reasons why they won so many championships."

It was earlier in that same regular season at Madison Square Garden, on December 23, 1979, against the other New York squad, that Taz and his teammates had their most infamous skirmish.

"What started it was the Rangers and the Rangers fans were very frustrated," explains O'Reilly. "I think the final score was 4-3; it was a one-goal game. Esposito had a breakaway for the Rangers in the last minutes of the game and I don't think he got a shot on net. I think he came down on Cheevers and the puck slid off his stick into the corner. He slammed the stick and broke it. So we're on our way home for Christmas, it's December 23rd and we've got three days off, which feels like two weeks during hockey season. It's three days off where you don't have to go to the rink and we've got a plane waiting for us, so we want out of there. But the buzzer goes, and we get on the ice to congratulate each other. We're headed down to get off the ice and some of the Rangers players started pushing and shoving us out of frustration, so there's a little bit of a melee going on. I didn't think it was going to turn into anything, and Stan Jonathan and one of the Rangers players were over against the side wall. The side wall glass was only two feet tall at the time, and this drunk fan standing up swung one of the hardest sucker punches you've ever seen. He, he just swung down and hit Stan right in the face, and he [Stan] covered up. The guy grabbed his stick, pulled it out of his hands and started swinging it like a machete. I was maybe 15 feet away and you know this guy is gonna hit Stan, steal his stick, and then disappear into the crowd, so I just sort of snapped, and I stepped over the glass as he was swinging the stick. I don't know what I was saying or thinking, but I went in and grabbed him around the waist and got him into a sort of a half nelson and I held him until the Madison Square Garden security came along and took him from me and arrested him. But when I had him, everybody [fans] closed in on me and then my teammates came over and chased everybody out. I felt like a quarterback in a pocket. I, you know, I looked up and I was just surrounded by black and gold."

O'Reilly received an eight-game suspension for leading the way. Peter McNab and Mike Milbury, famous for ripping a shoe off a Rangers fan and trying to whack him with it, both picked up six games.

He'd charge at me, and he looked like the front end of a Mack truck.

The ensuing time off for the players led to a magical encounter for team photographer Steve Babineau. With the next five Bruins games on the road, and the three players not traveling, it led to the perfect opportunity for some pickup hockey at the Garden.

"I played with the three of them and a few other people in a pickup game," Babineau remembers. "They broke into the electrician room and turned the lights on. O'Reilly is going crazy having a good time, but scaring the hell out of me. I'd go pick up the puck behind the net and bring it out to the circle and he'd charge at me, and he looked like the front end of a Mack truck. A few times I'd hide behind the net and he'd race in and he could go either way around after me. To me, he

*right:*

*Early in the 1979-80 season, left to right, Peter McNab, O'Reilly, and Mike Milbury at the old Garden.*

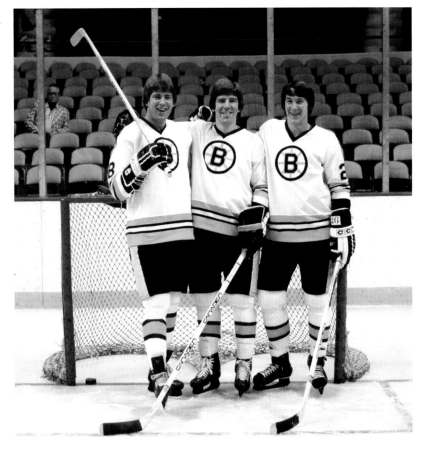

looked like my motor home. It was scary. One time, he dumped the puck, came down toward me doing the theme from *Dragnet*, 'duh-duh-duh-hh, duh-da-da-da-duhhhhh.' He did a baby flip in the corner just so I'd have to pivot and chase the puck with him following. It may have been the *Jaws* theme, like 'duhh-duhh, duh-duh, duh-duh, du-du, du-du, d-d,' faster and faster. He's following me and I'm wettin' my pants laughing and scared at the same time. It was unbelievable."

"I used to go down there a lot then, whether I had a slight injury and was left behind with the team, if the team went on the road, or I had a day off," O'Reilly recalls. "I was always at the Garden looking for ice, when we skated with some of the bullgang members [Zamboni drivers, ice men] and played pickup hockey. Even when I was coaching we were playing two-pass, you know, with anybody that wanted to come on the ice. We'd have our morning skate and then I would have the black aces stay out, the guys that weren't gonna dress. Sometimes it would be Jay Miller, or [Lyndon] Byers. We usually had an extra forward or an extra defenseman, so they needed to be out there and do some extra skating. We made them play two-pass with us.

"The other place I loved to go was the carpenter shop; that was one of my favorite places in the old Boston Garden," Taz continues. "It was just...I knew the guys, Paul, he was one of the top carpenters there at the time, and I'd go down and watch what he was working on and fixing up. I learned a few tricks from him and it was just a nice room. The carpenters' room was down in the corner, right by where the ramp came up and it had 8- or 10-foot-tall windows all around the two

*above:*

*O'Reilly turned himself into a great hockey player and became strong on his skates due to constant practice and use of ice time. His work ethic was as relentless as his desire to win.*

sides of it. So it was probably the brightest room in the building; it was like a solarium. So it was a nice place to go and hide for a little while."

O'Reilly's interest in carpentry continues today. He designed and helped rebuild his home on the North Shore, a multi-unit, five-story building, and most of the cabinetry within.

Since another taste of the NHL coaching ranks as an assistant with the Rangers from 2002 to 2004 after a 13-year hiatus, it would appear O'Reilly's desire to be involved has waned. He says he's looking to relax and enjoy retirement outside of Boston.

*below:*

*O'Reilly gets the best of Mike McEwen of the New York Rangers. Not that it was the case here, but if someone beat him in a fight, he'd fight 'em again.*

"I know when he went into New York, he has spoken of this, how difficult it was being an assistant coach on a team that had guys that he didn't think were giving it their all, and didn't care enough about playing this great game," confides Andy Brickley. "He felt like his hands were tied, that he couldn't approach them the way he would have been able to had he been a head coach in that situation."

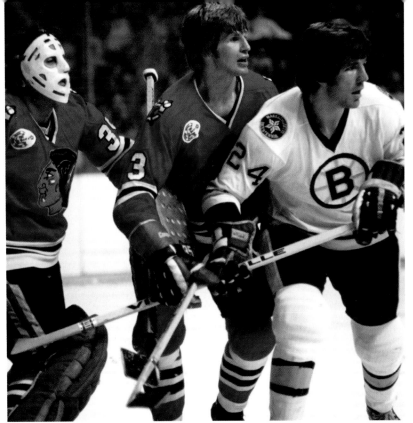

*right:*

*Blackhawks goaltender Tony Esposito being screened by O'Reilly and Chicago defenseman Keith Magnuson*

"I don't think the basic ingredients change a lot, but since I have been out of the game so long, except for the short stint in New York," O'Reilly explains, "I don't know the players anymore. I played for 12, 13 years before I coached the first time, and I knew the personnel in the whole League. The only ones I had to become familiar with were the draft picks that came up, and I was in the same boat as everybody else. But you know, there's a whole new breed of hockey player now, and with the new rule changes, I think there is more to the coaching than in the days of old when there was more of an emotional key to it. I think that's why Don Cherry was such a good coach. I think the right balance is somebody that's a good emotional motivator and somebody that can read personalities and the mood of the team, and somebody that's a real X-and-O technician. In my turn at the bat I had John Cunniff, and he was a great tactician. He just had the answers for everything—power play, penalty killing—and once we established our system, I was the guy that maintained the level, the level of input that we put into it."

Via humility, O'Reilly mentioned only Cherry as a solid emotional leader. The man he left off that short list was himself.

"He was my coach for one year," recalls Brickley. "Obviously I saw him play. Amazing that he would, from the very first minute of his NHL career to his last minute of his NHL career, he never stopped fighting. I don't mean dropping the gloves all the time. I mean fighting for every inch on the ice that he thought was his. And to have played for him as a

*left:*

*O'Reilly became captain of the Bruins in 1983-84 and held the honor for two seasons.*

coach, I mean, we had a great room. It was hard to get a word in edgewise with all the characters we had in our room, but Terry O'Reilly was our emotional focal point. That's unbelievable for a head coach. I mean he was so intense as a head coach, I can't imagine what he was like as a player. I didn't have that good fortune of playing with him. I did play against him, but he was our emotional leader as the head coach in the locker room and that's rare."

"As a coach, he was the same: passionate, passionate man for the sport of hockey and the will to win," adds Rick Middleton. "I watched some old clips not too long ago with him coaching and banging the glass. I always felt bad for the fans sitting in the first row because all of a sudden out of nowhere he'd just bang the glass, and they'd all jump."

I had the privilege to watch Terry as a player and I had the privilege to play under him when he was coach," adds Bob Sweeney, for six years a Bruins forward. "I thought Terry and John Cunniff as coaches were a great team, a great tandem. Terry was one of the best motivators that I ever came across. John Cunniff knew the game better than any coach that I ever played with. It was a great combination of motivation and tactics that I think brought the most out of us. That's the reason why in 1988 we went to the final. We may not have been the most talented team, but we were the best prepared team, we were the best conditioned team, and that's the reason we went all the way to the final."

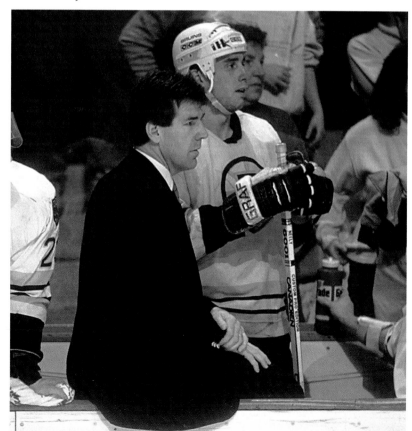

*left:*

*"Emotional leader as the head coach … and that's rare," describes Terry O'Reilly as the coach of the Bruins for almost three full seasons beginning in November 1986.*

O'Reilly's regular season coaching record finished up with 115 wins, 86 losses, and 26 ties. In the postseason, his teams lost in the first round, lost in the Stanley Cup final, and then lost in the second round.

For all of his efforts as a player and a coach and for his dedication to the "Black and Gold," O'Reilly received the ultimate honor on October 24, 2002: jersey retirement. Fittingly, he entered the event by wading through the fans in the stands, and then through the penalty box.

He was so intense as a head coach, I can't imagine what he was like as a player.

"It was a fantastic honor," O'Reilly recalls. "I had mixed feelings. It's a great honor to have my number up there, but I look at the guys that are up there—Bobby Orr, Phil Esposito, Ray Bourque, Cam Neely, Milt Schmidt—there's some amazing players up there. So I... sometimes I look up and think that I snuck in, and I look at some players that I played with—Brad Park, Rick Middleton, Wayne Cashman, you know, great players in their own right. And I don't see my career as being superior to theirs. In fact, they were my teammates and friends. So I wish everybody that I played with could be up there. But I'm not going to complain!" he chuckles.

"He's one of a kind. They threw the mold away," proclaims former Lunch Pail Gang teammate and tough guy John Wensink. "Talk about covering up for one another and leadership, he was absolutely number one. He's our oldest daughter's godfather and a super guy. Terry and I don't keep in touch that much, I'm not a big phone person. But it's funny. I hadn't seen Taz for a few years, we got together with the alumni in Phoenix, and it was like we never missed a beat. We just carried our conversation like we just had it yesterday, and to me that's a good friend."

*above:*

*Former Bruins coach Don Cherry with O'Reilly, the epitome of the Lunch Pail Gang, at O'Reilly's sweater retirement ceremony.*

Besides the wonderful long-term relationships and the jersey retirement, O'Reilly has a not-so-delightful reminder of his career: the pieces of Terry O'Reilly that really aren't Terry O'Reilly.

"Well, the teeth are all paid for," Taz says, laughing. "I did have bilateral hip replacement; it'll be three years in March, and they've been working pretty good, you know. It's amazing that if someone told me that I was going to have both my hips cut out of my body and replaced with metal, that I'd feel as good as I do…. But, it's a fad. Bobby has two new knees, Bobby Orr. Brad Park just had his second knee replaced in November of '07, so he's just getting back on his feet and getting more and more mobile. All just getting ready for the golf season."

*below:*

*Taz looks ahead and leaves Rob Ramage of the Blues in a bind.*

The injuries are just another long-term example of Terry O'Reilly paying the price—something his fans and his cohorts will never forget.

"Growing up here, and just watching Terry O'Reilly running around the ice throttling guys, I mean, every kid who grew up a Boston Bruins fan wanted to be Terry O'Reilly," proclaims Billerica, Massachusetts native and 17-year NHL veteran Tom Fitzgerald. "Number 24 was everybody's favorite player really—you take Bobby Orr, Phil Esposito and those guys—but everybody loved the way Terry O'Reilly played, because every time he stepped on the ice he gave it everything he had."

Hall of Fame defenseman and Bruins great Ray Bourque sums up Terry O'Reilly unequivocally: "The toughest player I ever played with and the best coach I've ever played for."

above:

*Fitting for "every fan's" favorite Bruin, O'Reilly entered the rink for his jersey retirement through the crowd and then through the penalty box.*

right:

*October 24, 2002, number 24 heads to the rafters. Evan and Connor, Terry's sons, assist with the effort.*

below:

*left to right, Don Cherry, Connor O'Reilly, Evan O'Reilly, Bobby Orr, Milt Schmidt, O'Reilly, John Bucyk, and Raymond Bourque.*

**TERRY O'REILLY** (RW) Niagara Falls, ON | #23, 24 | The embodiment of a Bruin

| BRUINS REGULAR SEASON STATISTICS | GP | G | A | Pts | PIM |
|---|---|---|---|---|---|
| 1971–1985 | 891 | 204 | 402 | 606 | 2,095 |
| Bruins Postseason Statistics | 108 | 25 | 42 | 67 | 335 |

# 7

# BRUINS LEGEND: RAY BOURQUE

*above:*

*A rare image of Ray Bourque wearing number 29, his training camp number prior to his rookie season in 1979-80.*

*left:*

*Bourque right after being named captain, still number 7, below the B's banners at the old Garden. Bourque was Bruins captain from 1985 to 2000, the longest tenure in team history. He shared the honor the first three seasons with Rick Middleton.*

Just three years after the departure of Bobby Orr, Bruins fans found themselves staring at a baby-faced teenager from Saint Laurent, Quebec. Ray Bourque, drafted eighth overall by the Bruins in 1979, would develop into the NHL's next iconic defenseman. There were many great D-men in the '80s, but Ray Bourque was in a league by himself.

For 21 seasons, Bourque donned the Spoked B, and Steve Babineau was on hand to capture all of the great moments.

"I've lost track of the records and of the record-breaking moments," Babs points out. "I have to check the old calendar and match things up all of the time. Let's see, was that the assists records photo, was this when he broke the Bruins scoring record, I remember this one, I remember that one. It goes on and on."

There is one simple way to summarize the various records. Ray Bourque is the all-time leading scorer among NHL defensemen: in assists (1,169), in goals (410), and in points (1,579).

"Those are the obvious things that people, fans, and everybody came to appreciate about Raymond," points out Don Sweeney, a longtime teammate and D partner. "He was an elite player, but they didn't necessarily realize the behind-the-scenes things he did day-to-day for his teammates—his approach to the game, his preparation, his commitment, every

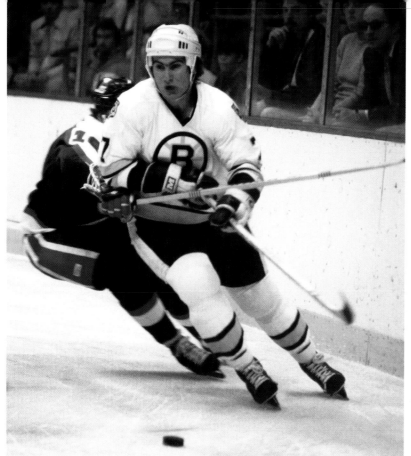

*left:*

*Bourque playing in his first NHL game on October 11, 1979, against the Winnipeg Jets at the Garden, being pursued by winger Larry Hopkins. Bourque scored in his first game.*

shift. When your best players are your hardest working players, it sets a precedent; it really sets a foundation for your organization. That's what he was. He was an absolute cornerstone. When you go to build a franchise you think about a few players, and he fits that bill."

In 1998, prior to leaving Boston and winning a Cup in Colorado three years later, Bourque was rated as the 14th greatest player of all time by *The Hockey News*, in its definitive list. The accolades had stacked up. A five-time Norris Trophy winner as the NHL's best defenseman, Bourque was voted to the midseason NHL All-Star Game a record 19 consecutive seasons. He retired with the second-most assists in NHL history. Bourque remains the Boston Bruins all-time leading scorer.

God knows if I was going to make the team or not, but if you were Bruins property, you were treated great by all the players.

"You also look at the unannounced things that he would do when a young kid would come to training camp," Sweeney continues. "He'd be the first one to walk over. Rather than have the kid look at his toes as he walked past, Ray would be sticking out his hand or inviting him over to dinner. It didn't matter—if you were wearing the sweater he was wearing, then you were a friend to him and a teammate. To me, those are the things that stood out an awful lot."

"One of the biggest pleasures for me was walking into my first training camp and having Ray Bourque walk up to me and say…and actually introduce himself," former Bruins defenseman Bob Beers describes. "I'm looking at him, thinking, 'I know who you are; you don't need to tell me who you are.' And it was tough to get over…being in awe of the guys around you."

above:

*Two practically identical poses, a decade apart. Bourque in 1986-87, and Bourque in 1995-96. Teammates are different, jersey number is different, the building is different, the helmet brand is different, and his stick blade is up as a veteran. Early shot: Keith Crowder is to the left. Later shot: Alexei Kasatonov is photo right.*

The common trait for Bourque and the other great Bruins players: an unconditional devotion to the Spoked B.

"It's tradition—a winning tradition—and pride," Bourque states emphatically. "I came here in 1979, and the year before they had lost the semi-finals to Montreal in overtime. They were a great team that had some great runs throughout the whole '70s and late '60s. They were really one of the dominant teams, a team rich in tradition and character and all the things you talk about with winning traditions: guys sticking up for each other, being one big family, really feeling for one another. From day one when I got here, I just remember walking into that locker room or meeting the guys just before camp and them making me feel like I was already part of the team. God knows if I was going to make the team or not, but if you were Bruins property, you were treated great by all the players. That started with the captain—that was Wayne Cashman back then—Gerry Cheevers, Jean Ratelle, Terry O'Reilly. Brad

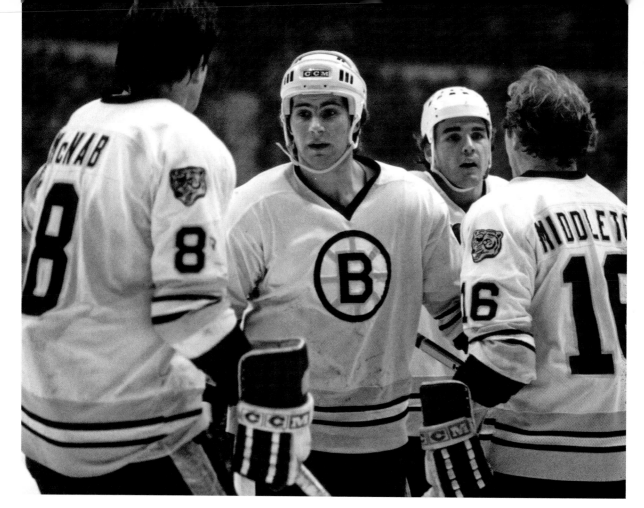

*above:*

*Bourque celebrates a goal early in his first season with teammates Peter McNab, Mike O'Connell, and Rick Middleton.*

Park was incredible with me. So many great players who had great careers, but that was just passed on from generation to generation. When you got here you felt that, and it was definitely something you passed on, and you tried real hard to make other players coming in feel that, because not all organizations have it."

Longtime Bruins public relations man Nate Greenberg witnessed some of that continuity firsthand.

"I didn't see Eddie Shore, but I did see a lot of Orr. He was with us for a few years, and I remember thinking how the Bruins were blessed with great defensemen," Greenberg recalls, "and then along comes Bourque. I always said Orr was the greatest player I ever saw—he revolutionized the game— but Bourque is certainly high up on the list. He was a horse from day one. He played great, and he played as much or more than any player ever. No one played more, no one influenced the game more, and he was right there in the mix. From the day he stepped on, to the day he finished, how many games did he miss to injury? He blocked shots, he did it all, and just kept playing. Especially near the end, he didn't have some of the great players other Bruins defensemen had, and he didn't win any Stanley Cups with the Bruins, but I'd put him up against any defenseman in the '80s and '90s."

"Bourque shot the puck from the point like Orr shot the puck from the point," Babineau states. "They got open and they cranked it. Other guys cashed in."

Kevin Paul Dupont, who has covered the Bruins for the *Boston Globe* for 30 years and continues to do so, offers up possibly the ultimate praise a Bostonian can offer.

"As I say, if you want to make a case, and I have before, better than Orr," Dupont starts, "better in that it was longer, and that it was damn near perfect every time. And to the last drop. I haven't seen anyone's career in any sport like that. Great from day one, great right to the end, and look at the years. To me, I hate to use 'body of work'; it was that entire dossier, every day. Even hurt, which was minimally… he virtually never missed, his conditioning incredible—our doctors at Mass General will tell you he blew out all aerobic testing—add dedication and a total professional. The entire length, the entire portrait, I've never seen anyone like that."

Bourque also handled his other team leadership responsibilities with patience and fortitude. As captain, he was available to the media every day after practice or a game, bar none.

*above:*

*Bourque one game after losing three front teeth during the 1999-2000 season.*

"He would laugh at himself, saying he was the most boring man in North America," Dupont adds, "but that said, he had a sense of when to say something, never controversial, never with a lot of edge to it, but every game, every practice, he'd accommodate the question. We've all heard the stupid questions, we've all asked them, but he'd take the time to answer it all. Absolute professional."

It's said that there is no greater honor than the honor bestowed upon one by his peers. The respect and fame earned in the game by Bourque was rarified. Babineau recalls instances where teammates and opponents alike, hockey players yet hockey fans at the same time, were in awe of Ray Bourque's career and his presence.

"I was working between the benches when Rob Ray of the Sabres leaned over and said, 'Try to get a picture of me and Ray on the ice,'" Babineau recalls.

It was late in Rob Ray's career, and late in Bourque's Boston existence.

"Rob Ray hadn't played all night," Babineau continues. "So I said, 'When? How?'"

"I'm going out in two shifts," Rob Ray answered.

"You'll probably have to hit 'em," Babineau suggested.

"I will, I will."

During the shift, Bourque carried the puck down the right wing boards to the Buffalo blue line just as a teammate stepped offside. The whistle blew and a moment later, Rob Ray ran into Bourque.

"I was following [Rob] Ray around in my lens, panning him," Babineau remembers. "The whistle went, and a good second or two later, [Rob] Ray comes over and pushes Bourque into the glass. A scrum, kind of melee, ensued, but I got his photo or two for him."

*above:*

*Bourque holding the Prince of Wales Trophy after defeating New Jersey in the conference finals in 1988.*

*below:*

*New Jersey Devil and future Bruin Bill Guerin with the big hook on Bourque as they race for a puck at the Fleet Center.*

*above:*

*Bourque leading the offensive charge at the Garden with center Tom Fergus.*

After the game, Babineau revealed the truth to the legendary defenseman while having some fun.

"Ray, what was the deal with Rob Ray? What was that all about?" Babineau asked, knowingly.

"Yeah, what the hell *was* that? I don't know," Bourque answered.

"I'll tell you what it was: he had set it up. He was trying to get me to take a picture of him with you."

"You're kidding me," Bourque responded with a grin.

Dave Shaw, who had played with Boston, and was later with Tampa Bay, did the same thing.

"Hey Babs," Shaw said as he leaned by the bench, "get a shot of me and Bourque together, would you? Right after the commercial is over."

"But Dave, you're a defenseman, he's a defenseman, you're on the opposite ends of the ice," Babs replied.

> To see his whole career unfold… when we first started shooting him, nobody knew that young Raymond Bourque was gonna turn into Ray Bourque, Hall of Famer.

"Don't worry about it. Now, before the draw," Shaw said. "I'd love a picture."

Sure enough, Shaw immediately skated over, leaned over to Bourque and said, "Ray, look at Babs; he's taking our picture."

Players as fans, like little kids, around a legend.

"To see his whole career unfold…when we first started shooting him, nobody knew that young Raymond Bourque was gonna turn into Ray Bourque, Hall of Famer," Babineau reflects. "He became that special guy, the core of the team.

Here's a guy who I was friends with as a rookie, becoming a star. He saw my family grow up and I saw his family grow up simultaneously. When he first came to my house, he didn't have any kids. He saw my kids, and then I watched *his* kids grow up."

During Bourque's rookie year, he and his wife, Christiane, spent two hours one afternoon looking at slides in Babineau's living room. It was the start of a two-decade-long dream for the photographer.

"One weekend there was a casual day at the Garden," Babineau brightens up, "and I got to skate with the team after practice. We were screwing around. Ray was a rookie. He sent me in on a breakaway against Rogie Vachon and I top-shelfed it. To this day, it's a highlight in my life. I didn't know much about him then, but I still have memories of that moment.

"The relationship I had with Bourque and his whole career was cool, number 7 with the A, to number 7 with the C, to number 77," Babineau continues. "I could ask him to take a picture anytime, anywhere, with anybody, and he'd say yes. It was unbelievable."

"Well, I'd like to say he [Babineau] was a kid, but he was a just a little older than me," Bourque points out. "He was taking pictures at every game, and I remember going to his house on more than one occasion, just to go through all of the pictures he had taken of me, for me to pick the ones I wanted to have, to sign for people, or just to collect. I went even for other pictures, action shots with other players, that I was looking for, to have for myself. Just an incredible amount of pictures, The stuff that he's taken was truly remarkable, and he shows you the other stuff, the other pictures from the other sports, and being a sports buff, it's pretty impressive. I couldn't imagine now, you know, going through all of his stuff."

One of the most memorable moments for both men occurred in 1996, when Boston and the new Garden (then called the Fleet Center) hosted the NHL All-Star Game. The Eastern Conference won the game 5-4 on Bourque's game-winning goal, and Ray was named the game's Most Valuable Player.

*above:*

*Ray Bourque waves to the berserk Bruins faithful after winning the All-Star Game MVP honors at the Fleet Center in 1996. One of his most memorable and emotional moments for Bourque in his career, and for photographer Babineau in his 35 years.*

*below:*

*Photographer Steve Babineau with Ray Bourque during a practice scrimmage at the Garden during Bourque's rookie season.*

Brad McCrimmon

"To be the All-Star photographer, me and my son Brian hired by the League, and to have Ray win the MVP—it was fantastic," Babineau smiles. "Chris Bourque [Ray's son], then a young teenager, was in the room after the game. It was another moment for both our families, a family tie."

"He's got many, many pictures of me. I know that," Bourque adds. "I remember after my first year or two, having grown up in Montreal, trying to get some pictures that Guy Lafleur and Larry Robinson would be in. I found a great picture of Guy Lafleur and I crossing sticks on the ice. Babs is the one who took that and I've got that one on my wall."

Another fellow French-Canadian who enjoyed a big night at the Garden: Mario Lemieux.

"Mario's first game in the NHL was at the Garden and I shot that," remembers Babineau, "and his last regular season game the first time he retired was at the Garden as well. For 'Mario Night,' Ray presented him with a big lounge chair, and a seat from the old Garden. It was a special moment for Ray and it was definitely cool for me."

With any long-term relationship, be it professional, personal, or otherwise, familiarity doesn't necessarily breed contempt; it simply breeds more familiarity.

Bourque with two of his French-Canadian favorites:

*above:*

Ray with childhood hero Guy Lafleur.

*right:*

Ray with long-time friend and contemporary superstar Mario Lemieux.

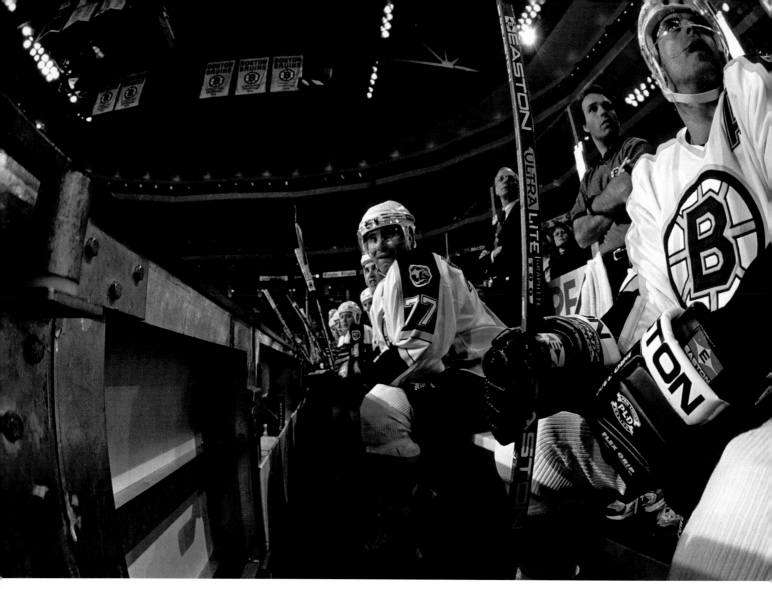

"They, the mainstays of the club treated me like a piece of furniture," Babineau points out. "I was always around. The conversations would go on whether I was standing there or not. It was relaxed, it was casual, and I had full access. If I had an idea, or needed an unusual photo, I'd just go up and say, 'Hey, can we do this photo?'

"I remember the last game during a non-playoff year," Babs continues, "We wanted to get the players getting dressed and doing their routine in the locker room. I wanted shots during the game, during the intermission. I sat in the dressing room right up until the guys went out. Don Sweeney was hurt, so I sat in his stall, next to Ray. I got Ray taping his stick, some of the other guys getting ready. I shot the equipment guys. Ray had a routine; he did his stick, did a heating pad, and then came into the room. I'm in the room with Sammy [Sergei Samsonov] and Joe Thornton. Bourque walked in."

"OK Babs, let's get going, big game, let's get going, come on, big one!" Bourque mocked. "Gotta get the shots off! Gotta take some good ones."

"He was bustin' chops, having a good time, and treating me like one of the guys, and that was cool," Babs concludes.

Staged photos, or ones taken in a controlled environment, were common. However, a great majority of Babineau's Bourque shots were taken in the completely uncontrolled environment of a real game.

"Bourque got his teeth knocked out near the end of his career," Babineau says with a grin. "He looked like hell. Lost his top chops. I was sitting there at the end of the bench, and he looks over and gives me a big smile. He knew I was there and he made this big face and smiled at me. He'd skate by every once and a while, smile, and make a face. He was so comfortable on the ice, having a good time."

*above:*

*Ray Bourque skated his way to five Norris Trophies, given each season to the NHL defenseman with the greatest all-around ability. Only three other players have won it more times than Bourque.*

Without a doubt, Bourque experienced a very successful and enjoyable career in Boston. The only thing lacking was a Stanley Cup victory. Twice, the Bruins came close. Bourque's and Babineau's first final: 1988.

The Bruins lost Games 1 and 2 in Edmonton to the Oilers by scores of 2-1 and 4-2. Boston hosted Games 3 and 4.

"The biggest disadvantage was we were playing hockey in June," Babs points out. "No air conditioning, no ventilation, they were playing the games in a fog. I mean, both teams had to deal with the same thing, but from a photographic standpoint it was a nightmare, and I'm sure it was tough for some of the fans."

The Bruins lost Game 3 6-3 and were temporarily spared a Stanley Cup final sweep by the summertime conditions at the Garden. The power went out with the score tied 3-3, and the electricians couldn't get it up and running again. The photographers thought it was their fault. Some believed the electronic strobes, strung throughout the building to act as "flashbulbs" for the photographers, commonly utilized then and today, may have pushed the energy situation to the brink.

"We thought we had done something with the strobes," Babineau remembers. "We had strobes set up in the ceiling and there were a lot of photographers. Turns out it was a generator outside. Too many generators running, the ice pack, the whole thing, they couldn't get the lights back on. Although the individual player statistics were tallied and counted, the game was scrapped. The teams moved back to Edmonton where the Oilers completed the series with a 6-3 win."

*Chapter 7*

Two years later, Bourque led his team to the final again, against the same representative from the West (Clarence Campbell Conference). Again, the B's lost. This time, the series started in Boston.

*above:*

*Classic shot of the captain putting on the brakes behind his net at the old Garden for a quick change of direction.*

"Unbelievable atmosphere," Babineau reminisces excitedly. "Everyone was wearing yellow T-shirts, and screaming their heads off. It was the ultimate way to experience a hockey game in Boston, although it was super hot in the building."

The generators held up; in fact in Game 1, they worked overtime…triple overtime.

"We were still shooting film at that time, actual film, not digital," Babs points out, "and I was literally running out of it. The game kept going and going and I was down to my last few snaps. Petr Klima, who doesn't play at all in the game, shows up on the ice. He's gung ho and has his 'jet skis' well rested. He comes out and kills us."

*below:*

*One of the most famous set of jerseys in hockey history. Bourque third jersey at top, Garden style white 77 on left, All-Star jersey from Pittsburgh on right, and an old Bourque number 7.*

Klima, who had 25 goals for Edmonton in the regular season after being acquired in early winter from Detroit but had sat on the bench most of the night, came off the pine and scored the game winner (3-2) 115 minutes and 13 seconds into the marathon.

"[Glen] Wesley had a chance to score—a glorious chance he shot over the net [in the first OT]—and we fell short," remembers then Bruins head coach Mike Milbury. "We still had a really good feeling about ourselves. But I think part of it was [goalie] Andy Moog just couldn't recover from the Game-1 loss. In Game 2, [Bill] Ranford was younger and more athletic and at one point I looked up at the board and the shots were 16-4 in the middle of Game 2, and we were down 3-2. We had our chance, but in the end they grabbed the momentum by the horns, in particular their kid line in [Martin] Gelinas, and [Adam] Graves, and [Joe] Murphy, and damaged us in the later parts of the series. We lost to a team that just grabbed it and beat us. If we win Game 1 it becomes a different series, maybe not a winning series, but at least a much longer and closer series. Anything could have happened."

The Bruins lost Game 2 at home, won Game 3 in Edmonton, and then lost the next two, and the series, four games to one.

It marked the last Stanley Cup final for Ray Bourque with the Bruins.

*below:*

*Ray Bourque celebrates a goal against the Edmonton Oilers in the 1990 Stanley Cup Final.*

A decade later, with his career in its latter stages and the Bruins not a serious contender, Bourque requested a trade for a final legitimate opportunity at winning the Cup. Harry Sinden and the Bruins honored the request, and on March 6, 2000, Bourque and Dave Andreychuk were sent to Colorado, in exchange for Brian Rolston, Martin Grenier, Sammy Pahlsson, and a first-round draft pick. On June 9, 2001, after what turned out to be his last game, Bourque and the Avalanche hoisted the Cup.

"Everyone in Boston was happy for Ray," Babineau concludes. "I know I was happy for him, and now he's living back here again. This is home."

Four years ago, Babineau had a chance to close the circle with Bourque so to speak, to tie their careers all together, from his point of view. During a charity event, the annual Bruins Wives' Carnival, Steve had his wife, Anita, approach Ray for an autograph on a framed photograph. The shot had Bourque and Babineau standing together in front of a goal— the day rookie Raymond Bourque sprung Babineau for the breakaway.

"He was speechless, dumbfounded; he didn't know what to write," Babs recalls fondly. "He couldn't believe that photograph. Understandably, given everything he's done and been through, they forget this stuff. I'll never forget it."

*above:*

*These four Bruins all won the Calder Trophy as NHL Rookie of the Year. Left to Right: Derek Sanderson (1968), Bobby Orr (1967), Sergei Samsonov holding the Trophy (1998), and Raymond Bourque (1980).*

*below:*

*Bourque returned to Boston to face the Bruins as a member of the Colorado Avalanche on March 24, 2001, in a 4-2 Colorado victory. That's Steve Babineau getting shots of Bourque at ice level.*

Brian Babineau

*right:*

Phil Esposito returns the favor, handing Bourque his number 77 for retirement on October 4, 2001, 14 years after Bourque took number 7 right off his own back and delivered it to Espo for retirement.

*above:*

Bourque in his sweater, acknowledging the crowd prior to making his jersey retirement speech.

*right:*

Number 77 begins its journey skyward. Left to right: Ray's wife Christiane, and kids Melissa, Ryan and Chris, watch dad as he unveils the banner.

| Ray Bourque (D) Montreal, QC \| #7, 77 \| The NHL's all-time greatest scoring D-man | | | | | |
|---|---|---|---|---|---|
| **BRUINS REGULAR SEASON STATISTICS** | **GP** | **G** | **A** | **Pts** | **PIM** |
| 1979–2000 | 1,518 | 395 | 1,111 | 1,506 | 1,089 |
| Bruins Postseason Statistics | 180 | 36 | 125 | 161 | 151 |

# CHAPTER

# BRUINS LEGEND: CAM NEELY

*above:*

*Neely in his first season in Boston. He arrived via trade with Vancouver along with a first round draft pick (Glen Wesley) for Barry Pederson June 6, 1986.*

*left:*

*Cam Neely, inducted into the Hockey Hall of Fame in November 2005, named Vice President of the Bruins in September 2007.*

June 5, 1986: the Bruins trade Barry Pederson to the Vancouver Canucks for Cam Neely and a first-round draft choice, which turned out to be Glen Wesley. One could maybe see where Vancouver was coming from at the time; they were picking up a veteran forward who averaged 39 goals a season in the four years he was healthy in Boston. Meanwhile, in the prior campaign, as a Canuck, Neely had 14 goals and 126 penalty minutes in 73 games, and no points in three playoff games.

The change of scenery obviously served Neely and the Bruins very well. No one knew at the time that his number 8 would one day be hoisted to the rafters.

"I wore number 12 growing up [near Vancouver]," Neely says. "I liked Stan Smyl. I actually played with him in Vancouver where I wore number 21, 12 backwards. I had 21 in juniors in Portland, as well."

Neely's Winter Hawks team won the Memorial Cup, major junior's ultimate prize, in 1983, with Cam contributing 20 points in 14 playoff games.

"When I came to Boston I was handed number 8," Neely adds. "I asked if I could switch to 21 and they said no. 'Harry likes you in 8; you're wearing 8.'"

"Neely turns out to probably be my best move," ponders longtime Bruins general manager Harry Sinden. "I made some good ones, I made some bad ones, but that one turned out pretty darn good. I give the credit to the scouts; they told us to get him."

Barry Pederson chuckles when he gets mentioned as the "other side" of the deal.

"Well, it worked out very well for the Bruins here, not only with Cam as an individual but their team," Pederson says. "They played well late-'80s, early '90s, and he was a huge part of that. He took his game to the next level when he got here, and I didn't when I went to Vancouver. That's kind of where that broke down. But it was a losing environment there, and they [the media] took a lot of shots at the players who didn't get it done, and I didn't really, and that was fine." A classy and understanding mind-set from Pederson, who went to a bad team, while Neely arrived to one beginning an upswing.

*above:*

*Neely crashes the net of Florida Panthers goalie Mark Fitzpatrick. The spinning puck has risen high above the crease on end, the width of the puck covering the first "e" in Reebok.*

"I think part of the reason Cam turned into a great player was because of the playmakers the Bruins put around him," states Steve Babineau. "He was a great player, a typical bruising Bruins player, but he played with [Craig] Janney, and Dave Poulin, and then the ultimate playmaker in Adam Oates.

Flying down the wing became powering down the wing, and into the corners, and in front of the net.

"When I showed up, they put me with good players," Neely agrees, "and the old Garden was suited for my style of play."

"I had a chance to play with Cam when he showed up," recalls Rick "Nifty" Middleton. "He played with me and Thomas Gradin. Gradin was a very good centerman, a great playmaker. All Cam and I had to do was get open and he'd get us the puck. I just remember Cam flying down the wing."

Flying down the wing became powering down the wing, and into the corners, and in front of the net.

The Garden's small ice surface didn't leave much room for the faint of heart.

"He kind of reminds me of a cross between Terry O'Reilly and Mike Bossy," observes Babineau. "Prior to Cam, O'Reilly was the ultimate Bruin. Both of them could turn a game around with a body check and both of them were relentless. For Cam, though, add Bossy's scoring touch. He'd be deeper in the slot than Bossy, getting pummeled, but he could still control the puck and score. He had Bossy's finesse, but in much worse traffic. Throw in a Johnny-Bucyk-like hip check, a Bobby-Hull-like slapper and release, and leadership. He was the super-Bruin. Players would sit and watch him and then go out for their next shift."

Comparing him to a handful of players melded together might be fair, but comparing him to just one other guy probably isn't. His enforcer teammate and pal off the ice Lyndon Byers concurs.

"One of a kind," states Byers. "I think one of the biggest misconceptions, one of the biggest mistakes reporters and hockey people and fans make is they try to compare people to Cam, they try to compare Cam to people. There will never be another power forward in the game that scores 50 goals in 44

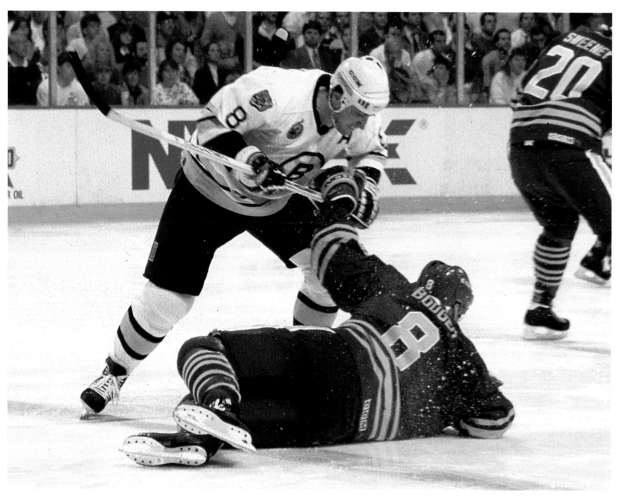

games. I still don't think he gets the accolades. We all respect him and we all know what he does, but there are all-stars and there are superstars, and so often it's 'he was a perennial all-star and tough as nails.' But I really and truly believe he is on a plane with the Gretzkys, the Messiers, the Lemieuxs, the Crosbys, the Orrs, and all those guys, as someone who reinvented—didn't reinvent—he *invented* superstar power forward. He was it. He's by himself; he's on a plateau by himself. It's pretty simple."

"He hit me a few times in practice," former defenseman Mike Milbury remembers, "and he'd just explode into you. I hadn't played with a guy who hit like that."

Neely's nickname became the appropriate "Bam Bam." He also later became known as Seabass, for his role in the 1994 film *Dumb and Dumber*, directed by his acquaintances the Farrelly brothers. These names set aside his original NHL moniker, "Tricky Dicky Hambone," given to him early in his career by Canucks centerman Gary Lupul. That nickname shortened to "Bone." Glove manufacturers used to stamp a dog bone-shaped emblem on his glove cuffs.

*above:*

*Neely was the consummate power forward, here disposing of, and following up on Doug Bodger of the Buffalo Sabres. That's Bob Sweeney (#20) photo right.*

"Cam was immensely strong and had great puck skills," former teammate Gord Kluzak adds. "People said he wasn't that great of a skater, but he'd always get there. They said he'd fit very well in the Boston Garden and boy did he ever."

The Garden was legendary for its small ice surface and its tight corners: no place to run, no place to hide. The hits, the chances, the goals came quickly.

Neely scored 36 goals his first season in Boston, then 42, then 37. By 1989–90, he powered his way to 55 goals and 92 points plus 117 penalty minutes. He actually became the super Bruin, every New England hockey fan's hero. Similar to Gordie Howe in his time, Neely was the best scorer and the most feared physical player on the ice as well.

In 1988, in just his second season in Boston, Neely endeared himself to Bruins fans another way: by helping the organization end a four-and-a-half decade long playoff drought against the Montreal Canadiens. The Bruins' last postseason series win against Montreal came in 1943, four games to one. Forty-five years later, after years of heartache at the hands of the Habs, the Bruins polished them off again in five games.

"That ended a long string of frustration against Montreal," points out Middleton. "I was still nervous when we were up 3-1 in that last game, but when Neely put us up 4-1, I knew we had it."

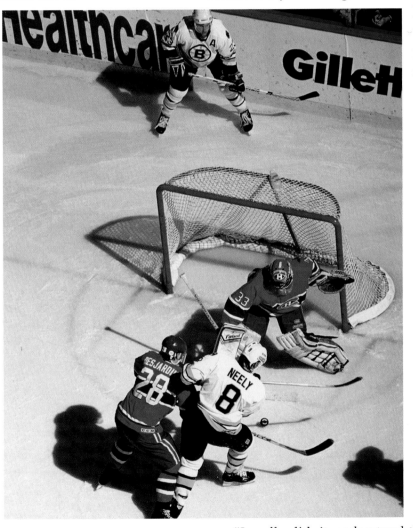

"I really didn't understand the full impact of beating them for hardcore, longtime Bruins fans, until we actually won the game," Neely thinks back. "And what it meant. When we showed up at Logan [Airport] and there were two to three thousand fans waiting, it was pretty special to be part of a team that could create that atmosphere, that we'd get that from a second-round win."

The Bruins made it to the Stanley Cup final, only to be swept by the Edmonton Oilers. Despite the loss, Neely had established himself as a bona fide scorer and a physical presence.

He would pummel people, and be pummeled; or at least opponents would try.

As the next few seasons unfolded, to slow down Neely, and to prevent the strong winger's physical domination from being one-sided in his favor, opponents stooped to cheap shots. The most notorious perpetrator: Pittsburgh defenseman Ulf Samuelson, who nailed Neely with an open-ice knee-to-knee hit that led to one injury, and who sparred with him countless other times. Their battles in the 1991 postseason, in a Conference final where the Bruins led two games to none at one point but was won by the Penguins, are infamous. A collision between the two late in the series led to Neely's chronic hip condition. Meanwhile, the fact that Samuelson consistently delivered cheap shots while wearing a visor, and the fact he'd never answer the bell and drop the gloves, drove Neely's old-time mentality crazy.

Neely expressed his dismay during an interview with NESN, produced at the time of his Hall of Fame induction.

*above:*

*Ulf Samuelsson (middle) being restrained by linesman Kevin Collins after yet another tussle with Neely. Samuelsson, who delivered a devastating open-ice knee-to-knee hit to Neely, along with countless other cheap shots, refused to drop the gloves. For this, Neely had little respect for his arch-enemy. That's Penguin Joe Mullen and Ray Bourque to the left.*

I never really respected a guy who played a certain way and didn't want to answer the bell.

"If you do not want to handle what is going to come because you chopped a guy, you slashed a guy, you cross-checked a guy; you know, you stuck a glove in the back of his head, his helmet, and pushed his helmet into his face," Neely starts, "then if you don't want to turn around and drop the gloves when the guy challenges you, then you shouldn't play that way. You know. He's got a face shield on. You play a certain way; I don't think you should wear a face shield if you're not going to back up what you're doing. You look at a lot of hockey players who play tough...if they get somebody mad, if somebody wants to go and drop the gloves, they're going to answer the bell. I never really respected a guy who played a certain way and didn't want to answer the bell."

Neely answered every bell, and overcame devastating knee and hip injuries to continue his career. Over two seasons, from 1991 through 1993, he played in only 22 games. He returned in 1993–94 and played as tough as ever, while essentially taking every other game off to rest his knee. He reached the 50-goal mark in 44 games played.

*below:*

*The Bruins score on Sean Burke of the Devils as Neely and New Jersey defenseman Randy Velischek head to the net, taken from the catwalk in the old Garden.*

*above:*

*Paul Coffey of the Red Wings jousts
with Neely in front of the net as they
await a shot.*

"It would be difficult in the history of the League, to find someone who combined what he did so effectively," Bruins president Harry Sinden was quoted as saying. "And that was scoring goals and being so powerful and the aggressive forward that he was. We've had a lot of great goal scorers who couldn't really live up to the other part. Cam had it...he had it all."

Rick Middleton adds, "Not many players could play that way—score and physically dominate."

And he did it on a knee and with a hip that was never again one hundred percent.

"His rehab was a lesson in perseverance I won't forget," Sinden states.

On top of "legend" status, Neely earned the Masterton Trophy in 1994 for his efforts. Each season, the Professional Hockey Writers' Association delegates the award to the NHL player who "best exemplifies the qualities of perseverance, sportsmanship, and dedication to hockey." That year's decision would fall under the "no-brainer" category.

Babineau remembers being in awe of some of the battles Neely went through.

"He'd be getting the hell beaten out of him in front. He'd lose his cool on occasion but mostly he'd keep his cool. Sometimes I'd pull the camera away just to watch the battle.

It was laughable sometimes—elbows, high sticks."

Tongue in cheek at the time, Babineau would warn Neely of the other side effect of his fracases.

"Don't get hit in the head or face, because you'll have to wear a shield. Those shield photos aren't going to sell," Babineau would say with a grin.

Because of a broken nose or an eye injury, maybe an average of once every year or two, Neely would actually have to don the shield for a couple games. He couldn't wait to take it off.

When asked which photograph of himself he liked best, Cam netted an unusual request.

"Goal, hit, or fight? Maybe all three 'mooshed' together in a collage or something like that. That would be cool," Neely says. "I remember Babs always being around, lurking in the corners. I remember him standing on that huge ladder taking the team pictures.

"It's hard to get those photos of those physical plays," Neely adds.

Babineau managed to get them, and he managed to get plenty of them.

"I think players should request certain kinds of shots ahead of time, instead of 'let me see what you have,'" Neely suggests. "There is one shot, where I'm celebrating a goal; I've got my stick in the air… that one stands out. It shows a lot of emotion." The Bruins used the image on a poster.

For Neely, as a Bruin, emotion stemmed from pride, and pride stemmed from tradition. Those two elements went hand in hand with old-school accountability.

"Original Six, so much history, so much pride to wear that jersey," Neely says with a smile. "It's expected that you embrace that tradition. When I walked in, we had guys like Ray Bourque, who led by example. He worked really hard. The best guy in the League day in and day out, and he had the work ethic. There's a correlation between working hard and having a great career.

"Bobby Orr was around and he'd sometimes walk into the dressing room and that was really cool," Neely adds. "Johnny Bucyk was around. They'd always come in and you'd always feel proud to be a Bruin."

"Neely was the consummate player, the toughest guy I ever played with," reflects Ken Hodge Jr., who joined the Bruins in 1990. "I was fortunate. I remember coming to my first game. I was number 10 at the time, and I saw 8 [Neely] next to me and Carpenter's number, I can't remember the number, but that was the line. 'Who am I playing with and what am I doing?!' I remember Cam saying to me, 'I don't want the puck in the defensive zone; I want the puck in the offensive zone. That's the only thing you have to remember.' 'OK, Mr. Neely,'" he remembers with a smile. "But Cam was a great guy, and we see him quite a bit, at the golf tournaments and involved now, and it's nice to see him able to do well."

*above:*

*Best way to break a horse? Ride 'em or rope 'em. Calgary Flames defenseman Dana Murzyn wraps and rides a power forward next to the net.*

"My favorite games were afternoon games on Saturday," Neely told NESN. "Get up, eat, get dressed, and go to the rink and play. Night games, you have the morning skate, you eat, you sleep, there's so much time to think of the game. Afternoon games at the Garden were the best, and an opportunity for people to bring their kids to the game. I loved the atmosphere."

"When I first played in the League with Calgary, I played against Neely so I really don't think I truly saw really what a great player he was," says former Bruins forward Tim Sweeney.

*above:*

*Ottawa goaltender Don Beaupre disappears under the weight and power of Neely. Senators' defenseman Sean Hill turns for the puck.*

"I saw him score a lot of goals and I saw him score a lot of goals on one knee too, because I was there for the end of his career and he was terrific—your prototypical power forward that really worked hard on and off the ice. It was a privilege to play him, but you really noticed it in Boston when you saw him doing it day in and day out."

Twice Neely played in the Stanley Cup final with Boston, the second time in 1990. They lost to the Oilers in five games.

"Game 1, triple overtime loss took some wind out," Neely said years later. "We were definitely better in '90 than '88. It's frustrating to this day that we didn't have a better series there."

After the '91 Conference final, Neely's Bruins would never again advance past the first round. Five years later, the damaged inflicted to his limbs was irreversible; there would be no more incredible rehabilitations.

"My right hip injury is a permanent disability which will prevent me from ever returning to professional hockey," a choked-up Neely announced on September 5, 1996.

Neely finished with 344 goals in 525 games with Boston, and is the franchise's all-time leading playoff goal scorer.

*above:*

*Cam Neely: A picture speaks a thousand words.*

*left:*

*A warrior rests in the penalty box. Neely's pounding style led to 921 PIM with Boston, to go with 344 goals, and 590 points.*

Between his physical retirement and his jersey retirement in January of 2005, Neely devoted his time to starting a family, and to helping those in the community less fortunate than himself. He had remained single until after his playing days.

"At home it was get up and think about hockey, and on the road it was get up and think about hockey. That's what I liked," Neely asserts. "As a player, I saw early on, guys were married and missed a lot of family stuff. When I wanted to start a family, I wanted it to be after the career, because I didn't want to miss [all of the] 'firsts.'"

Meanwhile, tragedy affected the Neely family as well. Cam lost both his parents, Marlene and Michael, to cancer. In 1995, Cam started the Neely Foundation, an effort he oversees with his brother, Scott. The basic mission statement: "Dedicated to helping patients and families deal with cancer."

Aside from raising funds and awareness for the Cancer Center at Tufts-New England Medical Center and its Floating Hospital for Children, Neely continues to expand the Neely House, a 15,000-square-foot, 16-apartment living area within the walls of the medical facility. It's a home away from home for families of cancer patients, particularly adolescent patients. Since 1997, thousands of people have stayed as guests,

"The best part about Cam, he's a better human being than he is a hockey player," maintains Lyndon Byers. "He takes care of his family, he takes care of his friends, and he takes care of strangers."

Byers's sentiment, and Cam's philosophy of "giving first," are best exemplified in Neely's Hall of Fame induction speech from November 2005. Excerpts focus as much or more so on

*left:*

*High scoring linemates Adam Oates and Neely celebrate a goal against Quebec Nordiques defenseman Craig Wolanin and goaltender Stephane Fiset.*

*below:*

*Adam Oates and Cam Neely. This photo ended up on the cover of the Bruins yearbook and on a Beckett hockey card magazine.*

being thankful and being a generous giver than they do on being a legendary hockey player.

"...I loved playing it [hockey] as a mite, a pee wee, a bantam, winning the Memorial Cup with the Portland Winter Hawks as a junior, and right through my time as a professional. However, there was that one brief instant in my life, a moment of misguided youth, when I actually wanted to quit hockey. I was 15 years old, playing my first year of midgets, all of my teammates were 16 and they were driving cars to and from games, while there I was heading home with Dad after games. I felt so out of place, I told my dad I wanted to quit, and my dad gave me one of life's great lessons: He said, 'Cam, you know what, you tried out for this team, and you made it. You took someone else's spot, and I want you to honor your commitment and finish the year.' He continued, 'If you don't want to sign up next year, that's your choice.' No yelling, no screaming, just a valuable opportunity to grow up and make my own decision. To say the least, I'm very glad that I continued and I'm profoundly indebted to my dad for that great lesson in life on commitment. To my brother, Scott, [and] sisters, Christine and Shaun, you deserve an enormous amount of thanks for the support you have given

> I remember well the gift of giving by the fans; their support extended beyond the game.

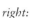

*right:*

*Cam and younger brother Scott pose with the Prince of Wales Trophy in 1988 after the Bruins advanced to the Stanley Cup finals. The brothers presently work closely in handling the family's charitable endeavors, including the Neely Foundation for Cancer Research.*

*below:*

*Neely celebrates a goal at the Garden.*

me over the years. My mother and father, my biggest supporters, I know you're watching today and are here with us today. I love you and I miss you. Their gift of giving is another life lesson, which is very much an important aspect of my life to this day. I thank them from the bottom of my heart.

"...They also gave me the opportunity to work hard every day, compete toward a common goal, and honor the tradition of all who wore the Bruins jersey. My teammates and I all knew that the name on the front meant a lot more than the name on the back. My memory of these gifts and opportunities mean the world to me, especially on a day like today. I remember well the gift of giving by the fans; their support extended beyond the game. I will never forget their compassion during my personal battles, with the illness of my parents, or with my professional battles with injury. I thank them deeply and sincerely. While I'm gratified today to be recognized for hard work and achievement, I also know this was part of my life's work. As we examine our lives, and certainly we all come from different walks of life, different parts of the world, we do share a common humanity. We believe that life's purpose is to give to others whenever possible. Sometimes it's an event that reaches deep within us that causes us to give back. Personally, after I lost both my parents after their courageous battles with cancer, a direction in my life became abundantly clear. I realized many more things about my life in my parents' passing. As a professional athlete, I have been given so much, but today, I have satisfaction from giving back. I want to give back to those who have helped me, who stoked my dreams. I want to give back to family and friends and others that have

*above:*

*The Bruins were led offensively in the early nineties by two men: Ray Bourque and Cam Neely. The dejected Red Wing on the right is future Neely linemate Adam Oates.*

encouraged me. I want to give back to those who I may have the privilege and responsibility to help in their time of need. Many have helped me along the way, and it's my honor and responsibility to return the favor. As you all know, and I have learned well from you, there is no better gift than giving. I thank you again for this terrific lesson, I will never forget it…"

"The Bruins didn't send me to his induction," recalls Babineau, "but I do remember being in the dressing room with him before his jersey was retired. The current Bruins at the time all came over and shook his hand and then he led them out on to the ice. He skated out, which was rare for one of those jersey retirements. It was cool; he took a lap around the ice while the team followed him and went to the bench. It was a big night for a guy who represents the ultimate Bruin."

In September 2007, Cam Neely was officially re-introduced into the Boston hockey community as a Bruins vice president. Neely works closely with the general manager and the hockey staff to evaluate players and their performance. He once again finds himself the face of the franchise, a responsibility he welcomes, with a chance to restore and re-affirm dedication to, and the tradition of, the Spoked B.

Left to right: Wife Paulina Neely, daughter Ava, and son Jack, Bruin Shaone Morrisonn leaning over (obscured), Jeff Jillson, and Cam.

above:

Hollywood celebrity and friend Michael J. Fox toasts Cam on his jersey retirement night, January 12, 2004. Bruins on the bench left to right: Glen Murray, Nick Boynton, Andrew Raycroft, and Joe Thornton. Standing are equipment manager Peter Henderson and assistant coach Norm Maciver.

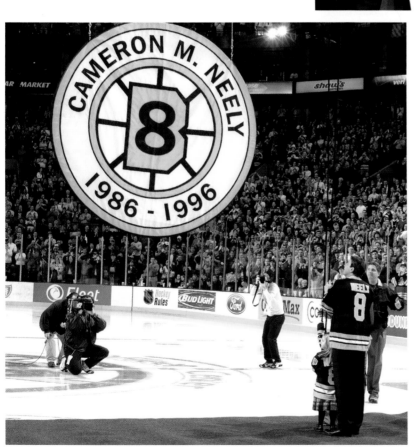

left:

Cameron Michael Neely's number 8 gets hoisted.

Bruins Legend: Cam Neely

| **CAM NEELY** (RW) Comox, BC \| #8 \| Heart, more than stats, earned him the Hall | | | | | |
|---|---|---|---|---|---|
| **BRUINS REGULAR SEASON STATISTICS** | **GP** | **G** | **A** | **Pts** | **PIM** |
| 1986–1996 | 525 | 344 | 246 | 590 | 921 |
| Bruins Postseason Statistics | 86 | 55 | 32 | 87 | 160 |

# THE LUNCH PAIL GANG

*above:*

*After winning the Bruins Seventh Player Award for the 1977-78 season, Stan Jonathan gets an appreciative peck from head coach Don Cherry.*

*left:*

*Bobby Schmautz celebrates his game winning goal in overtime of Game-4 against Montreal in the 1978 Stanley Cup final on May 21st. The goal tied the series, but the Canadiens went on to win in six games.*

Even after Steve Babineau had become the Bruins' official photographer in 1977, he had never been in the team's dressing room. That changed suddenly one afternoon after practice at the Garden, midway through his first season.

The short little assistant equipment manager nicknamed "Tattoo," after the Fantasy Island character from the '70s, found Babineau standing near the glass along the far boards.

"You Steve Babineau?" he asked Babs.

"Yeah."

"Coach wants to see you in his office," came the demand.

"Oh my God," Babineau thought to himself, "what could this be all about?" The same interjection entered his mind again as the dressing room doors swung open, which for Babineau was like opening the doors to a shrine. He stared at the player stalls and then moved cautiously through the room.

"Coach, I'm Steve Babineau, the team photographer," Babs introduced himself as he stepped into the coach's office.

Head Coach Don Cherry, nicknamed "Grapes," had seen Babineau's blown-up, framed Bruins photographs lining the walls of the new season ticket holder social area, the Boards and Blades Club. He wanted copies of a few of those photos and he wanted to see others.

"Sure thing," Babineau agreed.

The two arranged to meet the next Sunday afternoon at Babineau's apartment in Medford. When the day arrived, Cherry and his wife, Rose, pulled up in a huge, black Lincoln Continental.

"The car seemed to take up the whole block," Babs recalls.

Cherry spent a few hours going through dozens, maybe even a couple hundred photos. He also told stories about his players, and did imitations of the way they skated.

During the 1970s, the Big Bad Bruins gave way, or morphed themselves, into the Lunch Pail Gang. The gang was still "bad," with guys like Stan Jonathan, Terry O'Reilly, and John Wensink, but they also had a collective team work ethic like none other. Coach Cherry loved his grinders as much as he had loved watching Bobby Orr. Character players like Mike Milbury, Bobby Schmautz, and Al Secord made his team complete. The Bruins flew around the ice and, more often than not, ran into anything that moved. They were tough, intimidating, and successful.

"It was great. Don Cherry was definitely a players' coach," points out Gary Doak, a Bruins defenseman for much of 14 seasons. "It was different than the Cup teams. We had a lot of guys that worked hard; we had 20 guys that would stick their nose in and do whatever Don wanted us to do. Back then it was rough and tough. We all chipped in and we played that style of hockey, and that's how it was back then. We had Jonathan and Wensink, Wayne Cashman, Schmautz, and we also had players

*above:*

*Don Cherry behind his desk in his office at the Garden, which he decorated liberally with personal hockey memorabilia.*

that could score goals, like Peter McNab and Rick Middleton. So we had a solid all-around team back then. It was great playing for him; a great coach and a great person."

"We played hard for him because he always had us ready to play," states 5-foot-8-inch, 175-pound battler Stan Jonathan. "We had good leadership with Chief and Wayne Cashman, and we believed in one another. Part of it was the guys, part of it was Don, but we didn't take s— from anyone!"

Jonathan scrapped his way to 751 penalty minutes for the team, with all of his 411 NHL games coming in Boston. A smaller man with a big heart, the prototypical Lunch Pailer, Jonathan was a player coach Cherry adored.

"Grapes was a guy who'd go out and have a beer with you," remembers former defenseman Milbury. "He used to make me drive to the rink with him, from Andover, where we lived about a half-mile apart. He'd pick me up in the morning of the game, we'd ride in, and he'd practice his pre-game speeches. I knew exactly what he was going to say before he said it because I had heard it four or five times on the way in. I took some grief for riding with the coach, but I really had no choice—he insisted that I ride with him. We'd ride back after the skate on the day of the game and he'd stop and have a couple of Budweisers, order some Chinese food—the specials for him, his wife, and his son—and then he'd go home and have a little Chinese food and a nap."

Cherry's gang came together in a variety of manners. Schmautz came in a trade from Vancouver in February of 1974. Jonathan came via the 1975 draft, as a sixth rounder, 86th overall. Mike Milbury was a non-drafted college player who signed as a free agent in November of 1974. Harry Sinden was the general manager at the time, the man responsible for building this prototypical working class Boston club.

*below:*

*Don Cherry coached exactly 400 regular season games for the Bruins. His team won or tied 295 of them.*

Wensink's initial pro deal involved a three-year contract with St. Louis. For a portion of that time, he was assigned to Rochester, New York, in the AHL, where Cherry was coach. After a back injury his second season, Wensink had spinal fusion surgery and missed a year of hockey. Potentially considered damaged goods, he didn't get re-signed by St. Louis. The Bruins picked up Wensink as a free agent in October 1976. Midway through his fourth overall season, he was called up to the Bruins. Wensink is forever grateful to Grapes.

"He was my first pro coach, and the way I played and the way he coached, obviously that was the perfect marriage," points out Wensink. "He just was a good guy, a players' coach. He was also the one who gave me the shot when he was with the Bruins and I was in the minors. For me, I know management at that time, ownership [probably had their doubts], and I had just come off a year of not playing after having spinal fusion done. The Bruins ended up signing me and it was sometime early January they called me up. Grapes was the one who made the call. He said, 'Get that guy up here.' I was fortunate enough to stay."

Rick Middleton, meanwhile, took some time getting out of Cherry's doghouse. Acquired for Ken Hodge in the spring of 1976, the long-haired goal scorer with an early-career propensity for ignoring the back end gradually learned his lesson and gained ice time.

"It was my third year in the League, but I didn't think I'd be coming to Boston and stepping into a lineup that was very solid, especially on the right side," says Middleton. "I mean, Cashman, Schmautz, O'Reilly. I wanted to play, I thought they would play me, but I also realized I had so much more to learn. I never really learned in New York; no one ever taught me about the complete game. That's why I always thank Don, because he did it by forcing me to either make it or break it, because if I didn't learn, I wouldn't have been playing. I ended up watching these guys [teammates] as he wanted me to, and then applying it on the ice, and it worked out.

## He just was a good guy, a players' coach.

"Not always, though," he continues. "I remember one time in Buffalo, I went back to watch my point—he used to say, 'Watch your point, kid'—I watched my point and my defenseman [to cover] was Bill Hajt, who scored two goals a year. The other guy was Danny Gare, who scored 50 goals a year. So I went to Gare, and he puts it back to Hajt, and he gets one of his two goals a year, and I didn't want to go to the bench, 'cause I knew what was coming. For the most part, after that I didn't make too many errors and when Don left, he had really set the groundwork for me to continue and to excel at the whole game, so I thank him for that."

"Grapes was a great coach. I loved playing for him," claims the Chief, John Bucyk, who finished his 21-year Bruins career in 1978. "He stood up for his players and he was a great guy to play for. He never took the credit. If we won, it was because the players played well; if we lost, he'd take the blame and say it was the coach's fault. He never took credit and [always] treated us well."

"Cherry's mantra was 'them against us,'" says PR guy Nate Greenberg. "It worked out quite well. He had a terrific team, obviously, and I think it was safe to say he was the right coach at the right time. He had a lot of veteran players, and he coached them, treated them like veterans—the perfect coach for them. He knew how to mold them, and the whole "Lunch Pail" thing worked. It was a little bit of a misnomer. You think of a lunch pail gang, you think of hard workers that do it all with maybe no talent, but these guys worked hard, and had quite a bit of talent. They had some damn good players and he [Cherry] did a terrific job. The right time and place for him."

*Boston Globe* writer Fran Rosa is credited with coming up with the "Lunch Pail" moniker.

*above:*

*Cherry at home in his basement, checks out photos from his playing days in Rochester.*

"It seems to me I was talking to someone about them and said, 'They're like working stiffs—get up and go to work and then go home,'" remembers Rosa. "And they said, 'Like a lunch pail guy,' and I said, 'Yeah, just like that.' I added gang because they were a team, and they were very much a team. It's funny because some of the players, I don't remember who exactly, almost resented the fact that I called them that, because they thought it implied that they had no talent; that they were just a bunch of working stiffs. It wasn't true. They had talent on those Cherry teams; the nickname just described the work they did."

134

Chapter 9

"The four years I was in Boston, it was the case of 20 guys, or however large the roster was, 20 guys wanting to back each other up," states Wensink. "I knew as an individual, if you were called to go out for the next shift or whatever, you went over the boards not wanting to let any of the other 19 guys down. I think that said a lot for our togetherness. It wasn't always fancy, we didn't try to entertain always, but we wanted to get a job done. I know myself, and I think a lot of the other guys would say the same thing, you didn't want to let the other guys down. We had some talent, guys like Middleton, Park, and Ratelle, these guys knew how to handle the puck and wheel and deal, but we also had a core group of guys...with limited talent and a great work ethic."

In his five seasons as coach, Cherry went 231-105-64. His winning percentage is the best in team history among coaches who handled the job for more than three seasons. Only Tom Johnson (two-plus seasons) and Armand Guidolin (two seasons), his immediate predecessors with the Big Bad Bruins, had better winning percentages in team history.

*below:*

*New York Ranger Phil Esposito having a difference of opinion with Bruin Brad Park. The two were swapped for one another in a multiplayer deal in 1975. Others involved from left to right: Mike Milbury, Terry O'Reilly, and Ranger Don Murdoch.*

In the postseason, Grapes was almost as impressive. His record was 31-24 in overall games. His problem: the Gang never won the big one. Twice the team reached the Stanley Cup final, in 1977 and 1978, only to be swept in four games and then lose in six, both times to the Canadiens.

"It's enough to make a grown man cry," states Terry O'Reilly, referring to Cherry's last crack at it, the 1979 playoffs, when the Bruins lost a semi-final series they were moments away from winning, once again to Montreal.

*above:*

*On the bench with Don Cherry, Rick Middleton, Peter McNab, Terry O'Reilly and John Wensink.*

O'Reilly refers to the infamous too-many-men-on-the-ice penalty late in Game 7. After Middleton scored to give the Bruins a 4-3 lead with about four minutes remaining in the game, a screwed-up line change led to the infraction at 17:26 of the third period.

Goalie Gerry Cheevers, sitting on the end of the bench that evening, recalls the play and the discussions that followed.

"There were only nine guys on the ice there," Cheevers jokes. "Johnny D'Amico made the call, the linesman. I saw him in the summer and I said, 'John…,' and he stopped me right away and said, 'I didn't want to call it after six, after seven, and then after nine I had to call it.'

"I was injured. I didn't play that game," Cheevers adds. "Gilbert played it and it was so frantic and the pace was so frantic, everyone got caught up in the game. I don't know who

*above:*

*The whole gang joins Wayne Cashman and Peter McNab (at top) in celebrating a goal against the Montreal Canadiens.*

[caused the penalty]. Even if I knew who, I wouldn't say anything, but when players came to the bench they had their position, center, left wing, right wing, and the guys were so caught up they didn't know who was up next and I think two or three guys jumped on."

O'Reilly believes the entire late third-period scenario could have been avoided much earlier.

"Well, I remember that game…we went into the dressing room at the end of two periods with a 3-1 lead," Terry recalls. "But I think, if I remember correctly—I've never gone back and looked at the video—I remember a play near the end of that second period where Peter McNabb passed it over to me. I think he was in the left corner of the Montreal end, he passed it out, and I took it and snapped it and hit the goalpost dead center. Ugh, I mean, if it hit the inside of the post it went in and we've got a 4-1 lead going into the third period. It hit the post dead center, came right back out to Don Marcotte, and he blasted it and it went right into Dryden. So we had two opportunities to extend our lead, but we didn't and they came back, as Montreal often did in those days. And Guy Lafleur scored a goal with a slap shot. I think the puck was on the blue line. He was just stepping into our zone and if I looked at the video again you'd see his stick in the back swing came so close it almost touched the boards. That's how far…he was so far over to the side, so far back, but you could not fault [goalie Gilles] Gilbert for that goal. It was a perfect shot, it was like a laser, two inches off the ice, right off the inside of the far post."

Lafleur, in reality, a bit closer to the top of the face-off circle, ripped the power play goal home with a minute and 14 seconds left in the third. Yvon Lambert scored the game winner at 9:33 of overtime on a feed from Mario Tremblay, and the Habs advanced to beat the New York Rangers in the Cup final.

So the playoff jinx against the Canadiens continued—a jinx that may have simply been a match-up issue, seen often in the regular season as well.

"We were in Montreal one time; we couldn't ever win there, so Grapes said, 'Hey, we're gonna change things up,'" remembers Milbury. "The night before the game, he says, 'You're coming with me,' so we go around the corner from the hotel to a little tavern and a few of us sit and drink beer and tell stories for about five hours. The next night we got the crap kicked out of us. He just laughed about it and said, 'At least we tried. We had to do something different.'"

"It was great," chimes Cheevers. "I think more than any time, you'd go out of your way to go to the rink because every day was a new adventure with Grapes. We had fun. The dressing room was fun, everything was very positive. I was maybe the only guy who had played with him in Rochester, so when he started barking, I kind of knew what he was really like. Every day was an adventure."

"They [the Bruins] never had much of a power play, and there was a game over in Minnesota, and I think the Bruins had something like eight power plays, and were zero for eight," remembers beat writer Rosa. "So after the game I went down to the dressing room to get a few quotes as we always did, and Cherry looks at me and says, 'Damn you!' And I said, 'What?' And he said, 'I'm trying to pay attention to the game, and all I can think about is that Rosa is going to come down and ask me what I'm going to do about the power play.' I said, 'Well Don, you had little to do if you were thinking about what I was going to ask you.' And Don said, 'What do you want me to do, go out

below:

*left to right: Gary Doak, John Wensink, Dwight Foster, Al Sims, Terry O'Reilly, Peter McNab (standing and cheering), Rick Middleton, Mike Milbury (standing on bench cheering), Bobby Schmautz, Stan Jonathan, Bob Miller, and coach Cherry behind the last two players.*

above:

*Stan Jonathan clocks Bob Murdoch of the Los Angeles Kings. LA goalie Rogie Vachon follows the puck.*

and shoot myself?' And I said, 'No...try practicing it.'

Rosa wrote the conversation into his story for the next morning and Cherry then talked about it on the radio.

"I guess he ripped me up a little bit," Rosa says, "I didn't hear it. So I went to practice at the Garden the next day and [I was a little worked up and] I said to Don, 'Were you giving me the business on the radio?' And he said, 'Yeah, sit down and I'll tell you why we don't practice it,' which he did. It was funny. How could I get mad?"

Humor on and off the air became a foreshadow for Cherry, a man who has developed into one of Canada's most popular, controversial, and talked-about persons because of his comments on the "Coach's Corner" intermission segment on the CBC's *Hockey Night in Canada* weekly telecast.

"It's like the basic fan on the street...When I go up to Canada and I run into my buddies, people up in Canada, they either like him or dislike him," points out Wensink. "Funny

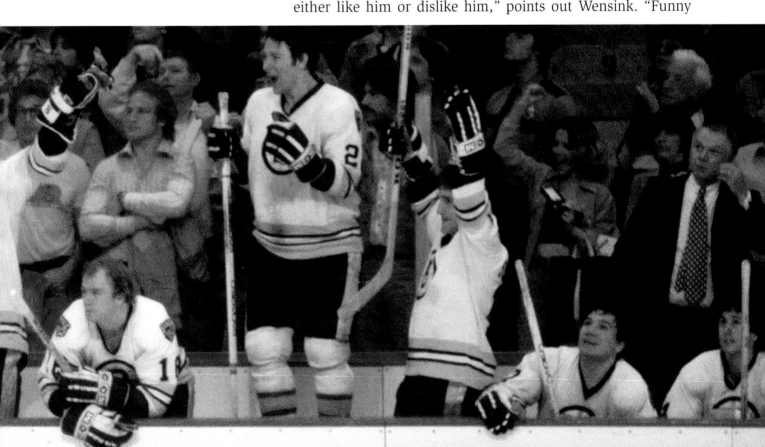

thing is, everybody watches him. The ones who like him watch him, because they're great followers of him; the ones that think he's off the wall, they want to listen and they do watch to hear what he has to say, to agree with him or disagree with him.

"The thing about it with him is, he may get a little carried away sometimes, no question, but the bottom line is, if you know the game at all or follow the game at all, he's not wrong. The way he gets there might be a little off-board sometimes, but he's right about pretty much everything he says. It may not be right at that moment—it may take a year or two—but eventually everyone says, 'Hey, that's exactly how it turned out.' He's not wrong very often, believe me."

More often than not, the controversy is somewhat playful and harmless. On other occasions, Cherry says something he's forced to take back. Nate Greenberg remembers one such occasion from Cherry's coaching days.

"He probably wanted it back after he said it, but one of the most controversial things…," recalls Greenberg. "We had played the Blackhawks where there was a stick deal, an incident, and the quote from Cherry was, 'The next time we're here we're gonna send Stan Mikita back to Czechoslovakia in a pine box.' He got all kinds of heck for it, and deservedly so, and he backed off of it later. [Then NHL president] Clarence Campbell called him and I think he recanted. He was always jousting with other teams."

*above:*

*Don Cherry wearing his Scottish red plaid, acknowledging the Garden faithful at the Last Hurrah in October 1995.*

Cherry, a relative unknown when he arrived from coaching in the minors, remains one of a kind, a promoter and a personality the NHL has lacked on the bench or on the ice since.

Stirring the pot was just another way to bring attention to himself and to his hockey team. Cherry, a relative unknown when he arrived from coaching in the minors, remains one of a kind, a promoter and a personality the NHL has lacked on the bench or on the ice since.

"When he left Boston he went to Colorado, and the first time he came back to Boston coaching another team, I think it might have been in the first period, he took his time out," recalls Rosa. "He took his time out to sign autographs around him. I said it was outrageous [at the time]."

*above:*

*"Media savvy" doesn't do enough to describe coach Cherry, a showman in every sense of the word. He's a fixture on* Hockey Night in Canada *on CBC television and considered one of Canada's most influential countrymen. Here, interviewed by Gail Granik of WBZ-4 Sports.*

"You never knew what was going to come out or what he was going to do," adds Greenberg. "Plus, he dressed then like he does now, almost, he had that unique style, and he was a show unto himself some nights. He really was, plus the team was successful. The act may not have gone over as well if the team was lousy. But it was perfect. He was a character and the team was good."

"Yeah, we were a very close team for quite a few years," says O'Reilly. "Wonderful place to play hockey. You know, it was a place where you look forward to going to work."

"Most of the guys on the team could call Grapes a friend," states Milbury. "We just had a ton of fun. Everyone around him realized they were enjoying a special time, and it wasn't just Grapes, it was the players, because he didn't have the same guys when he got tripped up in Colorado. But it was a pretty neat time and a great group of guys, all in all."

"Craziest guy?" responds Bucyk when asked. "Probably Bobby Schmautz, he was a bit whacky, and Cashman, he wasn't crazy but he was a team player and he would protect you. Yeah, Grapes had his moments, too."

"Grapes was a players' coach," adds Milbury. "He was no tactician. Our breakout play was to fire it around the boards and get it to our big wingers and we'd run over their defensemen. And it worked pretty effectively.

"He was with you or against you," Milbury continues. "If he was against you, chances are you weren't going to last very long. He was demanding in a sense that he wanted guys in good shape—we had some tough practices—and that you committed yourself physically. Beyond that, there wasn't a lot of high tech. Of course, it was a different era, too; there wasn't a lot of high-tech coaching going on either. You played hard or he was going to give it to you."

*below:*

*Wayne Cashman with time for a smile while being pinned to the boards by Toronto's Ian Turnball.*

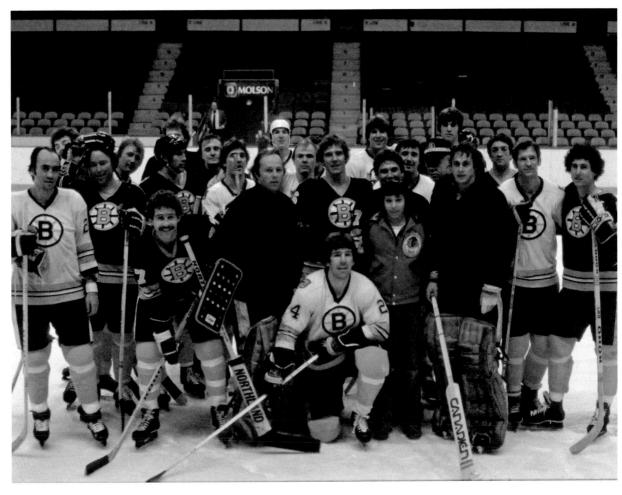

*above:*

*Casual spontaneity for the Lunch Pail Gang after practice at the Garden at the suggestion of coach Cherry: Left to right, those not totally obscured: Gary Doak in white, John Wensink craning his neck in back, Dick Redmond in black, face in back is Dennis O'Brien, moustache in front Dwight Foster, black helmet Al Sims, tall Tom Songin obscured in back, shorter face is Jim Pettie, stick blocking face of Bobby Schmautz, goalie Gerry Cheevers, white helmet above is Mike Milbury, Rick Middleton holding up the mouse ears, Al Secord in Spoked-B, Terry O'Reilly alone in front, behind the kid (Don's son Tim Cherry) is Stan Jonathan, Brad Park immediately behind, and Peter McNab behind them, coach Don Cherry with the hat on, Gilles Gilbert in front of him, tall Bill Bennett in back, Rick Smith, Jean Ratelle in white, and Bobby Miller.*

"He's a great guy and if he likes you, he'll go to the end of the world for you," Wensink adds. "As a coach that's how he was, too. If he liked you, unless you did something stupid, you were going to play.

He really is a great friend of mine, I wish him the best, and he's obviously done real well for himself. He's a good guy."

"It would have been nice to have been able to win one in the late '70s, and there was a couple there that could have been taken," concludes Cheevers. "We didn't take them, and it's disappointing in that respect, but there were other good teams. I think that's what happened a couple of those years."

Video highlights of the Lunch Pail Gang remain a consistent feature of the Bruins pre-game video presentation on the huge high-definition scoreboard above center ice to this day. A new generation of Boston supporters is constantly reminded of the personality and the work ethic of Cherry's Bruins. Meanwhile, the coach himself still publicly pulls for his old organization while on national television in Canada—all the result of a rare and enduring love affair between hockey players, a coach, and their fans.

# COACHES

*above:*

*During Babineau's tenure as team photographer, Harry Sinden twice filled in as interim coach, replacing Fred Creighton for the last seven games of season in 1979-80 and shown here, finishing the 1984-85 season after relieving Gerry Cheevers.*

*left:*

*Former Bruins coach Don Cherry presents Bruins head coach Pat Burns with the Jack Adams Award for NHL Coach of the Year in 1998. Cherry had won the award in Boston 22 years earlier.*

Including the legendary Art Ross, who ran the bench starting back in 1924, there have been 28 head coaches in the history of the Bruins. Steve Babineau has photographed and worked with 18 of them. Many of them had direct ties with the club as former players, while others came from outside the Bruins "family."

Considering all of the talents, personalities, and success stories tied into the Bruins coaching list the past 35 years, it may seem as though picking the most prominent bench-boss would be a difficult task. In reality, the selection is easy. Despite only coaching twice as an interim during that time period, for portions of two separate seasons, Harry Sinden commands the list. Maybe it's because as a hands-on general manager and Club president during most of the last three decades, his influence was often felt directly in the coach's office and in the dressing room. Or perhaps it's simply because of the vast depth of hockey knowledge he brought to the organization, as a former world championship player, Stanley Cup coach, and Hall of Fame executive.

"I have a great deal of respect for Harry—the longevity here in Boston, what he did for the Bruins and for the organization," states Ken Hodge. "We won a Stanley Cup. We won it with Harry. He was really the maestro of that team; he put the lines together. Granted, Milt Schmidt went out and made the trades then—that made everything possible—but Harry put everybody together in the right positions at the right time and right places. A tremendous coach and I have a great deal of

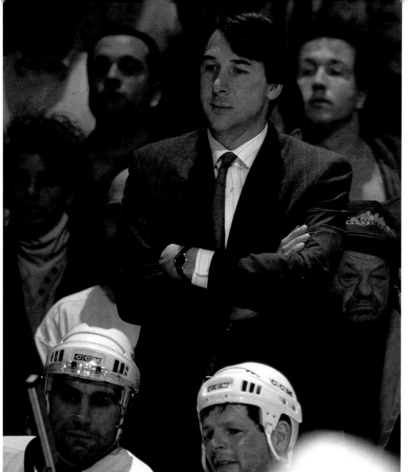

respect for him as a coach and a general manager and you've gotta respect what he's done for hockey here in New England and what he's done for the National Hockey League."

"The absolute best coach I ever played for was Harry," insists Mike Milbury. "I never had him very long, because he only pinch-hit on occasion when he fired a guy, but you could tell he was totally in charge. He knew what he was doing and it was a great learning experience to be a player with him and to later be a coach for him. He had so much experience going into it."

"Harry Sinden was the best coach I ever had in pro hockey," proclaims Phil Esposito, a man not very fond of Harry as a GM. "He really was. He recognized that I could score, and I remember him saying to me very early in my time with the Bruins, he said he was going to get me two wingers to get me the puck, and here's where he wanted me to play, by the hash marks, slot area, and he said they won't be able to get you there because you've got Orr at the point, and that's where I want you to be. That's sure worked best for me."

Oddly enough, it was Sinden's success as a coach that probably led him to have a quick hook as general manager. He had himself, his knowledge and expectations, to compare with everyone else. The coaching position, particularly in Sinden's latter years in charge, became a bit of a revolving door.

"I had four different coaches here," remembers former defenseman Frank Simonetti. "Gerry Cheevers, Harry Sinden, Butch Goring, and Terry O'Reilly. And that was over a time span of four years. The recipe isn't always right, every time. I think in coaching, the lifespan, and you still see it now, is two or three years if you're doing OK, but often times not longer than that. Gerry Cheevers had a three- or four-year run and

*above left:*

Hall-of-Fame goaltender Gerry Cheevers never enjoyed coaching as much as playing, despite good success during a nearly five season run. "I don't know if there's a best part about it," Cheevers states.

*above right:*

Cheevers with Gary Doak.

the team kind of stagnated—then Harry came in and coached for the rest of the season—then he selected Butch, a former player who lasted a couple seasons—and then they brought in Terry. To find the right player and coach combination isn't easy and certainly the Bruins can attest to that the last couple years and in the past."

Since Don Cherry, who actually played one playoff game for Boston in 1955, there have been 15 head coaches besides interim Sinden. Of the five with the most longevity, four were former Bruins players. This wasn't an unusual phenomena for the traditional clubs, to recruit and to stick with those with organizational ties. However, as coaching becomes more modernized, more technical and video oriented, and some would argue more generic, the emotional element becomes less of a factor around the League. The Bruin's latest GM Peter Chiarelli, with no previous ties to the club, has hired two head coaches with no previous ties. Bringing success and passion to the coaching position within an organization, simply because one possessed those elements as a player, no longer seems to matter as much over time.

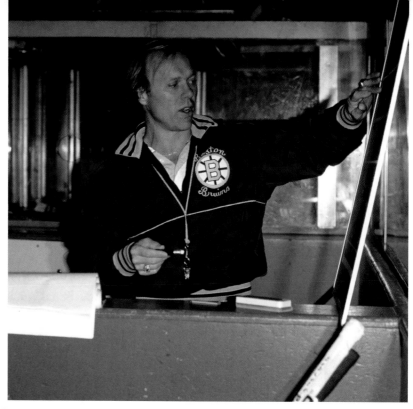

Goring took over the head coaching job in Boston the next season after wrapping up his 16-year NHL playing career in 1985. He played his final half season in Boston, after he was better known as an LA King, and well known as a New York Islander. He coached the Bruins for a total of 93 games.

*above:*

*Robert "Butch" Goring left the ice and immediately headed behind the bench in 1985. He coached 93 regular season games and three in the playoffs.*

"That's a good word for it—brief," Goring laughs. "We had a real good first year, and we had a lot of young guys over the two years that I did coach. It was my first coaching job. I had come right from playing, and I had a lot of fun with it. I was involved with Ray Bourque, which was a lot of fun. He was a great player and a great practice player. I was able to get Cam Neely's career going with him coming here, so that was a good experience for me. It was a tough ending for me because I was just getting started. I did learn some things along the way. I enjoyed the Boston Bruins when I played for them, and I certainly enjoyed the city. It was the start of a coaching career for me."

We had just beaten Montreal and eliminated them from the playoffs for the first time in 50 or 55 years.

General manager Harry Sinden replaced Goring 13 games into Butch's second season, in November of 1986.

"I liked Harry then and I still like Harry today," points out Goring. "You know, he was a tough general manager because he was very much hands-on, but when we got together and talked hockey, he was always a pleasure to be with and I always respected what he needed to do. That was part of his job. I don't have to agree with it or like it, but I understand what he did. We've still maintained a friendship to this day. I always got along with Harry; he's a great hockey guy."

*above:*

*O'Reilly and John Cunniff were a dynamic coaching duo. A South Boston native, Cunniff was a Boston College All-American, the Beanpot MVP twice, the eventual head coach of the New Jersey Devils, and a long-time coach and developer of talent for the United States national team. He died of throat cancer in May, 2002.*

*below:*

*Needham native, high school scoring phenom, and Former WHA scoring star Robbie Ftorek coached the Bruins for almost two full seasons. His tenure ended in March of 2003, when he was replaced on an interim basis by GM Mike O'Connell.*

Sinden went from firing one passionate hockey man to hiring the ultimate in passionate Bruins: Terry O'Reilly.

"Butch Goring was the first coach [for me] for a brief stint," recalls then defenseman Al Pedersen. "That's when Terry O'Reilly and John Cunniff came on board, and then after that was Mike Milbury along with Gordie Clark and Ted Sator."

Many ex-players would agree with Pedersen's assessment of O'Reilly and Cunniff, a dynamic hockey duo.

"They were both old school," says Pedersen. "It's sad that John's not with us anymore. He lived...everything he did was hockey, that guy. He was amazing in terms of being dedicated to the game. Terry's just Terry; he was a fair, intense guy. When you played for him you wanted to make sure you left it all out on the ice."

"Terry was my first professional coach here in Boston," remembers longtime Bruins defenseman Don Sweeney. "There was no more inspirational leader than him. He coached the same way he played. His emotions were right there in front of you; you knew what was required of you each and every night: go out and play for the [name on the front of the] jersey and not the name on the back. He bled Boston Bruin hockey. To me, being the player I was, being a player that had to

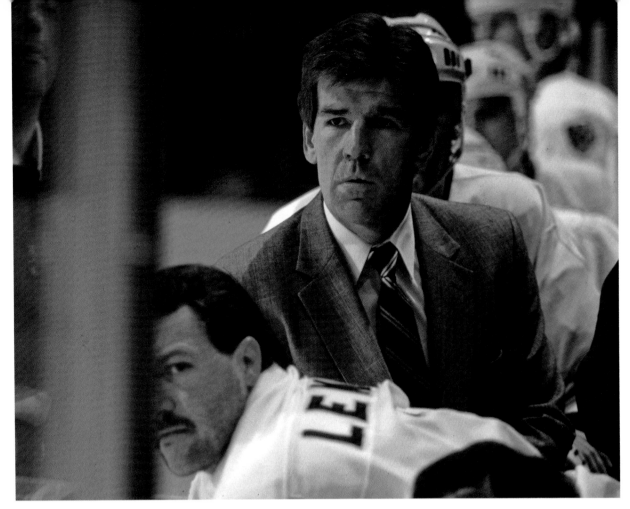

compete each and every night, he was probably the perfect coach for me. He took the things that I could do and had me work on the things that I couldn't do. He really helped me learn how to pass the puck at the NHL level, and just on being a competitive guy each and every night, and that's what he expected of all his players."

"He worked very hard as a coach," adds Hall of Fame forward Cam Neely. "He certainly knows the game. I know guys would certainly try to be accountable for him, because if you didn't give anything but that, he'd let you know."

O'Reilly's feather-in-the-cap coaching moment came in 1988 when his team beat the Montreal Canadiens in the second round of the playoffs, to end a lengthy head-to-head drought.

"When we beat Montreal, we had a two-goal lead and I was looking up at the clock and there was 24, 30 seconds left, and I was still worried, because in my career we had never beaten Montreal in the playoffs," O'Reilly recalls. "And it got down to nine seconds, and I was standing there on the bench as the head coach, thinking, 'They can't score two goals in nine seconds.' Maybe I was getting over-confident. The clock ran down and I remember jumping on the ice, realizing that we had just beaten Montreal and eliminated them from the playoffs for the first time in 50 or 55 years."

O'Reilly's Bruins lost in the Stanley Cup final that year to Edmonton, just as head coach Mike Milbury's Bruins would lose two years later. The two had that unfortunate result in common, and a coaching intensity in common as well.

"They had their own ways of motivating," remembers goalie Reggie Lemelin, who played for both. "They were players' coaches in that they wanted you to succeed. They were on your side, and they were great guys."

Often, it's not a single game or series that defines a coach, it's a single moment—a fact best represented by Steve Kasper. Nine years a forward for Boston, Kasper took over the coaching reins in 1995. He finished his first season nine games above .500. The next season the Bruins finished 19 games below .500. Along the way, Kasper left an unfortunate benchmark by benching Cam Neely and Kevin Stevens during a game in Toronto. It's what he's remembered for.

*above:*

*Mike Sullivan was victimized by the organization's post-lock-out decisions in 2005-06. A division champ' the year prior to the work stoppage, a completely revamped roster finished last in the division the following season of play. A change at general manager brought an end to Sullivan's tenure after his second season.*

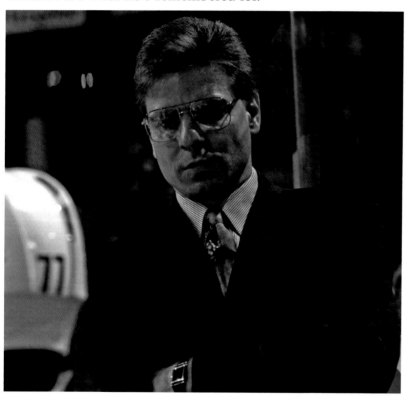

*left:*

*It's believed Steve Kasper was only following orders from above when he benched Cam Neely and Kevin Stevens in a game versus Toronto, a move he's remembered for, and which overshadows an excellent career as a Bruins centerman in the eighties.*

"I was on the team when Neely got benched, and Kevin Stevens, too," recalls then Bruins forward Tim Sweeney. "I think Kasper—he was a new coach—was trying to gain a little bit of respect by saying no one is playing very well, you guys aren't playing very well. I think what really struck me that was really weird about that was, not only did they dress to play, but then they never played. I think that's what really irked a lot of people because, hey, it's one thing to sit them

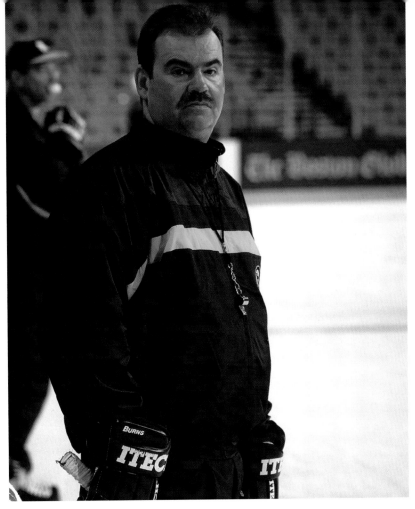

*above:*

*Pat Burns won the Jack Adams Award as top NHL coach three times with three different Original Six teams, including Boston in 1997-98. He's the only three-time winner of the Award.*

in the stands, but it's another thing to sit them on the bench the whole game." [Was the benching actually ordered by Harry Sinden? If so, the coach never spoke up, took the heat, and eventually lost his job.]

Kasper was replaced by Pat Burns in the spring of 1997, the same year a young Swede began his lengthy playing career as a Bruin in Boston.

"I think all of them [coaches] have had an effect in one way or another," states Bruins forward P.J. Axelsson. "I had Pat Burns when I first got here. He helped me to prepare to play every night. It was different coming from Sweden where you play 36 games or 40 games to 82 games so that was different, and he helped me out with that. The Swedish League was real defensive, so the coach that we had in Sweden before I got here was really defensive minded, so that helped me a lot, especially coming over and having Pat Burns as coach, because he was really defensive."

"I was really intimidated by Pat Burns that first season I was allowed to shoot between the benches," recalls Steve Babineau. "He had this stare, a really intense stare. I had to take his photo from between the benches for the yearbook and I finally had to just go up and ask him, because I didn't want to snap his picture without asking. I had an experience in Toronto when he was coaching the Leafs where he yelled at me for taking strobe pictures during practice, so I was a little cautious with him."

Burns's tenure in Boston ended as the new millennium began. A string of six, semi-rapid-fire coaching changes have followed. Inconsistency in a position as important as head coach can be challenging not just for a hockey club's players, but for its front office staff as well. Every personality brings new quirks, rules, and temperaments to the organization.

Often, it's not a single game or series that defines a coach; it's a single moment.

"We've been really lucky—I think Claude Julien is the 13th or 14th coach since I've been here and they've all treated me well," says Heidi Holland, who joined the club's media department in the mid-80s. "For a PR person they've all been great. You know, some [media people] have issues with Mike Keenan, but he never met a microphone he didn't like, so for a PR person that was great. Brian Sutter had his Western Canadian farm boy ways and thoughts. Some of his quotes would make you think twice, but I was very lucky with all of the coaches over the years. They were great to deal with. Kasper was good to me. Obviously, media wasn't his favorite thing to do, but he knew the Boston market and he knew the Boston media from playing here for so many years, and he was fine."

"It was easy with guys like Kasper, O'Reilly, Cheevers, and Milbury because they had been players, they all knew me, and they always saw me around the room," points out Babineau. "They knew what I had to do; they understood what I was up to. I could even get pretty good set-up shots from them. Although they were coaches with the team, they were still players in my mind.

"Keenan was a little different. He took down all of the archive photos in the dressing room—Orr, Shore, stuff like that," adds Babineau, "and he even had a weird thing about the team picture. I had taken about 25 of these things, and right after I had everyone set up that year for the photo, he stood up and

*above:*

*"Iron" Mike Keenan replaced Burns eight games into 2000-01 and lasted just the one season. As of June 2008, he's held the head coaching position with eight different NHL teams.*

above:

*Dave Lewis earned renown as an assistant in Detroit under Scotty Bowman, helping to win three Stanley Cups. As Bowman's successor with the Wings, he didn't meet with similar head coaching success. In 2006-'07 in Boston, his team finished six games below .500 and failed to make the playoffs.*

below:

*Armand "Bep" Guidolin took over with 26 games remaining in the 1972-73 season for legendary Canadiens and Bruins defenseman and defending Cup winning coach Tom Johnson. The former Boston Braves (AHL) coach found the act too tough to follow, or more accurately, his players did.*

started critiquing the set-up and where everyone was sitting. It became a joke after that. Every time I had a set-up photo of any sort, I'd laugh and say, 'Did Keenan approve this?'"

Two factors most often affect coaches more than anything else. The first one can prevent a career from burgeoning: a former player realizes that coaching, aside from the competitive element of compiling wins and losses, isn't the same as playing. The camaraderie vanishes, or at least is completely different, and the pressure and the frustration of not being able to control matters on the ice becomes overwhelming. Coaches are hired to be fired, and very few retire on top.

"I don't know if there is a best part about it," states legendary Bruins goalie and former coach Gerry Cheevers. "I figured it out after I took the job, that every year, there were all but one who failed. The only guy that succeeded was the guy who won the Cup. There was one success and however many failures. As a player, you could shake off a loss and prepare yourself for the next game. As a coach, to me it was a much tougher deal. I wouldn't be playing the next game. Playing, I'd jump right back in. As a coach, I took it harder, and I don't think I was programmed for it. Instead of dealing with it yourself, you're looking at it through 40 eyes."

The other factor that can't be controlled is being hired after a legend or a huge success has moved on.

The first example would be former Bruins player Armand "Bep" Guidolin, who followed the last two coaches to win Cups in Boston, the combination of Harry Sinden and then Tom Johnson.

"Bep used to whistle," exclaims Esposito. "He used to whistle at us, and one night he was whistling and I wouldn't come off the ice. And he got angry at me and he said, 'Don't you hear me?' I said, 'I'm not a dog so don't whistle. I'm not going to answer to a whistle. My father used to whistle and I'd come a-runnin', so I'm not answering to a whistle no more.' He and I really didn't get along all that much. I really didn't think he was that great a coach."

Was Bep actually a bad guy or a bad coach? Maybe the new face, the adjustment, contributed to Espo's, and other players' potential dislike. Guidolin coached 104 games in Boston and 21 more in the playoffs. He moved on despite winning more than 73 percent of his games.

Example two is Fred Creighton, who had an impressive winning percentage as well (63.7), one that would earn a coach a lengthy stay anywhere else. Unfortunately for him, Creighton replaced the irreplaceable: Don Cherry.

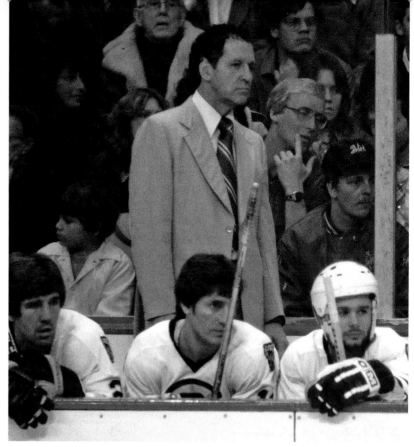

*above:*

*Fred Creighton had the disadvantage of following larger-than-life Don Cherry as the head coach of the Bruins. He lasted seven games short of a full season despite an excellent winning percentage.*

"What I remember about Fred Creighton is that he was kind of a quiet guy. I kind of remember that," says then Bruins forward Al Secord. "I think the toughest part was following the act of Don Cherry. Don was the kind of guy...he approached it as a very simple game. What I liked about the guy [Cherry] was, he let the older guys run the team. The older guys knew when to cut loose and have a good time; they knew when to shut it down. They kept the younger guys in line, and they taught you how to be a team player all the time. The team was very close, they took care of each other, and we didn't have any problems. If a guy created a problem and it got all the way to Don, he was shipped out pretty quick.

"I think after Don Cherry being such a character, and I think also [because] he was the best coach I ever had, I think [for Fred] it was such a tough act to follow. I mean, he took over pretty much right after Cherry was fired, and I think that was the thing—it just wasn't the same thing," Secord adds.

Timing of tenure is uncontrollable, more a matter of circumstance than an actual element to the job.

For fans in Boston, regardless of when a bench boss is hired, physicality must be part of the coaching formula. Even in this most modern incarnation of the rules and game, the elements that mean the most to Bruins fans are pretty straightforward: Combine winning with toughness. Rough 'em up on the ice, while you're roughing 'em up on the scoreboard. Simple advice for any Bruins coach.

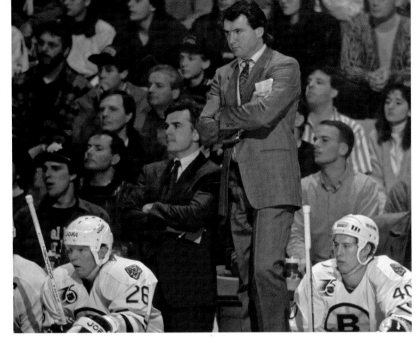

*right:*

*It may be unfair to state Rick Bowness is a better assistant coach than he is a head, although in nine different seasons with five different clubs, he's only led a team to the playoffs once. That was in his lone Boston season, 1991-92, when the B's were swept by eventual Cup champ Pittsburgh in the third round. He was replaced by Brian Sutter after the one season.*

Coaches whose tenures included or began after 1973-74, the season in which Steve Babineau took his first professional photo at a Bruins game.

| REGULAR SEASON STATISTICS | GP | W | L | T/OTL | W% |
|---|---|---|---|---|---|
| **Rick Bowness** \| 1991–1992<br>Fired after 1992 playoff sweep at the hands of the Penguins | 80 | 36 | 32 | 12 | .525 |
| **Pat Burns** \| 1997–2000<br>Coach of the year in three cities: Montreal, Toronto, and Boston | 254 | 105 | 103 | 52 | .516 |
| **Gerry Cheevers** \| 1980–1985<br>Reluctant to coach despite success behind bench | 376 | 204 | 126 | 46 | .604 |
| **Don Cherry** \| 1974–1979<br>Now considered one of Canada's most famous and influential persons | 400 | 231 | 105 | 64 | .658 |
| **Fred Creighton** \| 1979–1980<br>Simple problem of following a larger-than-life legend | 73 | 40 | 20 | 13 | .637 |
| **Robbie Ftorek** \| 2001–2003<br>High school star in Needham; 1972 U.S. Olympian | 155 | 76 | 52 | 27 | .577 |
| **Butch Goring** \| 1985–1986<br>Straight from the ice to the bench | 93 | 42 | 38 | 13 | .522 |
| **Armand "Bep" Guidolin** \| 1972–1974<br>Started as a player at age 16 in NHL; still youngest ever | 104 | 72 | 23 | 9 | .736 |
| **Claude Julien** \| 2007–2008<br>Took injury-plagued team to turnaround season and playoffs | 82 | 41 | 29 | 12 | .590 |
| **Steve Kasper** \| 1995–1997<br>Disliked for benching Neely & Stevens in Toronto | 164 | 66 | 78 | 20 | .463 |
| **Mike Keenan** \| 2000–2001<br>"Iron Mike"; hired by Sinden, fired by O'Connell | 74 | 33 | 28 | 13 | .538 |
| **Dave Lewis** \| 2006–2007<br>Won multiple Cups as an assistant coach in Detroit, but didn't translate | 82 | 35 | 41 | 6 | .463 |
| **Mike Milbury** \| 1989–1991<br>Last to coach Bruins to the Stanley Cup Final | 160 | 90 | 49 | 21 | .628 |

| REGULAR SEASON STATISTICS | GP | W | L | T/OTL | W% |
|---|---|---|---|---|---|
| **Mike O'Connell** \| 2003<br>Brief stint to figure out Sullivan was replacement for Ftorek | 9 | 3 | 3 | 3 | .500 |
| **Terry O'Reilly** \| 1986–1989<br>Coach when Bruins snapped 45-year playoff drought to Canadiens | 227 | 115 | 86 | 26 | .564 |
| **Harry Sinden** \| 1966–1970, 1980, 1985<br>Greatest GM never to win Stanley Cup; won as coach in 1970 | 327 | 153 | 116 | 58 | .557 |
| **Mike Sullivan** \| 2003–2006<br>Victim of poor post-lock-out financial strategies of team hierarchy | 164 | 70 | 56 | 38 | .543 |
| **Brian Sutter** \| 1992–1995<br>Fired the same day the Celtics fired Chris Ford | 216 | 120 | 73 | 23 | .609 |

# 11

# MASKED MEN

*above:*

*Gerry Cheevers's stitch-art is arguably the most famous mask design in hockey history. Simplistic yet barbaric, the stitch marks indicate where the goaltender would have been hit. "That would have been my face," laughs Cheevers.*

*left:*

*A focused Andy Moog makes a glove save. Acquired from Edmonton in March of 1988, Moog backstopped the Bruins to the Stanley Cup final in 1988 and 1990.*

Of the goaltenders on the Bruins Hall of Fame list, an overwhelming majority made just a brief stop in Boston. Names like Harry "Apple Cheeks" Lumley [78 games with Boston], Jacques Plante [8 games], Terry Sawchuk [102 games], and Bernie Parent [57 games] are all more readily identifiable with other organizations. Only Cecil "Tiny" Thompson from the 1920s and '30s, Frank Brimsek from the 1930s and '40s, and Gerry Cheevers from the 1960s and '70s are legitimate black-and-gold Bruins. Cheevers is the only post-expansion netminder, and the only one from photographer Steve Babineau's era, to earn his way into the Hall.

The list of Bruins netminders who "stole the show" is short: Many simply held down the fort while a talented and feisty group of skaters in front of them, particularly defensemen, commanded much of the attention. Part of it may just be a coincidence, part of it may be impatience with development, or part of it could be the physical, low-risk style of play, which prevented goaltenders in Boston from consistently having to stand on their heads. For whatever reason, goalies fall behind blueliners and forwards in the Bruins annals of greatness.

When listing prominent Bruins netminders, mainly because he manned the crease for Boston's last two Cups, Cheevers's name first comes to mind.

His crease partner for those title runs, veteran Eddie Johnston, is the last to play every game of his team's season [all 70 in 1963–64], but as the Bruins climb into Cup contention in the late '60s, Cheevers emerged as the choice.

"He was very consistent," states former teammate John "Pie" McKenzie. "He helped win some very important games for us, a championship goalie."

"'Cheesie' was a big-game goaltender," proclaims Babineau. "When the game was on the line, he was there. He never wanted to practice; he'd take as few shots as he could. He didn't want to stand there and take slapshots, but in the game he was huge."

One could argue that Cheevers is not only the greatest Bruins goalie of the modern era, but the greatest goalie of all time. Only Frank "Mr. Zero" Brimsek, for two stints beginning in 1938, with one more win and nine more shutouts, has similar numbers. Cheevers had several fewer losses and a similar goals-against-average.

"Cheesie was fading out at the beginning of my career," adds Babineau, "but I remember from watching just as a fan and as a photographer what a great goalie he could be. Then of course, there's the mask."

Cheevers's mask artwork, made up of simple black stitch marks on the spots where the puck had made contact, has to

Cheevers's mask artwork, has to be hockey's greatest ever. "That would have been my face," states Cheevers.

*above:*

*Photographer Steve Babineau referred to Cheevers as a "cool cucumber." "He didn't like taking shots, he didn't like practice, he just liked to play." Here, before a game, Cheevers chats with goaltending Hall of Famer Johnny Bower, sitting alongside injured Leafs forward Darryl Sittler.*

be hockey's greatest ever. Despite the simplicity, it remains unforgettable and sends a strong message. It was assistant trainer John "Frosty" Forristall who first put the magic marker to Cheevers's mask.

"That would have been my face," states Cheevers, who began his career sans protection.

The goaltending carousel in Boston has been consistent throughout the years, thus making Cheevers an exception to the rule. Only five other men's names pop up when one thinks of decent consistency during the last three-and-a-half decades. The acrobatic Gilles Gilbert [277 Bruins games played] played a prominent role with the Lunch Pail Gang. Byron Dafoe [283 games] nailed down 25 shut-outs as a

*above:*

*Pete Peeters posing without his mask.*

*right:*

*Pete Peeters was the last Bruins goaltender to win the Vezina Trophy as the League's best keeper. To the goalie's left, that's a glimpse of former Bruin Peter McNab with Vancouver, seeking a scoring chance.*

Bruin at the turn of the millennium and was runner-up for the Vezina Trophy behind Dominik Hasek in 1999. But his teams only passed the first round of the playoffs once. Reggie Lemelin [183 games] had some big playoff wins and helped the team to the final twice. Andy Moog [261 games] fell into place right along with Lemelin, while the 1982-83 Vezina Trophy winner Pete Peeters [171 games] was the next closest thing to goaltending greatness.

In his fourth year in the League, his first in Boston after a trade from Philadelphia, Peeters put together a 31-game unbeaten streak, which fell one short of the NHL record of 32, set in 1971–72 by Cheevers. Peeters's streak ended on February 16th in Buffalo.

"Gerry was our head coach, and late in the game when we knew we were going to lose in Buffalo, he sent all of the guys off the bench out to me, to congratulate me and such," Peeters remembers. "That was a special moment and a great gesture I thought. He was a pretty special coach. As a former goalie, he helped me with the mental aspects, how to deal with the trials and tribulations.

Peeters and the Bruins made it to the conference finals that playoff season before bowing out to the eventual Cup champs, the New York Islanders.

These days, Peeters continues to take Cheevers's advice one step further, as the goalie coach for the Edmonton Oilers.

*above:*

*Gilles Gilbert was a fixture for the Bruins as a tandem goaltender. After arriving in 1973 he was the number one, then shared time and played behind Cheevers from 1975 to 1980. Toronto's "Cowboy" Bill Flett is looking for the rebound while Bruin Daryl Edestrand approaches. The photo is from the 1974-75 season.*

*Bill Ranford had two stints in Boston a decade apart. He was first drafted by the B's in 1985 as the 52nd overall pick. Both times he was traded, a goalkeeper came the other way as part of the deal, Andy Moog from Edmonton in March 1988, and Jim Carey from Washington in March 1997. Here, Ranford dons the B's "Bear-head" third jersey, referred to by some jokingly as the "Pooh jersey." Less than ferocious, the image wasn't based on the lovable character obviously, but on a bear painting that hung behind Harry Sinden's desk.*

*Gerry Cheevers departed Boston for the start-up World Hockey Assocation after the 1972 Cup. He returned in 1975. Here, Cheevers recovers from a save, with Cleveland Baron J.P. Parise on the doorstep.*

"I try to emphasize lateral motion; it's something I learned from [the late goaltending coach] Warren Strelow in Washington," Peeters says. "When things go south for a goalie, when he gets deep in his crease, when he goes in the tank, it's usually because he's lost his lateral motion. I wish I had understood that much earlier. When I played, I got traded every time I went in the tank."

Peeters had great years in Philly, Boston, and Washington, but remembers the Bruins with the most fondness.

"Our [Edmonton's] AHL affiliate is in Springfield [Massachusetts] now, so as goalie coach I'm able to sneak back to Boston now and again," Peeters says. "I have flashbacks of the great times, the people, the fans, and playing for Cheevers."

While Cheesie's career may be the Bruins' benchmark, and Peeters's single season is almost unmatched, the same can't be said for Cleon Daskalakis and his efforts. A Boston native who produced All-America numbers at Boston University, Cleon's pro career wasn't "all that." Cleon played a grand total of 12 NHL games for the Bruins, and as a local, he still gets teased by the other alumni about his career stats. Cleon remains a fixture in town, as the president for Celebrity Marketing, which handles philanthropic endeavors for pro athletes, and represents Hall of Famer Bruin Ray Bourque and other pro athletes.

"It was the fulfillment of a dream," states Daskalakis. "I grew up in Canton, Massachusetts. There's pictures of me when I'm 10 and 11 years old with a Bruins jacket on, and I always aspired to be Gerry Cheevers: that was my goal. I idolized him and Bobby Orr. When I was a kid, I dreamed of being the Bruins goaltender. In my high school yearbook under class predictions, they predicted that I'd be goalie for the Bruins. So, when the opportunity came, I was a free agent, the Bruins showed interest, and it worked out. I think it's almost hard to believe, hard to think about the dream of playing for the team you grew up with, but then to have that happen! I wouldn't change a thing—even though I didn't play much—to play in Boston.

"A lot of my friends were guys that were hurt a lot," Cleon continues. "Being a second or third goaltender, I'd spend time hanging out with the hurt guys, training at the same time, taking practice shots when they were recovering. That's part of the reason why Gord Kluzak and I are such good friends. He had injuries quite a bit while I was there."

Defenseman Kluzak was Daskalakis's best man at his wedding in Greece: the ultimate symbol of camaraderie on the ice—and off the ice.

While a number of position players from New England have had a huge impact on the Bruins' success over the years, it's simply not the case for goaltenders. The region has produced solid NHL netminders, but very few who have helped the Bruins. In fact, the list is short. For example, Jim Stewart, born in Cambridge, played one game for the B's, and Matt DelGuidice, from Connecticut, played 11. Only Olympic Gold Medalist Jim Craig and Dorchester native Jim Carey had definitive impacts, and the impacts were felt elsewhere or outside the NHL.

*above:*

*This photo was taken by amateur photographer Steve Babineau from his obstructed view seat in the stadium section of the old Garden. Netminder Eddie Johnston retired prior to Babs getting his press credentials and becoming a professional shooter. Based on ticket stubs, Babs believes he took this photo during the 1970-71 season.*

*right:*

*Dorchester native Jim Carey came from Washington in a trade that sent Bill Ranford to the Cap's in 1997. After Carey had won a Vezina Trophy in DC, his career slowly fizzled, it's believed mostly due to his lack of interest in playing the position.*

*below:*

*Jim Craig returned to his home town to sign with the Bruins in 1980-81 after playing just four games at the end of the previous season for the Atlanta Flames. The former Boston University Terrier won Gold with Team USA in 1980 with the "Miracle" team, but then his pro career was short. He played 23 games in all for Boston.*

Possibly, the goaltender who best represents Boston ideals is one of Boston's most recent. Tim Thomas isn't a New Englander—he's from Flint, Michigan—but he does represent the concepts of perseverance and hard work as well as anyone. By chance, Thomas ended up in the region playing college hockey at the University of Vermont. With teammates and future NHLers Martin St. Louis and Eric Perrin, Thomas helped lead the Catamounts to their first NCAA Frozen Four. From there, he was drafted by Quebec (Colorado), but was released by the Avalanche. After a brief stint in the Edmonton organization, Thomas headed overseas and played in Finland and in Sweden. After catching the eye of NHL scouts, he was signed by the Bruins as a free agent in 2001. By then he was already 27 years old.

"They decided to give me a chance," Thomas remembers, "and I had a really good camp. But when they broke camp, they kept two other goalies in Providence, including Andrew Raycroft, and I was under contract to the Bruins, headed back to Finland."

After a season there, Thomas returned to the Boston organization in 2002–03, where he was called up to the NHL for the first time, playing four games (three wins, one loss), including a win in his first start in Edmonton.

"I was very emotional coming off the ice [after] the first game," admits Thomas, smiling, "and *Hockey Night in Canada* pulled me aside for an interview, so I had to put on a straight face right away and pretend I wasn't that emotional."

The next blip for Timmy: the NHL lockout. He went back to Finland to become league MVP one season, and then came back to the Bruins, only to be shipped to Providence once again. Finally, midway through 2005–06, due to injuries in the lineup, Thomas earned a full-time gig. He signed a three-year contract that season after single-handedly helping the team stay in the playoff race in the weeks prior to the Olympic break.

"After getting called up in January, I ended up winning a lot of games and ended up winning the [Bruins] Seventh Player Award, so it was a season of highs and lows, that's for sure," says Thomas.

A new benchmark came in 2008, when he was named to the NHL Eastern Conference All-Star team. Thomas played the third period and ended up winning the game.

"I've hit a few milestones that I'm proud of," says Thomas, "but hopefully we can hit a few more."

Not bad for a kid whose childhood dream was to play for his local pro team, the Flint Generals of the IHL.

*above:*

*Andrew Raycroft looked like a world beater in 2003-04 before the NHL work stoppage, winning the Calder Trophy as rookie of the year. After the lockout he was a contract hold-out, he suffered an injury, and his time in Boston went downhill before being dealt to Toronto in the summer of 2006.*

One thing Thomas hasn't experienced on a regular basis is the thrill and intensity of the NHL playoffs. Aside from Cheevers, one of the Boston goalies whose seen more than most is Reggie Lemelin. Lemelin was the netminder in 1988 when the Bruins beat the Canadiens in the playoffs for the first time in 45 years.

"The whole playoffs were great," states Lemelin. "To me, it didn't mean the same as it did to the team, and some of the players, and to the organization. It was my first year in Boston, so I didn't feel the same thing that these guys felt playing Montreal—what it meant. I had played for Atlanta/Calgary for nine years. I hadn't been part of this rivalry and I came in with a different attitude and view. Beating Montreal was great, because I felt for the other guys on the team, and the management and the fans. I was happy for that part there, but as far as I was concerned, we hadn't won the Cup—we had beaten Montreal in the second round. It didn't mean as much to me, although it was an important step. For all of the fans around, it was as if we'd won the Stanley Cup. It was incredible."

For all of the fans around, it was as if we'd won the Stanley Cup. It was incredible.

The Bruins would go on to earn a chance at the Cup that season against Edmonton in the finals and again two seasons later, both times with Lemelin as one of the backstops.

"We had a better chance in the '90 series than we did in the '88," Reggie points out. "Nineteen eighty-eight—a lot of things happened along the way. It was crazy. It was the year of the doughnut thing with the ref [after a tough loss to Boston, New Jersey coach Jim Schoenfeld called referee Don Koharski a pig and told him to "have another donut"], the year the lights went out, and it was also the year we finally beat Montreal in the second round. Nineteen ninety—I thought we had a better hockey club, they [Edmonton] had lost Gretzky, they had lost Fuhr, some of their core players. The first game, we played a pretty good game. Glen Wesley [Bruins defenseman] missed the [wide open] net in the overtime. We were all

*below:*

*Along with Gilbert/Cheevers, the Reggie Lemelin/Andy Moog goaltending tandem was arguably one of the best two in Bruins history.*

*above:*

*On January 24, 1987, Steve Babineau, using flash strobes, snapped a photo of Reggie Lemelin of the Calgary Flames during pregame warm-up as Lemelin looked up at the ceiling of the Garden. Lemelin noticed the strobes, was spooked, and early in the first period asked the referee to tell Babs to stop taking pictures. He signed with Boston the next season and forgot the incident, much to the relief of the team's nervous photographer.*

standing on the bench thinking it was over; then it goes three overtimes and we lose. Then the next night, they had gained so much confidence they won the game pretty bad. From that point on we just never recovered. I really believe if we win that first game we're in good shape and it's maybe [a] different series."

During that playoff season, Lemelin experienced one of the goaltending quirks, or realities, of postseason hockey: when a coach [Mike Milbury] sticks with the goalie who won the most recent game. With Captain Ray Bourque injured and out of the lineup, Lemelin was replaced in Game 4 of the opening series against Hartford with the score 5-2 for the Whalers. Andy Moog came in, the Bruins scored four unanswered goals to win the game. Boston would go on to win the series in seven.

"He took over in that game and won, and we won again, and we went on to the next round against Montreal and we won in five games, and then we played Washington and won in four, and he was playing well, and we kept going, and that stuff happens," explains Lemelin. "He and we kept winning, so we go with it."

Most recently, Lemelin is a goaltending coach in the NHL for the Philadelphia Flyers. This, after a 15-year NHL career and 236 regular season wins.

"Toward the end, no question about it, I was always talking to the younger players. I didn't view the younger players as a threat to my career at that point, so I was always trying to help them by showing them the tricks and discussing the game with them," Coach Lemelin states. "I think that's why Andy and I had such a good relationship. He was six years younger than me when he joined the Bruins and I actually helped him out. It was my first year with the Bruins and he came in at the deadline, and we went all the way to the final, and we had a very healthy relationship. Two or three years later he took over."

If only Cleon Daskalakis had had Reggie as a teammate.

"I backed up Pete Peeters, Doug Keans, Pat Riggin, and Bill

*above:*

*Doug Keans played 154 games in net for the Bruins, a solid back-up during the mid-1980s. Here, Keans plays the puck up the boards, away from Montreal Canadiens Captain Bob Gainey.*

Ranford," lists Cleon. "One of my favorite goaltenders that I didn't get to play with was Reggie Lemelin. He was the type of goaltender…me as a young guy, I really could have benefited from him. He's so intelligent about the position, about the game, not only the physical elements but also the mental aspects of the game. He always jokes with me and says, 'You'd have had an amazing career if I was around,' and I know that. He had an ability to break things down, and teach, and had perseverance. He's the one goalie I wish I had played with. I think he would have made a difference in my career. I didn't miss him by that much, maybe a couple years."

Lemelin responds with laughter. "I've seen him play some alumni games and I started to play some alumni games and several times I'd say to him, 'How did you not make it big? You've got a lot of good stuff in your game.' I'm not sure if I could have helped him—I wasn't there then—but maybe."

*below:*

*Sussex, England, native "Lord" Byron Dafoe manned the crease for the Bruins for five seasons beginning in 1997. He lost only 104 of the 283 games he played in Boston, and tallied 25 shut-outs.*

1. *Robbie Tallas*   2. *Vincent Riendeau*   3. *Cleon Daskalakis*   4. *Pat Riggin*   5. *Blaine Lacher*   6. *Dave Reece*   7. *Jim Pettie*

8. John Grahame  9. Ken Broderick  10. Craig Billington  11. Marco Baron  12. Daniel Berthiaume

left:

*Surfer dude [now minister] John Blue from Huntington Beach, California, and the more successful veteran Jon Casey from Grand Rapids, Minnesota, gave it their best effort for the B's during the 1993-94 campaign. Both moved on right after, the flopper Blue played 5 more NHL games, Casey played 43 more.*

Goalies whose careers included or began after 1973-74, the season in which Steve Babineau took his first professional photo at a Bruins game.

| BRUINS REGULAR SEASON STATISTICS | GP | W | L | T/OT | GAA | SO |
|---|---|---|---|---|---|---|
| **Alex Auld**—Thunder Bay, ON | 23 | 9 | 7 | 5 | 2.32 | 2 |
| #29 | 2007–2008 | Two-career shut-out losses, in shoot-outs | | | | | | |
| **Scott Bailey**—Calgary, AB | 19 | 6 | 6 | 2 | 3.42 | 0 |
| #39 | 1995–1997 | Victimized by a four-goal Mario Lemieux night | | | | | | |
| **Mike Bales**—Prince Albert, SK | 1 | 0 | 0 | 0 | 2.40 | 0 |
| #30 | 1992–1993 | Scored goal two seasons ago in German pros | | | | | | |
| **Marco Baron**—Montreal, QC | 64 | 31 | 24 | 5 | 3.40 | 1 |
| #31, 33 | 1979–1983 | Pro debut in same game as Jim Stewart | | | | | | |
| **Yves Belanger**—Baie Comeau, QC | 8 | 2 | 0 | 3 | 3.48 | 0 |
| #31 | 1979–1980 | Cheevers injury opened the door for him | | | | | | |
| **Daniel Berthiaume**—Longueuil, QC | 8 | 1 | 4 | 2 | 3.16 | 0 |
| #31, 50 | 1991–1992 | 2-17-1 in Ottawa's inaugural season | | | | | | |
| **Craig Billington**—London, ON | 35 | 15 | 14 | 3 | 3.35 | 1 |
| #1 | 1994–1996 | 15-year NHL career as the ideal back-up | | | | | | |
| **John Blue**—Huntington Beach, CA | 41 | 14 | 16 | 7 | 2.94 | 1 |
| #39, 45 | 1992–1994 | Face injury with surfboard one summer | | | | | | |
| **Ken Broderick**—Toronto, ON | 20 | 9 | 8 | 1 | 2.61 | 1 |
| #31 | 1973–1975 | Team Canada; '64 Olympics; no medals | | | | | | |
| **Ross Brooks**—Toronto, ON | 54 | 37 | 7 | 6 | 2.64 | 4 |
| #30 | 1972–1975 | Tied NHL mark with 14-game win streak, '73-'74 | | | | | | |
| **Jim Carey**—Dorchester, MA | 29 | 8 | 15 | 1 | 3.52 | 2 |
| #30 | 1996–1998 | Vezina in Washington; didn't like his job | | | | | | |
| **Jon Casey**—Grand Rapids, MI | 57 | 30 | 15 | 9 | 2.88 | 4 |
| #30 | 1993–1994 | Dubbed "Technicolor 5-hole" by writer | | | | | | |
| **Gerry Cheevers**— St. Catharines, ON | 416 | 229 | 101 | 74 | 2.89 | 26 |
| #30 | 1965–1972, 1975–1980 | Two Stanley Cups and a legendary mask | | | | | | |

| BRUINS REGULAR SEASON STATISTICS | GP | W | L | T/OT | GAA | SO |
|---|---|---|---|---|---|---|
| **Tim Cheveldae**—Melville, SK | 2 | 0 | 1 | 0 | 3.23 | 0 |
| #31 | 1996–1997 | Goal partner in Detroit named Alain Chevrier | | | | | | |
| **Jim Craig**—North Easton, MA | 23 | 9 | 7 | 6 | 3.68 | 0 |
| #30 | 1980–1981 | Hero of Team USA Olympic Gold in 1980 | | | | | | |
| **Byron Dafoe**—Sussex, England | 283 | 132 | 104 | 40 | 2.30 | 25 |
| #34 | 1997–2002 | "Lord Byron" Vezina finalist in 1999 | | | | | | |
| **Cleon Daskalakis**—Boston, MA | 12 | 3 | 4 | 1 | 4.86 | 0 |
| #35 | 1984–1987 | Better known as Ray Bourque's PR man | | | | | | |
| **Matt DelGuidice**—West Haven, CT | 11 | 2 | 5 | 1 | 3.87 | 0 |
| #33, 70 | 1990–1991 | East Haven Comets; then University of Maine | | | | | | |
| **Manny Fernandez**—Etobicoke, ON | 4 | | | | | |
| #35 | 2007–2008 | Arrived from Minnesota with bad knee | | | | | | |
| **Brian Finley**—Sault Ste. Marie, ON | 2 | 0 | 1 | 0 | 3.05 | 0 |
| #60 | 2006–2007 | Sixth overall pick in 1999, Nashville | | | | | | |

| BRUINS REGULAR SEASON STATISTICS | GP | W | L | T/OT | GAA | SO |
|---|---|---|---|---|---|---|
| **Norm Foster**—Vancouver, BC | 3 | 2 | 1 | 0 | 4.57 | 0 |

#29, 36 | 1990–1991 | Won 1986 National Title with Michigan State

| | GP | W | L | T/OT | GAA | SO |
|---|---|---|---|---|---|---|
| **Gilles Gilbert**—St. Esprit, QC | 277 | 155 | 73 | 39 | 2.95 | 16 |

#1 | 1973–1980 | Traded for fellow goalie Rogie Vachon in 1980

| | GP | W | L | T/OT | GAA | SO |
|---|---|---|---|---|---|---|
| **John Grahame**—Denver, CO | 76 | 29 | 30 | 9 | 2.77 | 4 |

#30, 47 | 1999–2003 | Won Calder Cup in 1999, Ron's son

| | GP | W | L | T/OT | GAA | SO |
|---|---|---|---|---|---|---|
| **Ron Grahame**—Victoria, BC | 40 | 26 | 6 | 7 | 2.76 | 3 |

#31 | 1977–1978 | Traded to LA for '79 draft pick, Ray Bourque

| | GP | W | L | T/OT | GAA | SO |
|---|---|---|---|---|---|---|
| **Jeff Hackett**—London, ON | 18 | 8 | 9 | 0 | 3.21 | 1 |

#30 | 2002–2003 | Goalie coach with Avalanche

| | GP | W | L | T/OT | GAA | SO |
|---|---|---|---|---|---|---|
| **Doug Keans**—Pembroke, ON | 154 | 83 | 46 | 13 | 3.33 | 4 |

#31 | 1983–1988 | Took over starting job from Pete Peeters

| | GP | W | L | T/OT | GAA | SO |
|---|---|---|---|---|---|---|
| **Blaine Lacher**—Medicine Hat, AB | 47 | 22 | 16 | 4 | 2.80 | 4 |

#31 | 1994–1996 | '92 Lake Superior State National Champs

| | GP | W | L | T/OT | GAA | SO |
|---|---|---|---|---|---|---|
| **Reggie Lemelin**—Quebec City, QC | 183 | 92 | 62 | 17 | 3.09 | 6 |

#1 | 1987–1993 | In net to beat Habs in '88 to break jinx

| | GP | W | L | T/OT | GAA | SO |
|---|---|---|---|---|---|---|
| **Joey McDonald**—Pictou, NS | 7 | 2 | 2 | 1 | 2.68 | 0 |

#31 | 2006–2007 | March win in NJ kept brief playoff hopes alive

| | GP | W | L | T/OT | GAA | SO |
|---|---|---|---|---|---|---|
| **Mike Moffat**—Galt, ON | 19 | 7 | 7 | 2 | 4.29 | 0 |

#30 | 1981–1984 | Won the Buffalo series in 1982 playoffs

| | GP | W | L | T/OT | GAA | SO |
|---|---|---|---|---|---|---|
| **Andy Moog**—Penticton, BC | 261 | 136 | 75 | 36 | 3.08 | 13 |

#35 | 1987–1993 | On 3 Cup winners in Edmonton

| | GP | W | L | T/OT | GAA | SO |
|---|---|---|---|---|---|---|
| **Pete Peeters**—Edmonton, AB | 171 | 91 | 57 | 16 | 2.99 | 9 |

#1 | 1982–1986 | Won '83 Vezina, with 31-game unbeaten streak

| | GP | W | L | T/OT | GAA | SO |
|---|---|---|---|---|---|---|
| **Jim Pettie**—Toronto, ON | 21 | 9 | 7 | 2 | 3.68 | 1 |

#31 | 1976–1979 | Prominent role in Plimpton book *Open Net* in '77

| | GP | W | L | T/OT | GAA | SO |
|---|---|---|---|---|---|---|
| **Felix Potvin**—Anjou, QC | 28 | 12 | 8 | 6 | 2.50 | 4 |

#29 | 2003–2004 | "Felix the Cat" fought goalie Ron Hextall

| | GP | W | L | T/OT | GAA | SO |
|---|---|---|---|---|---|---|
| **Bill Ranford**—Brandon, MB | 122 | 52 | 49 | 14 | 3.19 | 6 |

#30 | 1985–1987, 1995–1997 | Won Smythe Trophy with Edmonton vs. Boston

| | GP | W | L | T/OT | GAA | SO |
|---|---|---|---|---|---|---|
| **Tuukka Rask**—Savonlinna, Finland | 4 | 2 | 1 | 1 | 3.25 | 0 |

#40 | 2007–2008 | "Finnish Flash" obtained for Raycroft

| BRUINS REGULAR SEASON STATISTICS | GP | W | L | T/OT | GAA | SO |
|---|---|---|---|---|---|---|
| **Andrew Raycroft**—Belleville, ON | 108 | 43 | 46 | 10 | 2.62 | 3 |

#1 | 2000–2006 | Calder Trophy hold-out; then injury

| | GP | W | L | T/OT | GAA | SO |
|---|---|---|---|---|---|---|
| **Dave Reece**—Troy, NY | 14 | 7 | 5 | 2 | 3.32 | 2 |

#29, 30 | 1975–1976 | Sole victim of Darryl Sittler's 10-point game

| | GP | W | L | T/OT | GAA | SO |
|---|---|---|---|---|---|---|
| **Vincent Riendeau**—St. Hyacinthe, QC | 29 | 10 | 12 | 2 | 3.00 | 1 |

#37 | 1993–1995 | First North American NHLer to jump to Russia

| | GP | W | L | T/OT | GAA | SO |
|---|---|---|---|---|---|---|
| **Pat Riggin**—Kincardine, ON | 49 | 20 | 16 | 9 | 3.36 | 1 |

#1, 30 | 1985–1987 | Started career with Atlanta Flames

| | GP | W | L | T/OT | GAA | SO |
|---|---|---|---|---|---|---|
| **Roberto Romano**—Montreal, QC | 1 | 0 | 1 | 0 | 6.00 | 0 |

#1 | 1986–1987 | Arrived from Pittsburgh for Pat Riggin

| | GP | W | L | T/OT | GAA | SO |
|---|---|---|---|---|---|---|
| **Philippe Sauve**—Buffalo, NY | 2 | 0 | 0 | 0 | 5.85 | 0 |

#35 | 2006–2007 | His goalie father Bob a B's archrival in Buffalo

| | GP | W | L | T/OT | GAA | SO |
|---|---|---|---|---|---|---|
| **Paxton Schafer**—Medicine Hat, AB | 3 | 0 | 0 | 0 | 4.68 | 0 |

#1 | 1996–1997 | 10 minor league teams; 3 NHL games

| | GP | W | L | T/OT | GAA | SO |
|---|---|---|---|---|---|---|
| **Steve Shields**—Toronto, ON | 36 | 12 | 13 | 9 | 2.75 | 0 |

#31 | 2002–2003 | Journeyman; wore Cheevers's testimonial mask

| | GP | W | L | T/OT | GAA | SO |
|---|---|---|---|---|---|---|
| **Jordan Sigalet**—New Westminster, BC | 1 | 0 | 0 | 0 | 0.00 | 0 |

#57 | 2005–2006 | Played goal with multiple sclerosis

| | GP | W | L | T/OT | GAA | SO |
|---|---|---|---|---|---|---|
| **Peter Skudra**—Riga, Latvia | 25 | 6 | 12 | 1 | 3.33 | 0 |

#35 | 2000–2001 | NHL for eight seasons, then to Russian League

| | GP | W | L | T/OT | GAA | SO |
|---|---|---|---|---|---|---|
| **Jim Stewart**—Cambridge, MA | 1 | 0 | 1 | 0 | 15.00 | 0 |

#31 | 1979–1980 | Called up same day as M. Baron; started; lost

| | GP | W | L | T/OT | GAA | SO |
|---|---|---|---|---|---|---|
| **Don Sylvestri**—Sudbury, ON | 3 | 0 | 0 | 2 | 3.53 | 0 |

#30 | 1984–1985 | ECAC 1st-Team All-Star with Clarkson

| | GP | W | L | T/OT | GAA | SO |
|---|---|---|---|---|---|---|
| **Robbie Tallas**—Edmonton, AB | 87 | 26 | 35 | 10 | 2.85 | 3 |

#35 | 1995–2000 | Heart attack while playing in Finland

| | GP | W | L | T/OT | GAA | SO |
|---|---|---|---|---|---|---|
| **Tim Thomas**—Flint, MI | 165 | 73 | 62 | 20 | 2.80 | 6 |

#70, 30 | 2002–2008 | Two-time 7th Player Award winner

| | GP | W | L | T/OT | GAA | SO |
|---|---|---|---|---|---|---|
| **Hannu Toivonen**—Kalvola, Finland | 38 | 12 | 14 | 5 | 3.33 | 1 |

#33, 54 | 2005–2007 | Ankle injury sidetracked progress

| | GP | W | L | T/OT | GAA | SO |
|---|---|---|---|---|---|---|
| **Rogie Vachon**—Palmarolle, QC | 91 | 44 | 30 | 12 | 3.47 | 2 |

#1 | 1980–1982 | End of career with B's; had three Cups with Habs

| | GP | W | L | T/OT | GAA | SO |
|---|---|---|---|---|---|---|
| **Kay Whitmore**—Sudbury, ON | 5 | 1 | 2 | 0 | 5.32 | 0 |

#31 | 2000–2001 | 26th overall pick for Hartford in 1985

CHAPTER

# 12

# BLUELINERS

*above:*

*In a photo taken at the Hartford Civic Center, Brad Park skates away from Hartford Whaler forward Jordy Douglas. "Park is the best defenseman never to win the Norris," touts photographer Steve Babineau.*

*left:*

*Boston defensemen Garry Galley and Don Sweeney celebrate a goal. Galley came via free agency in 1988 and stayed three-and-a-half seasons while Sweeney was a near lifer, spending all but 63 of his 1,115 NHL games in Boston. He later moved to the Bruins front office.*

The characteristics that define most Bruins defensemen over the years are somewhat generic: play hard, hit, fight. Characteristics New Englanders would want in any hockey player. Or maybe so many Boston defensemen simply seem generic, because for so long, five or six of them on the roster would be residing in a shadow of greatness— greatness which, intended or not, took the spotlight off everyone else.

Eddie Shore, Bobby Orr, Ray Bourque: the first blueliners to pop into everyone's mind the moment the words "Bruins" and "defenseman" are mentioned in the same sentence. Believe it or not, there have been many other fine defensemen working the blue line for the Bruins over the past 35 years.

Brad Park for example played 501 games with Boston, 1,100-plus in the NHL, and his plaque resides in the Hall of Fame.

"Basically, Park was hated by the Bruins fans for a time there when he played for the Rangers," remembers Steve Babineau. "He and Orr were rivals. I remember them fighting one night. Until Bobby got hurt and Park came in as the savior replacement, Boston fans didn't like him. They did actually

*left:*

*In his first year with the team, Brad Park is shown wearing a B's road jersey with the 1976 U.S. bicentennial patch on the shoulder. Taken at the Montreal Forum on one of Babineau's first road excursions, the man back right is legendary bilingual Habs PA Announcer Claude Mouton.*

overlap for about a dozen [ten] games. I remember them working together at the point on the power play. Back and forth, back and forth, and finally one of them blasted it home."

"Brad was a great teacher, mentor, and a guy who showed us how to play the game, and how to handle ourselves outside the game," states Ray Bourque.

"Park was an unbelievable passer! Just unbelievable. He'd get it up to the blue line and then he'd make a seeing-eye pass to someone up-ice," Babineau says. "I remember him making passes to Jean Ratelle and Bobby Schmautz. Park's remembered for having that big goal against Buffalo [Park scored a game-7 overtime winner on April 24, 1983, against Buffalo to win the division final]. He was like a professor. It seemed like he was able to slow the game down."

I remember them working together at the point on the power play. Back and forth, back and forth, and finally one of them blasted it home.

Park spent eight seasons with the Bruins. He and the other Hall of Famers weren't the only D-men to enjoy lengthy, prosperous careers in Boston.

Maritimer Don Sweeney played all but 63 games of his 16 NHL seasons in Boston as a steady partner to Bourque and others.

"I came in at a time with some guys that had been around this organization for a while," says Sweeney, "and [they] felt like the Spoked B was tattooed on their ass, so to speak. That's how I learned, and I carried that with me."

*above:*

*It's believed Hall-of-Fame defenseman Ray Bourque spent more shifts during his career with Don Sweeney than with any other defenseman. Here, the two lace up in the "new" Garden Bruins dressing room.*

Since Sweeney entered the League in 1988, just 20 years ago, the attitude and devotion surrounding a team and its emblem has changed dramatically, probably more so than anything else because of the money involved and the level of free agency. It's a tendency that can be overcome.

"With the changeover and some of the younger players coming in, some of those things go by the wayside," Sweeney explains. "The onus is on older players to make guys understand and appreciate what it means to wear that [sweater], and point to the guys that have done it before them. For a period of time there, I thought that had waned a bit, but now being involved with the organization in a different capacity [Director of Hockey Operations and Player Development], and seeing Cam back here, and knowing the direction the GM wants to take things, *is* going to take things, and the way the

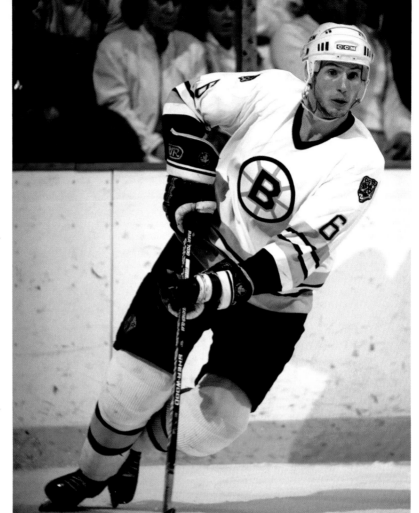

*left:*

The Bruins selected Glen Wesley 3rd overall in the 1987 draft out of Portland of the Western League. He spent seven seasons with Boston before being traded to the Hartford/Carolina organization in the summer of 1994. He won a Cup with the Hurricanes in 2006 and retired in May, 2008 after 21 NHL seasons.

*right:*

The Bruins were looking for another great defenseman when they chose big Gord Kluzak of the Western League Billings Bighorns as the first overall pick in the 1982 draft, ahead of forward Brian Bellows, and ahead of future Hall-of-Fame defensemen Scott Stevens and Phil Housley. Knee problems shortened Kluzak's career to 299 games.

coach handles things day to day, I think guys are starting to garner a greater appreciation for that. For me, that says an awful lot about where our organization is headed."

Sweeney played college hockey at Harvard, making him well aware of the Bruins' tradition, via osmosis across the Charles River.

I remember walking into the locker room for the first time at training camp, and to see all of those sweaters hanging there!

Meanwhile, many others obtained a love, devotion, and respect for the Spoked B simply by growing up near Boston. Not unlike Ontario natives playing for the Maple Leafs, certain Quebec natives playing for Montreal, or a kid from Windsor playing for the Red Wings, the hockey hotbed that is New England produces an endless list of Bruins fans who become Bruins.

"It was extra special for me and for any kid growing up in Boston to play locally," says 1980s Bruins defenseman Frank Simonetti. "To have an opportunity to play for your hometown team it was—certainly to play in the NHL was a treat—but to play for your hometown team was extra special."

Regional connections, college ties, and simple respect for hockey history affected others.

"It was a dream come true," admits Mike Milbury. "I played at Colgate and I really didn't have any anticipation of a professional career. I didn't get drafted. They used to have what they called a negotiation list, and each team could put four players on their negotiation list. They could drop a name, add a name; it was another one of those quasi-slavery rules. So after a tournament in Syracuse, Boston put me on their list. At the end of my senior year I got called up to the old Boston Braves and played a few games with them, and based on how I did there, they [the B's] gave me a tryout. My first day of training camp, eight o'clock practice for the veterans and I was on at ten. I was there two hours ahead to be ready."

"My childhood years were through the '70s, and I watched the Bruins, and that's when they were the Big Bad Bruins and I loved watching them," says Pennsylvania native Bob Beers, who spent 77 games as a defenseman with Boston. "So to have the ability to put that jersey on...I remember walking into the locker room for the first time at training camp, and to see all of those sweaters hanging there! I never got to play in any exhibition games that year. When I actually got to play in my first game it was down in Hartford and I walked into the locker room and you see all the sweaters hung nicely, the equipment guys did everything right; you walk in there and you see that, and you see that jersey and that was...it really hit. The feeling was unbelievable, and then you start to see the guys filter into the locker room...you realize it's for real."

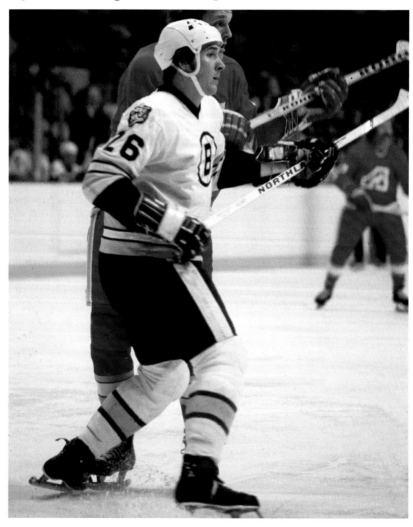

*below:*

*Mike Milbury, out of Colgate University and fresh off two years with Rochester in the American League, joined the Lunch Pail Gang and head coach Don Cherry in 1976. He went on to play more than 750 games as a Bruin.*

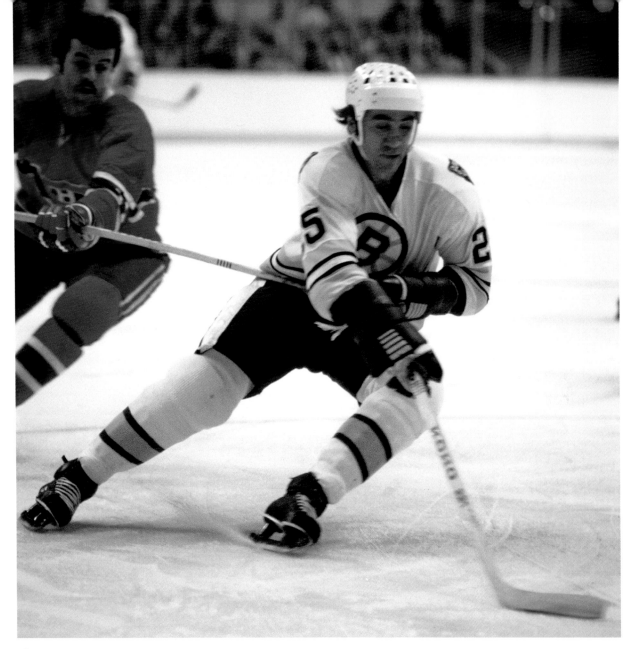

*above:*

*Gary Doak, known as "Sammy" because according to teammate Eddie Johnston, when they first came up, Doak had a nose like rat-packer Sammy Davis Jr. As is often the case in hockey, the name stuck in perpetuity. Doak, who won a Cup with the B's in 1970, is being chased by Canadiens left wing Yvon Lambert.*

"Boston was the greatest place to play," says longtime D-man Gary Doak, who like Sweeney, Milbury, Simonetti, and Beers, remains in the area. "I played in Vancouver, Detroit, and New York, but out of all those cities, Boston is a big city, but it's also a small city you can get around easy. We'd go to the North Shore, be at the rink in 15 minutes. We practiced up on 114 at the Danvers twin rinks. Everything was pretty unique. The people and fans of New England, you won't find a better group of fans than right here in Boston."

"I think being on an Original Six team is special in itself," states 333-game Bruins' defenseman Al Pedersen. "Not only at home but on the road, people come to see the Original Six teams. To be a part of the history of Boston sports...there's definitely more pressure playing in a town like Boston, but it made you better, and it made you appreciate the sport and the city that much more."

Pride in city, pride in team, and pride in emblem were characteristics shared by Pedersen and Sweeney, whose careers in Boston overlapped.

"I always felt this was going to be a difficult place for teams to come in and steal two points from," Sweeney points out, "and you knew when you went into certain buildings that you were in for a tough night. That's what it stood for to be a member of the Boston Bruins. We had a pack mentality and [coach] Mike Milbury described it as a pack mentality. It was a team mentality; it wasn't ever about one guy. You were able to call out teammates, and the pride and the heart, for me, stood out first and foremost."

Sweeney played more of his games with Ray Bourque than he did with anyone else. He shares the aforementioned common appreciation for one of the game's all-time greats.

"A lot of young players got a chance to play with Raymond, but it seems like more of a crutch, because obviously he can

*below:*

*Strike one on Bourque, with Sweeney playing catcher. How this puck ended up where it did, with Ray trying to grand slam it out of the zone while Don is standing right next to him is anyone's guess. Goalie Andy Moog is poised behind them.*

*Dallas Smith, being chased by North Stars Tom Reed (#20) and ex-Bruin Murray Oliver (#10). Smith helped the Bruins win two Cups and spent all but 29 of his 890 NHL games with the Bruins.*

dominate the game and you can just kind of play off of that, and he could cover up for a lot of your mistakes," Sweeney explains. "I did get the opportunity to play with him for an extensive period of time and after that, where I was acclimated into the League, I felt like I was contributing rather than just being on the ice just to take up time as a young player. That was a real pleasure because we were matched against the top lines and he took that to heart. That challenge to him— he knew he'd put up points, he knew he'd be on the power play—was to come out of the night as a plus against the top lines in the League. That was a challenge I think both of us really, really enjoyed. That was probably the highlight for me, that period of time, getting to play with him exclusively."

That challenge was to come out of the night as a plus against the top lines in the League.

"By that point [with me], 30-plus minutes a night, he [Bourque] played with everybody," Pedersen adds. "Unselfish. I thought he was the epitome of team player. To see a guy play with the energy and passion that he did night in and night out, it was just amazing. I was fortunate to be a part of that, to play with one of the best players of all time."

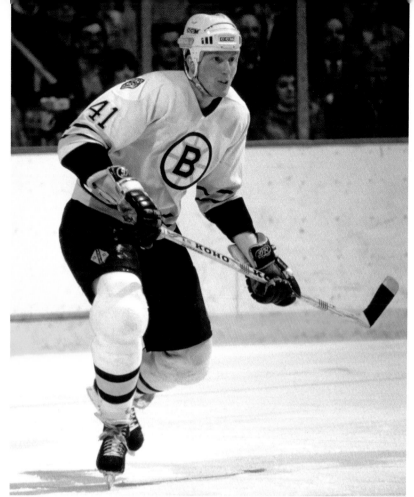

*left:*

*Al "Beach" Pedersen, known as an excellent shot-blocker, about to go down on two knees to do just that. Big and fearless; two qualities Al used to make it his forte. His sarcastic nickname came from being pale in comparison to most.*

*right:*

*A high priced free agent acquisition in 2006, Zdeno Chara immediately became the Bruins captain. A Norris Trophy finalist in 2008, Chara brings size, skill, and a temper to the Bruins blueline, a triple threat Boston fans love.*

*below:*

*Reed Larson came to Boston following ten seasons as a Red Wing. His wicked hard, high slap shot made goalies nervous. He had 77 points in 141 Bruins games.*

Pedersen, who wrapped up his NHL playing career in 1994, was a Bruin who had a tight relationship with the Bruins photographer. Pedersen also had one of the team's great nicknames.

"Babs was like part of the team," Pedersen says. "He was there such a long time. What I liked about him, he went about his business very professionally; you didn't really know he was around, but he was always around. He's a class act."

"My nickname was 'Beach,'" Pedersen continues. "Back in Medicine Hat in juniors when I came up I was a skinny bugger, 6-foot-3, 165 pounds, and white as a ghost. The older guys, tough guys, 19- or 20-year-olds, they used to call me 'Casper' and all that, but then they started calling me Beach because they said I'd never been to one. It stuck. People still call me Beach."

Pedersen is obscure compared to Bourque, to most everyone except Bourque himself. To Ray, and the same could be said for Bobby Orr, the names Pedersen, Beers, Hawgood, Larson, Simmons, and others, all meant as much as the names Bourque and Orr. Each man went to battle wearing the Spoked B; each man protected his net, his zone, and his teammates. Therein lies what it means to be a Bruin, and to man the Boston blueline together.

1. *Andrew Alberts*  2. *Al Sims*  3. *Bob Beers*  4. *Left to right, back row:  Mike Milbury, Gord Kluzak, Assistant coach Gary Doak, Randy Hillier, Jim Schoenfeld.  Front row:  Mike O'Connell, Ray Bourque, Guy Lapointe wearing number five (briefly).*
5. *Rick Smith*  6. *Brian Leetch*

7. *Left to right, back row: Jim Wiemer, Gord Kluzak, Al Pedersen. Front row: Garry Galley, Assistant coach Ted Sator, Glen Wesley.* 8. *Dick Redmond* 9. *David Shaw* 10. *Carol Vadnais* 11. *Brad McCrimmon* 12. *Frank Simonetti*

Defensemen whose careers included or began after 1973–74, the season in which Steve Babineau took his first professional photo at a Bruins game. A handful of defensemen have been moved to the enforcer list.

190

*above:*

*The Euro Connection from left to right: Alex Kasatonov, Mats Thelin, Michael Thelven, and Mattlas Timander.*

| BRUINS REGULAR SEASON STATISTICS | GP | G | A | Pts | PIM |
|---|---|---|---|---|---|
| **Johnathan Aitken**—Edmonton, AB | **3** | **0** | **0** | **0** | **0** |
| #49 | 1999–2000 | One of the three 1st round picks for Wesley | | | | | |
| **Andrew Alberts**—Minneapolis, MN | 184 | 1 | 18 | 19 | 231 |
| #41 | 2005–2008 | Four years at BC; work in progress | | | | | |
| **Bobby Allen**—Weymouth, MA | 50 | 0 | 3 | 3 | 12 |
| #38 | 2006–2008 | On BC National Championship—2001 | | | | | |
| **Bob Beers**—Pittsburgh, PA | 77 | 3 | 11 | 14 | 53 |
| #22, 34, 43 | 1989–1992, 1996–1997 | Bruins radio color commentator | | | | | |
| **Bryan Berard**—Woonsocket, RI | 80 | 10 | 28 | 38 | 64 |
| #34 | 2002–2003 | Unlikely career after blinded in right eye | | | | | |
| **Nick Beverley**—Toronto, ON | 82 | 1 | 10 | 11 | 28 |
| #6, 27 | 1966–1967, 1969–1970, 1971–1974 | NHL Captain, head coach, GM, and scout | | | | | |

| BRUINS REGULAR SEASON STATISTICS | GP | G | A | Pts | PIM |
|---|---|---|---|---|---|
| **John Blum**—Detroit, MI | 169 | 5 | 22 | 27 | 443 |
| #33 | 1983–1986, 1987–1988, 1989–1990 | Big hitter at Michigan; fought a lot early in NHL | | | | | |
| **Paul Boutilier**—Sydney, NS | 52 | 5 | 9 | 14 | 84 |
| #34 | 1986–1987 | Survived fight with Nilan during bench-clearer | | | | | |
| **Nick Boynton**—Etobicoke, ON | 299 | 22 | 62 | 84 | 399 |
| #44 | 1999–2006 | Two-time 1st round draft pick | | | | | |
| **Rich Brennan**—Schenectady, NY | 7 | 0 | 1 | 1 | 6 |
| #59 | 2002–2003 | Hockey East 1st team at BU, 35 goal Junior year | | | | | |
| **Sean Brown**—Oshawa, ON | 81 | 1 | 6 | 7 | 164 |
| #23 | 2001–2003 | B's 1st rounder in '95; last playing in Germany | | | | | |
| **Zdeno Chara**—Trencin, Slovakia | **157** | **28** | **66** | **94** | **214** |
| #33 | 2006–2008 | At 6-foot-9, tallest player in NHL history | | | | | |
| **Denis Chervyakov**—Leningrad, Russia | 2 | 0 | 0 | 0 | 2 |
| #43 | 1992–1993 | One of 1st Russians B's allowed on club | | | | | |
| **Paul Coffey**—Weston, ON | 18 | 0 | 4 | 4 | 30 |
| #74 | 2000–2001 | Hall-of-Fame career wound down in Boston | | | | | |
| **Mark Cornforth**—Montreal, QC | 6 | 0 | 0 | 0 | 4 |
| #40 | 1995–1996 | Now wins World Pond Hockey titles | | | | | |
| **Alain Cote**—Montmagny, QC | 68 | 2 | 9 | 11 | 65 |
| #26, 33, 37, 40 | 1985–1989 | Had Milbury's number until Mike unretired | | | | | |
| **Kevin Dallman**—Niagara Falls, ON | 21 | 0 | 1 | 1 | 8 |
| #58 | 2005–2006 | Never drafted; regular shifts in LA | | | | | |
| **Albert T. DeMarco**—Cleveland, OH | 3 | 0 | 0 | 0 | 0 |
| #19 | 1978–1979 | "Ab" played for 7 NHL teams; B's last | | | | | |

| BRUINS REGULAR SEASON STATISTICS | GP | G | A | Pts | PIM |
|---|---|---|---|---|---|
| **Nathan Dempsey**—Spruce Grove, AB | 17 | 0 | 1 | 1 | 6 |
| #29, 21 | 2006–2007 | One of Chiarelli's ex-Senators | | | | | |
| **Gary Doak**—Goderich, ON | 609 | 20 | 81 | 101 | 656 |
| #25 | 1965–1970, 1972–1981 | Would block slap shot with face to help team | | | | | |
| **Dale Dunbar**—Winthrop, MA | 1 | 0 | 0 | 0 | 0 |
| #45 | 1988–1989 | BU'er, knee injury ended career in Finland | | | | | |

| BRUINS REGULAR SEASON STATISTICS | GP | G | A | Pts | PIM |
|---|---|---|---|---|---|
| **Darryl Edestrand**—Strathroy, ON | 215 | 8 | 37 | 45 | 195 |
| #6 | 1973–1978 | One of few to win decision in fight with Orr | | | | | |
| **Dave Ellett**—Cleveland, OH | 136 | 3 | 26 | 29 | 92 |
| #44 | 1997–1999 | Owns a team in the Central League | | | | | |
| **Andrew Ference**—Edmonton, AB | 85 | 2 | 16 | 18 | 81 |
| #21 | 2006–2008 | Visited Africa with Right to Play charity | | | | | |
| **Mike Forbes**—Brampton, ON | 32 | 0 | 4 | 4 | 15 |
| #6 | 1977–1978 | Oilers took him from B's in expansion draft | | | | | |
| **Garry Galley**—Montreal, QC | 257 | 24 | 82 | 106 | 322 |
| #28 | 1988–1992 | Spectacular O.T. winner vs. Habs in 1990 | | | | | |
| **Hal Gill**—Concord, MA | 626 | 20 | 77 | 97 | 588 |
| #75, 25 | 1997–2006 | Jaromir Jagr's personal nemesis; good on PK | | | | | |
| **Jonathan Girard**—Joliette, QC | 150 | 10 | 34 | 44 | 46 |
| #55, 46 | 1998–2003 | Prospect career cut short by car accident | | | | | |
| **Sergei Gonchar**—Chelyabinsk, Russia | 15 | 4 | 5 | 9 | 12 |
| #55 | 2003–2004 | Pre-lock-out deadline deal; then gone | | | | | |
| **John Gruden**—Virginia, MN | 59 | 0 | 7 | 7 | 28 |
| #29, 36 | 1993–1996 | Not the coach of the Tampa Bay Buc's | | | | | |
| **Doug Halward**—Toronto, ON | 65 | 3 | 9 | 12 | 14 |
| #26, 29 | 1975–1978 | Puck mover with knee and phlebitis issues | | | | | |
| **Ken Hammond**—Port Credit, ON | 1 | 1 | 0 | 1 | 2 |
| #55 | 1990–1991 | RPI National Champions' Captain in 1985 | | | | | |

| BRUINS REGULAR SEASON STATISTICS | GP | G | A | Pts | PIM |
|---|---|---|---|---|---|
| **Greg Hawgood**—Edmonton, AB | 134 | 27 | 51 | 78 | 160 |
| #35, 38, 39, 40 | 1987–1990 | "Hawgy Hockey"; puck rusher | | | | | |
| **Matt Hervey**—Whittier, CA | 16 | 0 | 1 | 1 | 55 |
| #43 | 1991–1992 | Schooled in '92 playoffs by Jagr | | | | | |
| **Randy Hillier**—Toronto, ON | 164 | 3 | 30 | 33 | 253 |
| #23 | 1981–1984 | Heavyweight body checker | | | | | |
| **Shane Hnidy**—Neepawa, MB | 43 | 1 | 4 | 5 | 41 |
| #34 | 2007–2008 | "The Sheriff"; another former Senator | | | | | |
| **Marty Howe**—Detroit, MI | 78 | 1 | 11 | 12 | 24 |
| #27 | 1982–1983 | Son of "Mr. Hockey"; brother of Mark | | | | | |
| **Matt Hunwick**—Sterling Heights, MI | 13 | 0 | 1 | 1 | 4 |
| #48 | 2007–2008 | Won World Junior title with Stuart in 2004 | | | | | |
| **Gord Hynes**—Montreal, QC | 15 | 0 | 5 | 5 | 6 |
| #47 | 1991–1992 | Played 12 playoff games in '92; 3 points | | | | | |
| **Al Iafrate**—Dearborn, MI | 12 | 5 | 8 | 13 | 20 |
| #43 | 1993–1994 | "The Planet" with hardest shot in hockey | | | | | |
| **Richard Jackman**—Toronto, ON | 2 | 0 | 0 | 0 | 2 |
| #43 | 2001–2002 | Part of a revolving door period for B's | | | | | |
| **Jeff Jillson**—North Smithfield, RI | 50 | 4 | 10 | 14 | 35 |
| #23 | 2003–2004 | Drafted by the Sharks at the Fleet Center | | | | | |
| **Milan Jurcina**—Liptovsky Mikulas, Slovakia | 91 | 8 | 6 | 14 | 74 |
| #68 | 2005–2007 | "Jerky" gassed by Dave Lewis | | | | | |
| **Alex Kasatonov**—Leningrad, Russia | 63 | 3 | 14 | 17 | 45 |
| #6 | 1994–1996 | Twilight years after greatness in Russia | | | | | |
| **Chris Kelleher**—Cambridge, MA | 1 | 0 | 0 | 0 | 0 |
| #48 | 2001–2002 | Freshman for National Title at BU, 1995 | | | | | |
| **Gord Kluzak**—Climax, SK | 299 | 25 | 98 | 123 | 543 |
| #6 | 1982–1991 | First overall pick in 1982; knee problems later | | | | | |
| **Pavel Kolarik**—Vyskov, Czech Rep. | 23 | 0 | 0 | 0 | 10 |
| #72 | 2000–2002 | 10 seasons including title; Czech League | | | | | |

| BRUINS REGULAR SEASON STATISTICS | GP | G | A | Pts | PIM |
|---|---|---|---|---|---|
| **Jarno Kultanen**—Luumaki, Finland | 102 | 2 | 11 | 13 | 59 |
| #64 \| 2000–2003 \| "B's best D-man"—Keenan | | | | | |
| **Zdenek Kutlak**—Budejovice, Czech Rep. | 16 | 1 | 2 | 3 | 4 |
| #39 \| 2000–2001, 2003–2004 \| Big lefty; happy playing at home | | | | | |
| **Guy Lapointe**—Montreal, QC | 45 | 2 | 16 | 18 | 34 |
| #5, 27 \| 1983–1984 \| Caused uproar by wearing Clapper's number 5 | | | | | |
| **Reed Larson**—Minneapolis, MN | 141 | 25 | 52 | 77 | 196 |
| #28 \| 1985–1988 \| The wickedest of high slapshots | | | | | |
| **Matt Lashoff**—East Greenbush, NY | 30 | 1 | 6 | 7 | 12 |
| #49 \| 2006–2008 \| Plays a mean blues guitar | | | | | |
| **Dominic Lavoie**—Montreal, QC | 2 | 0 | 0 | 0 | 2 |
| #37 \| 1992–1993 \| Accomplished fighter elsewhere | | | | | |

| | GP | G | A | Pts | PIM |
|---|---|---|---|---|---|
| **Jay Leach**—Syracuse, NY | 2 | 0 | 0 | 0 | 7 |
| #48 \| 2005–2006 \| Posed on cover of *Rhode Island Magazine* | | | | | |
| **Grant Ledyard**—Winnipeg, MB | 69 | 6 | 15 | 21 | 39 |
| #36 \| 1997–1999 \| Undrafted; played for nine NHL clubs | | | | | |
| **Brian Leetch**—Corpus Christi, TX | 61 | 5 | 27 | 32 | 36 |
| #22 \| 2005–2006 \| Ended Hall-of-Fame career with bad knee | | | | | |
| **Ray Maluta**—Flin Flon, MB | 25 | 2 | 3 | 5 | 6 |
| #23, 27 \| 1975–1977 \| Unenviable task of filling Orr's shoes/skates | | | | | |
| **Paul Mara**—Ridgewood, NJ | 59 | 3 | 15 | 18 | 95 |
| #23 \| 2006–2007 \| Belmont Hill trained, 7th overall pick, 1997 | | | | | |
| **Brad McCrimmon**—Dodsland, SK | 228 | 17 | 37 | 54 | 325 |
| #29 \| 1979–1982 \| As Red Wing, almost strangled Lazaro | | | | | |
| **Dan McGillis**—Hawkesbury, ON | 90 | 5 | 24 | 29 | 75 |
| #6 \| 2002–2004 \| Hockey East 1st Team twice at Northeastern | | | | | |
| **Kyle McLaren**—Humboldt, SK | 417 | 34 | 90 | 124 | 370 |
| #46, 18 \| 1995–2002 \| Second youngest player in NHL as rookie | | | | | |
| **Larry Melnyk**—Saskatoon, SK | 75 | 0 | 12 | 12 | 123 |
| #33 \| 1980–1983 \| On ice with Park for Game-7 winner vs. Buffalo | | | | | |

| BRUINS REGULAR SEASON STATISTICS | GP | G | A | Pts | PIM |
|---|---|---|---|---|---|
| **Mike Milbury**—Brighton, MA | 754 | 49 | 189 | 238 | 1,552 |
| #28, 26 \| 1975–1987 \| Led Walpole in scoring; then D at Cornell | | | | | |
| **Ian Moran**—Cleveland, OH | 55 | 2 | 6 | 8 | 40 |
| #18 \| 2002–2006 \| Renowned yapper with chronic knee problems | | | | | |
| **Shaone Morrisonn**—Vancouver, BC | 41 | 1 | 7 | 8 | 18 |
| #28 \| 2002–2004 \| B's 1st rounder; 19th overall in 2001 | | | | | |
| **Gord Murphy**—Willowdale, ON | 106 | 8 | 20 | 28 | 126 |
| #28 \| 1991–1993, 2001–2002 \| Broke an ankle falling down some stairs | | | | | |
| **Anders Myrvold**—Lorenskog, Norway | 9 | 0 | 2 | 2 | 4 |
| #14, 41 \| 1996–1997 \| Norwegian trailblazer in NHL | | | | | |
| **Graeme Nicolson**—North Bay, ON | 1 | 0 | 0 | 0 | 0 |
| #29 \| 1978–1979 \| Played 41 games with the Colorado Rockies | | | | | |
| **Jeff Norton**—Acton, MA | 3 | 0 | 1 | 1 | 2 |
| #33 \| 2001–2002 \| Cardinal Cushing Academy; then Michigan | | | | | |
| **Dennis O'Brien**—Port Hope, ON | 83 | 4 | 11 | 15 | 138 |
| #28 \| 1977–1980 \| Solid 6th defenseman | | | | | |
| **Mike O'Connell**—Chicago, IL | 424 | 70 | 198 | 268 | 312 |
| #20 \| 1980–1986 \| As GM, traded Joe Thornton to San Jose | | | | | |
| **Sean O'Donnell**—Ottawa, ON | 232 | 5 | 47 | 52 | 275 |
| #27, 21 \| 2001–2004 \| Went on to win Cup in Anaheim | | | | | |
| **Brad Park**—Toronto, ON | 501 | 100 | 317 | 417 | 553 |
| #22 \| 1976–1983 \| Best defenseman never to win the Norris Trophy | | | | | |
| **Allen Pedersen**—Fort Saskatchewan, AB | 333 | 4 | 31 | 35 | 408 |
| #41 \| 1986–1991 \| Personal friends with team photographer | | | | | |
| **Peter Popovi**—Koping, Sweden | 60 | 1 | 6 | 7 | 48 |
| #23 \| 2000–2001 \| Gentle giant; ended with five seasons in Sweden | | | | | |
| **Petr Prajsler**—Hradec Kralov, Czechoslovakia | 3 | 0 | 0 | 0 | 2 |
| #52 \| 1991–1992 \| Hradec Kralov's greatest Bruin ever | | | | | |
| **Stephane Quintal**—Boucherville, ON | 158 | 8 | 19 | 27 | 219 |
| #21 \| 1988–1992 \| Bruins picked him so Quebec couldn't | | | | | |
| **Dick Redmond**—Kirkland Lake, ON | 235 | 36 | 79 | 115 | 124 |
| #6 \| 1978–1982 \| Brother of 50-goal scorer Mickey | | | | | |
| **Stephane Richer**—Hull, QC | 21 | 1 | 4 | 5 | 18 |
| #25 \| 1992–1993 \| The other Stephane Richer | | | | | |

| BRUINS REGULAR SEASON STATISTICS | GP | G | A | Pts | PIM |
|---|---|---|---|---|---|
| **Barry Richter**—Madison, WI | 50 | 5 | 13 | 18 | 32 |
| #46 \| 1996–1997 \| Member of B's last worst overall team | | | | | |
| **Jamie Rivers**—Ottawa, ON | 64 | 4 | 2 | 6 | 45 |
| #31 \| 2001–2002 \| Piled up points in Sudbury, before seven NHL teams | | | | | |
| **Gord Roberts**—Detroit, MI | 124 | 6 | 18 | 24 | 145 |
| #14 \| 1992–1994 \| Beat B's with Minnesota North Stars in 1981 | | | | | |
| **Jon Rohloff**—Mankato, MN | 150 | 7 | 25 | 32 | 129 |
| #38 \| 1994–1997 \| Turnover in NJ led to 1995 playoff loss | | | | | |
| **Jim Schoenfeld**—Galt, ON | 39 | 0 | 2 | 2 | 20 |
| #13 \| 1983–1984 \| As rookie with Buffalo, started brawl with Cashman | | | | | |
| **Jeff Serowik**—Manchester, NH | 1 | 0 | 0 | 0 | 0 |
| #49 \| 1994–1995 \| Runs hockey academy in Boston area | | | | | |
| **Yevgeny Shaldybin**—Novosibirsk, USSR | 3 | 1 | 0 | 1 | 0 |
| #62 \| 1996–1997 \| Softer than butter sittin' in the sun | | | | | |
| **David Shaw**—St. Thomas, ON | 176 | 14 | 27 | 41 | 229 |
| #34 \| 1992–1995 \| Won Memorial Cup with Kitchener in 1982 | | | | | |
| **Jonathan Sigalet**—Vancouver, BC | 1 | 0 | 0 | 0 | 4 |
| #50 \| 2006–2007 \| Played with brother Jordan in Providence | | | | | |
| **Al Simmons**—Winnipeg, MB | 10 | 0 | 1 | 1 | 21 |
| #26 \| 1973–1974, 1975–1976 \| Also had one game with California Golden Seals | | | | | |
| **Frank Simonetti**—Melrose, MA | 115 | 5 | 8 | 13 | 76 |
| #21 \| 1983–1988 \| Shoulder injury shortened career | | | | | |
| **Al Sims**—Toronto, ON | 310 | 22 | 48 | 70 | 172 |
| #20, 23, 29 \| 1973–1979 \| Bobby Orr's partner during Al's rookie year | | | | | |
| **Jiri Slegr**—Jihlava, Czech Rep. | 68 | 9 | 26 | 35 | 83 |
| #71 \| 2003–2006 \| Cup winner, Olympic Gold, World Champ | | | | | |
| **Brandon Smith**—Hazelton, BC | 30 | 3 | 4 | 7 | 10 |
| #53 \| 1998–2001 \| A favorite of coach Pat Burns; strong work ethic | | | | | |
| **Dallas Smith**—Hamiota, MB | 861 | 54 | 248 | 302 | 936 |
| #8, 20 \| 1959–1962, 1965–1977 \| 7th Player Award winner; "strong as an ox" | | | | | |
| **Rick Smith**—Hamilton, ON | 513 | 36 | 125 | 161 | 391 |
| #10, 23 \| 1968–1972, 1976–1980 \| Scored 1st goal of Final Game 4 in 1970 | | | | | |
| **Steve Staios**—Hamilton, ON | 66 | 3 | 8 | 11 | 75 |
| #48 \| 1995–1997 \| Cup Final run with Edmonton in 2006 | | | | | |
| **Paul Stanton**—Boston, MA | 71 | 3 | 7 | 10 | 54 |
| #25 \| 1993–1994 \| Back-to-back Cup wins with Pittsburgh | | | | | |
| **Brad Stuart**—Rocky Mountain House, AB | 103 | 17 | 31 | 48 | 62 |
| #6 \| 2005–2007 \| Wife wanted him "elsewhere" | | | | | |
| **Mark Stuart**—Rochester, MN | 114 | 5 | 6 | 11 | 105 |
| #45 \| 2005–2008 \| Captain of USA World Junior Champs in '04 | | | | | |
| **Don Sweeney**—St. Stephen, NB | 1,052 | 52 | 210 | 262 | 663 |
| #32 \| 1988–2003 \| Bourque's long-time defensive partner | | | | | |
| **David Tanabe**—White Bear Lake, MN | 54 | 4 | 12 | 16 | 48 |
| #55 \| 2005–2006 \| Slowed by wrist injury | | | | | |

| BRUINS REGULAR SEASON STATISTICS | GP | G | A | Pts | PIM |
|---|---|---|---|---|---|
| **Mikhail Tatarinov**—Angarsk, USSR | 2 | 0 | 0 | 0 | 2 |
| #28 \| 1993–1994 \| Top offensive D-man in Russia | | | | | |
| **Mats Thelin**—Stockholm, Sweden | 163 | 8 | 19 | 27 | 107 |
| #27 \| 1984–1987 \| Swedish "goon"; played with an edge | | | | | |
| **Michael Thelven**—Stockholm, Sweden | 207 | 20 | 80 | 100 | 217 |
| #14, 22 \| 1985–1990 \| Versatile; knee injury hurt career | | | | | |

| | GP | G | A | Pts | PIM |
|---|---|---|---|---|---|
| **Mattias Timander**—Solleftea, Sweden | 146 | 2 | 23 | 25 | 52 |
| #47, 37 \| 1996–2000 \| Best season with Flyers in 2004 | | | | | |
| **Patrick Traverse**—Montreal, QC | 37 | 2 | 6 | 8 | 14 |
| #63 \| 2000–2001 \| Involved in rare Boston-to-Montreal trade | | | | | |
| **Carol Vadnais**—Montreal, QC | 263 | 47 | 134 | 181 | 433 |
| #10 \| 1972–1976 \| Added for Cup run in February, 1972 | | | | | |
| **Darren Van Impe**—Saskatoon, SK | 220 | 15 | 56 | 71 | 216 |
| #45, 20 \| 1997–2001 \| Distant relative of "Bully" D-man Ed | | | | | |
| **Dennis Vaske**—Rockford, IL | 3 | 0 | 0 | 0 | 6 |
| #29 \| 1998–1999 \| Captain of '99 Providence Calder Cup Champs | | | | | |
| **Terry Virtue**—Scarborough, ON | 4 | 0 | 0 | 0 | 0 |
| #71 \| 1998–1999 \| Providence '99; beat them with Hartford '00 | | | | | |
| **Philip Von Stefenelli**—Vancouver, BC | 27 | 0 | 4 | 4 | 16 |
| #41 \| 1995–1996 \| BU, Detroit Viper with Samsonov | | | | | |
| **Aaron Ward**—Windsor, ON | 85 | 6 | 10 | 16 | 72 |
| #44 \| 2006–2008 \| Three-time Stanley Cup winner | | | | | |
| **Eric Weinrich**—Roanoke, VA | 22 | 1 | 5 | 6 | 10 |
| #27 \| 2000–2001 \| Came in deal from Montreal; traded for Traverse | | | | | |
| **Glen Wesley**—Red Deer, AB | 537 | 77 | 230 | 307 | 421 |
| #26 \| 1987–1994 \| The "Buckner" of missed empty nets, '90 | | | | | |
| **Dennis Wideman**—Kitchener, ON | 101 | 19 | 25 | 44 | 97 |
| #6 \| 2006–2008 \| Scored franchise's 18,000th goal | | | | | |
| **Jim Wiemer**—Sudbury, ON | 201 | 11 | 47 | 58 | 259 |
| #30, 36 \| 1989–1994 \| Solid 5th or 6th defenseman | | | | | |
| **Jason York**—Nepean, ON | 49 | 1 | 7 | 8 | 32 |
| #25 \| 2006–2007 \| Part of the GM Peter Chiarelli Ottawa connect | | | | | |
| **Joe Zanussi**—Rossland, BC | 68 | 1 | 8 | 9 | 38 |
| #29 \| 1975–1977 \| Went with Phil Esposito to NYR in trade | | | | | |
| **Rick Zombo**—Des Plaines, IL | 67 | 4 | 10 | 14 | 53 |
| #34 \| 1995–1996 \| Comic book artist; shares birthday with author | | | | | |

# 13

# SCORERS

*above:*

*To the most modern generation of Bruins fans, "Jumbo" Joe Thornton was the face of the franchise from the time he was drafted 1st overall by the Club in 1997, to the time he was traded in November of 2005. He tallied 454 points with the Bruins.*

*left:*

*From 1992 to 1997 Adam Oates led the Bruins in scoring during four of his five full seasons in Boston and also led them in scoring in four of their five playoff runs. He's the Bruins 13th all-time leading scorer.*

As exhibited by our list of legends, it would appear that just being a talented scorer in Boston isn't enough. One also needs to be tough as nails, and as physical as possible. Johnny Bucyk's hips, Cam Neely's fists, Terry O'Reilly's entire body: testaments to the key combination of grit and "game." Phil Esposito by the way, was no pushover in his day, at 6-foot-1, 205 pounds. Even a more recent scoring machine, the man who found his way to San Jose, Joe Thornton was known as "Jumbo Joe." He didn't necessarily use his size as others have or would have, but his big body and skill were well respected. To the latest generation of Bruins fans, his trade away in November of 2005 from the team that drafted him first overall in 1997, remains the benchmark moment of trauma. Thornton is a potential Hall of Famer.

If not physically dominant, another way to earn a quick trip into the hearts of Bruins fans is to simply use what one has in the most aggressive way possible. Fearless, reckless at times, and feisty, are all qualities readily appreciated.

Ken Linseman originally earned his nickname "the Rat" for his bent-over skating style, but getting into opponents' faces, playing with an angry streak, and lighting the lamp all the while, didn't hurt his cause or seem inappropriate to his moniker. Linseman was a scoring forward with an attitude.

"Bobby Clarke gave me the nickname when I started in Philly because I scurried around the ice, I darted around, plus I was a disturber," Linseman points out. "Clarke had a nickname for everybody, and I did skate bent over quite a bit, like I was on four legs."

*left:*

*Ken Linseman's nickname "The Rat" and his reputation as a shift disturber probably leaves him under-rated as a point producer. He scored 807 points in 860 NHL games. He spent six seasons in Boston in the late-eighties.*

The former 1st round pick of the Flyers spent four years in Philly, two years in Edmonton where he won a Cup, and then the next six seasons in Boston.

"I was a second line center wherever I went; then I'd get bumped," Linseman points out. "In Edmonton, Gretzky was the number one center; I was two. When they moved Messier to center, I became expendable. I wasn't a third line guy because our line usually scored quite a bit. So I became the second line center in Boston. I was happy to get back to the [United] States, and was fortunate to play with three really good teams."

I grew up playing street hockey every day that I wasn't on the ice.

These days, the former "hockey rodent" with 256 NHL goals and 1,700 penalty minutes is now a "wet rat." In his spare time, Linseman travels the world surfing with his friends and with his son.

Realistically, despite physicality being the preferred characteristic for Bruins fans, an overwhelming majority of great goal scorers and playmakers are not going to have a nasty streak and rack up penalty minutes. Most will use speed, skill, and guile.

Boston's poster-boy for craft and talent as a goal scorer is Rick Middleton. Middleton wasn't a physical thumper, but he's the former Bruin most often mentioned as the one who should be in the Hall of Fame, but isn't. He was just 17 points short of being a point-a-game man over the course of his entire 1,005-game NHL career. Of those points, 448 were goals, while he added 100 more points in the playoffs. "Nifty" was truly just that, and like so many playmakers and scorers, he learned the game by growing up with a stick in his hand.

*above:*

*Rick Middleton is the best Bruin, and arguably one of the finest NHLers ever, not inducted into the Hockey Hall of Fame. Here he attacks the net on Pittsburgh netminder Greg Millen.*

"I think a lot of it started...it was born on the street," explains Middleton. "I didn't grow up on ponds; I grew up playing street hockey every day that I wasn't on the ice. Even taking shots in the summer in the driveway with some buddies, I was in love with the sport, and I was the guy that always called everyone. I grew up in what was a new suburb of Toronto at the time, and it seemed like every boy in the neighborhood was the same age, so we had great teams and great games. If anyone has ever played street hockey with a ball, it's hard to carry the ball, because it sticks. There's nothing worse than a frozen tennis ball, so I learned not to keep it on my stick, you want to keep it ahead of you. I think it just morphed onto the ice for me, and I ended almost liking it better with the puck ahead, bouncing every which way. I felt better than controlling it. I think it was a subconscious thing, but I think street hockey is how I developed a touch with the puck. I never had the big shot from the outside; I always had to work in close. I had to go around defensemen that really didn't like me too much and that was my game. Get in close, score some goals, and make people look foolish. I'm actually surprised I lasted as long as I did."

He lasted 14 NHL seasons, the last 12 in Boston, and like so many others who fall in love with the city and its surroundings, he's still here.

"My kids were born here," Nifty says, "so I felt like I put down some roots. I got a great offer from a buddy of mine to start working ["a real job"] six months after I retired and I just love the area and the people. It's a great sports town, probably greater than any other sports town, particularly right now. I'm from Canada, from Toronto, [so] it's not that far to go home."

One of Middleton's businesses since retiring involves the introduction of his frozen dessert product, "Nifty-16 Dessert Bars," referring to his nickname and his jersey number. He brought the idea from Canada, where Nanaimo Bars, named after the alleged town of their origin—Nanaimo, British Columbia—are popular. He created his own recipe and distributes them to stores himself, and a portion of the proceeds go to area youth hockey programs.

The nickname on the box is from an unknown origin.

"I honestly don't know [where my nickname came from]," Nifty states. "Some players have taken credit for it. Gerry Cheevers said he was the one who gave it to me. I just think it was an adjective given to me, which was put in the paper after I scored a couple of goals and it kind of stuck."

Another of Middleton's businesses is television, where he analyzes the NHL hockey action during Boston Bruins games on NESN. His cohort, and another former Bruins scorer, is color commentator Andy Brickley. "Brick" did a year of radio work after his retirement from hockey prior to joining the TV ranks, where

*below:*

*Middleton in front of the net wearing the captain's C, a distinction he shared for three seasons with Ray Bourque. Middleton, shown battling with future Bruin Rick Zombo, is the 4th all-time leading scorer in Bruins history.*

*above:*

*Glen Murray wore #44 early on, after being drafted by the Bruins 18th overall in the 1991 entry draft. The goal scorer left in a trade to Pittsburgh in August 1995, only to return in a trade via Los Angeles in 2001. As of spring 2008 he had one year left on his contract.*

he remains today. A Massachusetts native, being involved with the Bruins organization on and off the ice over the years remains a dream come true.

"I had the advantage of having been a pro for about seven or eight years before I came to Boston, which was huge," Brickley explains. "The reason I bring that up is because I've seen Bostonians that have played for the Bruins early in their career and it's difficult. If you have a certain level of immaturity, to play for your hometown team, the team you idolized growing up, it becomes tough to handle. So I had that going for me, number one, and I also saw other players come to Boston and put that sweater on, and put that emblem on their chest, and it changed the way they played. Garry Galley's a classic example. It just elevates your game. You have the benefit of playing with guys like Bourque and Neely, to see how they prepared and how they got ready—not that you don't have that on other teams, but it was just another level. For me, having grown up in Boston, I idolized the Bruins and everybody that played for the Bruins, whether they were a finesse guy or a tough guy or someone in between. They were all your heroes. So you knew there was a place for you even if you didn't play like Terry O'Reilly.

"Those were the proudest moments, the best four years of my professional hockey career, and this was coming from New Jersey where we had something special happening," Brickley continues. "It was nice to be a part of that, but Boston was a whole newer level of playing the game. I thought it elevated my game, it made me a better player, a more complete player, a more accountable player, because of the tradition that was in place. I think every player should get traded to New York [Rangers] for their salary to go up, and every player should get a chance to play in Boston so their talent level and their understanding of the game goes up."

Every player should get a chance to play in Boston so their talent level and their understanding of the game goes up.

Sixteen-year NHLer Robert "Butch" Goring, a New York resident, finished his playing career in Boston immediately before his coaching career began here in 1985. He played 39 games, and scored just 13 of his 375 career goals as a member of the Bruins. He previously spent the bulk of career in Los Angeles and then with Cup winning teams on Long Island.

"I enjoyed playing here. Good hockey guys—Kenny Linseman, Bourque, and O'Reilly," says Goring. "It was a little different perspective, playing with them after playing with the Islanders [where he spent five-plus seasons and had won four Cups], but I enjoyed my time here and I was sad to go."

Ken Hodge, another Bruins scorer with a New York connection—he was traded to the Rangers for Middleton in

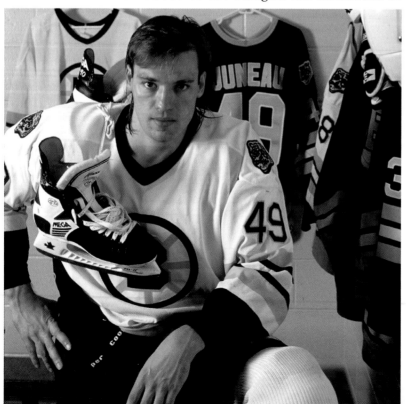

left:

*Joe Juneau, originally drafted by the Bruins in the 4th round of the 1988 entry draft, had 70 assists his first full season in Boston, still an NHL single season record for a left wing. Like Adam Oates, Juneau earned All-America honors while attending Rensselaer Polytechnic Institute*

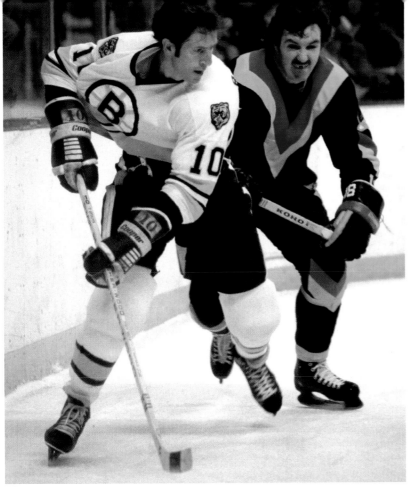

*above:*

*Vancouver Canucks defenseman John Grisdale gives Jean Ratelle the stick. Known more for his time in New York with the Rangers, the classy French-Canadian Ratelle spent his final six NHL seasons with Boston, retiring in 1981.*

*right:*

*Boston's 7th all-time leading scorer Ken Hodge battles with Buffalo Sabres defenseman Larry Carriere. Long-time Hodge/Phil Esposito linemate Wayne Cashman skates in the background. The Sabre with the helmet and sideburns is winger Craig Ramsay, who became a Bruins assistant coach in 2007.*

1976—returned to Boston in retirement, after beginning to raise a family here during his nine stalwart seasons with the B's.

"What I'm even prouder about is that all three of my boys got a chance to play at the old Garden, which to me is quite an accomplishment," reflects Hodge. "They all played high school and college hockey at the old Garden, which is quite nice."

One of them, Hodge's namesake, actually made it onto the Garden ice wearing the beloved Spoked B.

"For me the thrill was that first game, that first little step," remembers Kenneth D. Hodge. "It was maybe about two inches, [but] it felt like about five miles when I first got on the ice for that first warm-up. It was a thrill just to be there and get the opportunity to play in the Garden and to play where my dad played. That first goal as a Bruin was just an absolute thrill and you couldn't...I didn't care about the paychecks the first couple years; I just wanted to be there.

"[The game] was against Quebec and Bobby Carpenter came down the middle of the ice and took a shot and I got the rebound and I was fortunate to get a little bit of a seam," he continues, recalling his first goal. "I think it was Ron Tugnutt, not the game he saved 75 shots, but it was one of his lesser games, and I was able to get that goal and it felt great. I remember going back to the bench and thinking I finally got it. It took me about four or five games to get that goal and it was a relief."

Although not as prolific as Dad in the short term or in the long, Ken did score 30 goals and add 29 assists in his best NHL season, 1990–91.

The younger Hodge played college hockey at Boston College with another Boston scorer with apparent NHL family ties. However, for Tim Sweeney, the assumed direct bloodlines to two other Bruins didn't actually exist. Tim, a prolific scorer in college who ended up earning 291 NHL games, is not directly related to defenseman Don, or to another former B.C. forward, Bob. One would have to return to Ireland to find any family relationship between the Sweeneys.

"My biggest moment as a Bruin actually was the first game I played as a Bruin in the Boston Garden," reflects Tim. "As a

*A man with a heavy wrist shot, Brian Rolston scored 101 goals during his four-plus seasons in Boston. He was cut loose and headed to Minnesota via free agency during the Club's lock-out purge.*

*right:*

*Unfairly renowned for being part of the trade that brought Cam Neely from Vancouver, Barry Pederson had prolific scoring abilities. Boston's first round, 18th-overall pick in 1980 spent five-plus seasons with the Bruins. He had 76 points in 79 games his first season with the Canucks.*

kid growing up in this area, it is probably what a lot of kids dream to do, so I think the first game I ever played in the Boston Garden was probably my biggest moment as a Bruin."

Home grown or not, the aura of the Original Six, the tough old Bruins, and the Garden, proved to be an allure for many a young hockey player. Barry Pederson was born in Big River, Saskatchewan, and played juniors in British Columbia, but the Boston Garden was a magnet.

"The biggest moment for me was the Bruins being able to continue to turn things around after I got here, continue in the right direction," states Pederson, the Bruins first-round pick in 1980. "I had a chance to play with Rick Middleton and it was a thrill to go out there every night and have an opportunity to contribute offensively."

Pederson tallied more than a point a game for the Bruins over 379 games, but is best known to some for being a part of the trade with Vancouver that brought Cam Neely to Boston. For Pederson, now another TV hockey analyst between periods for NESN, it didn't take anything at all off his Original Six experience.

"It was a great thrill. Growing up even in Western Canada, I was a Bruins fan," Pederson states, "a Bobby Orr fan, fan of the Big Bad Bruins. It was a big thrill to be drafted by the Bruins, come into the old Garden, and it was a lifelong dream that I was very fortunate to have lived."

1. Left to right.  Dmitri Kvartalnov, Adam Oates, Joe Juneau  2. Anson Carter  3. Tom Fergus  4. Left to right: Jozef Stumpel, Shawn McEachern, Mariusz Czerkawski, Ray Bourque  5. Jason Allison  6. Steve Heinze and Ted Donato

7. *Left to right: John Carter, Bob Sweeney, coach Mike Milbury, Bobby Carpenter, Andy Brickley* 8. *Marco Sturm and Phil Kessel* 9. *Normand Leveille* 10. *Bill Guerin* 11. *Left to Right: Rick Middleton, Barry Pederson, Mike Krushelnyski*

*left:*
*Marc Savard, Glen Murray and Phil Kessel celebrate a goal against the Montreal Canadiens in game six of the Eastern Conference quarterfinal at the TD Banknorth Garden.*

Scorers and playmakers whose careers included or began after 1973–74, the season in which Steve Babineau took his first professional photo at a Bruins game.

| BRUINS REGULAR SEASON STATISTICS | GP | G | A | Pts | PIM |
|---|---|---|---|---|---|
| **Rick Adduono** (C)—Thunder Bay, ON | 1 | 0 | 0 | 0 | 0 |
| # \| 1975–1976 \| Longevity as minor/junior league coach | | | | | |
| **Jason Allison** (C)—North York, ON | 301 | 105 | 189 | 294 | 242 |
| #14, 41 \| 1996–2001 \| Slow but unstoppable below the dots | | | | | |
| **Dave Andreychuk** (LW)—Hamilton, ON | 63 | 19 | 14 | 33 | 28 |
| #38 \| 1999–2000 \| Captain of the Cup winner in Tampa | | | | | |
| **Ralph Barahona** (C)—Long Beach, CA | 6 | 2 | 2 | 4 | 0 |
| #37 \| 1990–1992 \| Big scorer at Wisconsin Stevens Point | | | | | |
| **Shawn Bates** (C)—Melrose, MA | 135 | 14 | 14 | 28 | 44 |
| #17 \| 1997–2001 \| Four Frozen Fours and a title at BU | | | | | |
| **Clayton Beddoes** (C)—Bentley, AB | 60 | 2 | 8 | 10 | 57 |
| #37 \| 1995–1997 \| Shoulder injury ended career in Alaska | | | | | |
| **Bill Bennett** (LW)—Warwick, RI | 7 | 1 | 4 | 5 | 2 |
| #7 \| 1978–1979 \| One of three to wear Espo's number after Espo | | | | | |
| **Paul Beraldo** (RW)—Hamilton, ON | 10 | 0 | 0 | 0 | 4 |
| #30, 37 \| 1987–1989 \| National teamer with Canada and Italy | | | | | |
| **Patrice Bergeron** (C)—Quebec City, QC | 239 | 72 | 117 | 189 | 72 |
| #37 \| 2003–2008 \| Missed 72 games with concussion | | | | | |
| **Zdenek Blatny** (LW)—Brno, Czech Rep. | 5 | 0 | 0 | 0 | 2 |
| #89 \| 2005–2006 \| Former Finnish and Czech Leaguer | | | | | |
| **Brandon Bochenski** (RW)—Blaine, MN | 51 | 11 | 17 | 28 | 20 |
| #10 \| 2006–2007 \| Half-step too slow as NHL scorer | | | | | |
| **Brad Boyes** (C/RW) Mississauga, ON | 144 | 39 | 64 | 103 | 53 |
| #26 \| 2005–2007 \| 40+ goals first season in St. Louis | | | | | |
| **Andy Brickley** (LW/C) Melrose, MA | 177 | 37 | 76 | 113 | 38 |
| #25 \| 1988–1992 \| Top-rate TV color commentator | | | | | |

| BRUINS REGULAR SEASON STATISTICS | GP | G | A | Pts | PIM |
|---|---|---|---|---|---|
| **John Byce** (C)—Madison, WI | 21 | 2 | 3 | 5 | 6 |
| #42 \| 1989–1992 \| Played with Mike Richter at University of Wisconsin | | | | | |
| **Anson Carter** (LW)—Toronto, ON | 211 | 70 | 73 | 143 | 102 |
| #11, 33 \| 1996–2000 \| No NHL work; headed to Swiss League | | | | | |
| **John Carter** (LW)—Winchester, MA | 185 | 33 | 41 | 74 | 120 |
| #8, 31, 32 \| 1985–1991 \| Sinden gave Neely his number | | | | | |
| **Bob Carpenter** (C)—Beverly, MA | 187 | 63 | 71 | 134 | 175 |
| #11 \| 1988–1992 \| "Can't miss kid" from high school to NHL | | | | | |
| **Stanislav Chistov** (F) Chelyabinsk, Russia | 60 | 5 | 8 | 13 | 36 |
| #13 \| 2006–2007 \| Former 5th overall pick, Anaheim | | | | | |
| **Dave Christian** (RW)—Warroad, MN | 128 | 44 | 38 | 82 | 49 |
| #27 \| 1989–1991 \| Hockey stick family; 1980 US Olympian | | | | | |

| BRUINS REGULAR SEASON STATISTICS | GP | G | A | Pts | PIM |
|---|---|---|---|---|---|
| **Robert Cimetta** (LW/RW)—Toronto, ON | 54 | 10 | 9 | 19 | 33 |
| #14 | 1988–1990 | Boston's 1st rounder in 1988 | | | | | |
| **Gordie Clark** (RW)—Glasgow, Scotland | 8 | 0 | 1 | 1 | 0 |
| #28, 29 | 1974–1976 | Executive in Boston, New York | | | | | |
| **Geoff Courtnall** (LW)—Duncan, BC | 259 | 78 | 81 | 159 | 368 |
| #34, 32, 14 | 1983–1988 | Traded at deadline with 32 goals | | | | | |

| | GP | G | A | Pts | PIM |
|---|---|---|---|---|---|
| **Mariusz Czerkawski** (RW)—Radomsko, Poland | 100 | 23 | 22 | 45 | 45 |
| #19, 29 | 1993–1996, 2005–2006 | One of two Poles to play for B's | | | | | |
| **Bill Derlago** (C)—Birtle, MB | 39 | 5 | 16 | 21 | 15 |
| #14 | 1985–1986 | Fourth overall pick in 1978 draft for Vancouver | | | | | |
| **Ted Donato** (LW)—Boston, MA | 528 | 119 | 147 | 266 | 297 |
| #46, 21, 40 | 1991–1999, 2003–2004 | Coaches Harvard, his alma mater | | | | | |
| **Todd Elik** (C)—Brampton, ON | 90 | 17 | 45 | 62 | 56 |
| #20 | 1995–1997 | 10 years in Europe after 8 in NHL | | | | | |
| **David Emma** (C)—Cranston, RI | 5 | 0 | 0 | 0 | 0 |
| #52 | 1996–1997 | Bishop Hendricken School | | | | | |
| **Tom Fergus** (C)—Chicago, IL | 289 | 98 | 138 | 236 | 138 |
| #28 | 1981–1985 | Made Bruins at age 19 in 1981 | | | | | |
| **Ron Flockhart** (C)—Smithers, BC | 4 | 0 | 0 | 0 | 0 |
| #36 | 1988–1989 | Later coached Reno in the WCHL | | | | | |
| **Dwight Foster** (RW)—Toronto, ON | 252 | 51 | 82 | 133 | 165 |
| #27, 20 | 1977–1981, 1985–1987 | Bruins 1st rounder in 1977 | | | | | |
| **Lee Goren** (RW)—Winnipeg, MB | 35 | 4 | 1 | 5 | 14 |
| #37 | 2000–2001, 2002–2003 | Spoiled BC's Frozen-4 in 2000, UND | | | | | |
| **Thomas Gradin** (C)—Solleftea, Sweden | 64 | 12 | 31 | 43 | 18 |
| #10 | 1986–1987 | Neely's first center | | | | | |
| **Bill Guerin** (RW)—Worcester, MA | 142 | 69 | 60 | 129 | 213 |
| #13 | 2000–2002 | Two-time 7th Player Award winner | | | | | |
| **Brett Harkins** (C)—Cleveland, OH | 45 | 4 | 15 | 19 | 8 |
| #40, 65 | 1994–1997 | "Minor League Mario" | | | | | |

| BRUINS REGULAR SEASON STATISTICS | GP | G | A | Pts | PIM |
|---|---|---|---|---|---|
| **Eric Healey** (LW)—Hull, MA | 2 | 0 | 0 | 0 | 2 |
| #40 | 2005–2006 | Career AHLer after scorer at RPI | | | | | |
| **Steve Heinze** (RW/LW)—Lawrence, MA | 515 | 131 | 108 | 239 | 275 |
| #45, 23 | 1991–2000 | Career ended by concussions | | | | | |
| **Andy Hilbert** (C/LW)—Lansing, MI | 38 | 3 | 3 | 6 | 18 |
| #29, 16 | 2001–2004 | Demanded one-way deal; got "go-away" | | | | | |
| **Kenneth R. Hodge** (RW)—Birmingham, England | 652 | 289 | 385 | 674 | 620 |
| #8 | 1967–1976 | Two-time 50-goal scorer | | | | | |
| **Ivan Huml** (LW)—Kladno, Czech Rep. | 49 | 6 | 12 | 18 | 36 |
| #36 | 2001–2004 | Played in Czech, Swede, and Fin Leagues | | | | | |
| **Craig Janney** (C)—Hartford, CT | 262 | 85 | 198 | 283 | 44 |
| #22, 23 | 1987–1992 | Clutch goal vs. NJ in '88 playoffs | | | | | |
| **Bobby Joyce** (LW)—St. John, NB | 115 | 26 | 38 | 64 | 78 |
| #27 | 1987–1990 | Led NHL rook's with 8 goals in '88 post | | | | | |
| **Joe Juneau** (C/LW) Pont-Rouge, QC | 161 | 51 | 142 | 193 | 72 |
| #23, 49 | 1991–1994 | Juneau capitol of 49th state, thus 49 | | | | | |
| **Petr Kalus** (RW)—Ostrava, Czech Republic | 9 | 4 | 1 | 5 | 6 |
| #47 | 2006–2007 | Traded to Wild in deal for Manny Fernandez | | | | | |
| **Sheldon Kennedy** (RW)—Elkhorn, MB | 56 | 8 | 10 | 18 | 30 |
| #33 | 1996–1997 | With Swift Current when bus crashed | | | | | |
| **Phil Kessel** (C/W)—Madison, WI | 152 | 30 | 36 | 66 | 40 |
| #81 | 2006–2008 | Won Masterton Trophy in 2007 | | | | | |
| **Dmitri Khristich** (LW)—Kiev, Ukraine | 161 | 58 | 79 | 137 | 90 |
| #12 | 1997–1999 | 19-year career in Russia and NHL | | | | | |
| **Mike Knuble** (RW)—Toronto, ON | 307 | 69 | 76 | 145 | 164 |
| #26 | 1999–2004 | Lost after lock-out during roster purge | | | | | |
| **Chuck Kobasew** (RW)—Vancouver, BC | 83 | 23 | 18 | 41 | 54 |
| #12 | 2006–2008 | Broken leg kept him out of '08 post season | | | | | |
| **Andrei Kovalenko** (RW)—Balakovo, Russia | 76 | 16 | 21 | 37 | 27 |
| #51 | 2000–2001 | 20-year pro in Russia and NHL | | | | | |

| BRUINS REGULAR SEASON STATISTICS | GP | G | A | Pts | PIM |
|---|---|---|---|---|---|
| **David Krejci** (C)—Sternberk, Czech Rep. | 62 | 6 | 21 | 27 | 22 |
| #46 \| 2006–2008 \| Emerged late in 2008 season | | | | | |

| BRUINS REGULAR SEASON STATISTICS | GP | G | A | Pts | PIM |
|---|---|---|---|---|---|
| **Mike Krushelnyski** (LW/C)—Montreal, QC | 162 | 51 | 65 | 116 | 100 |
| #33, 25 \| 1981–1984 \| Eight playoff goals as rookie | | | | | |
| **Dmitri Kvartalnov** (LW)—Voskresensk, USSR | 112 | 42 | 49 | 91 | 26 |
| #10 \| 1992–1994 \| First Russian with Bruins | | | | | |
| **Bobby Lalonde** (C)—Montreal, QC | 133 | 14 | 37 | 51 | 59 |
| #19 \| 1979–1981 \| Nine + NHL years despite 5-foot-5 stature | | | | | |
| **Robert Lang** (C)—Teplice, Czechoslovakia | 3 | 0 | 0 | 0 | 2 |
| #45 \| 1997–1998 \| Three Olympic medals with Czechs | | | | | |
| **Brian Lawton** (LW)—New Brunswick, NJ | 8 | 0 | 0 | 0 | 14 |
| #29 \| 1989–1990 \| First American to be first overall pick | | | | | |
| **Steve Leach** (RW)—Cambridge, MA | 293 | 76 | 83 | 159 | 501 |
| #27 \| 1991–1996 \| Matignon High School; four straight state titles | | | | | |
| **Tommy Lehmann** (C)—Stockholm, Sweden | 35 | 5 | 5 | 10 | 16 |
| #20 \| 1987–1989 \| Opted for last seven years in Sweden | | | | | |
| **Normand Leveille** (LW)—Montreal, QC | 75 | 17 | 25 | 42 | 49 |
| #19 \| 1981–1983 \| Cerebral hemorrhage ended career | | | | | |
| **Ken Linseman** (C)—Kingston, ON | 389 | 125 | 247 | 372 | 746 |
| #13 \| 1984–1990 \| "The Rat" was 1988 playoff scoring leader | | | | | |
| **Morris Lukowich** (LW)—Speers, SK | 36 | 6 | 12 | 18 | 31 |
| #12 \| 1984–1986 \| Older brother Ed is a curling legend | | | | | |
| **Mikko Makela** (LW)—Tampere, Finland | 11 | 1 | 2 | 3 | 0 |
| #42 \| 1994–1995 \| Runs hockey camps in Alberta | | | | | |
| **Eric Manlow** (C)—Belleville, ON | 11 | 0 | 1 | 1 | 2 |
| #57 \| 2000–2002 \| Still kickin' around the AHL in '08 | | | | | |
| **Cameron Mann** (RW)—Thompson, MB | 89 | 14 | 10 | 24 | 40 |
| #10 \| 1997–2001 \| Failed 1st round pick, won Calder Cup | | | | | |
| **Daniel Marois** (RW)—Montreal, QC | 22 | 7 | 3 | 10 | 18 |
| #33 \| 1993–1994 \| Peaked in '89–90 with 76 pts for Toronto | | | | | |
| **Tom J. McCarthy** (LW)—Toronto, ON | 75 | 32 | 34 | 66 | 37 |
| #19 \| 1986–1988 \| 10th overall pick—Minnesota 1979 | | | | | |

| BRUINS REGULAR SEASON STATISTICS | GP | G | A | Pts | PIM |
|---|---|---|---|---|---|
| **Shawn McEachern** (LW)—Waltham | 110 | 26 | 35 | 61 | 56 |
| #14, 17 \| 1995–1996, 2005–2006 \| Boston University; Stanley Cup in Pittsburgh | | | | | |
| **Andrew McKim** (C)—St. John, NB | 36 | 1 | 4 | 5 | 4 |
| #45 \| 1992–1994 \| Three seasons with Berlin Polar Bears | | | | | |
| **Peter McNab** (C)—Vancouver, BC | 595 | 263 | 324 | 587 | 111 |
| #8 \| 1976–1984 \| Great bloodlines; father Max a legend | | | | | |
| **Rick Middleton** (RW)—Toronto, ON | 881 | 402 | 496 | 898 | 124 |
| #16 \| 1976–1988 \| Selling Nifty–16 Dessert Bars | | | | | |
| **Sandy Moger** (C)—Hundred Mile House, BC | 132 | 27 | 23 | 50 | 116 |
| #45 \| 1994–1997 \| NCAA Champ at Lake Superior State | | | | | |
| **Doug Morrison** (RW)—Vancouver, BC | 23 | 7 | 3 | 10 | 15 |
| #11, 23, 38 \| 1979–1982, 1984–1985 \| Brother Mark has even fewer GP | | | | | |
| **Joe Mullen** (RW)—New York, NY | 37 | 8 | 7 | 15 | 0 |
| #11 \| 1995–1996 \| First American-born 500-goal scorer | | | | | |
| **Joe Murphy** (RW)—London, ON | 26 | 7 | 7 | 14 | 41 |
| #43 \| 1999–2000 \| Apparently once told coach "I'm too tired to go" | | | | | |

| BRUINS REGULAR SEASON STATISTICS | GP | G | A | Pts | PIM |
|---|---|---|---|---|---|
| **Glen Murray** (RW)—Halifax, NS | 570 | 206 | 180 | 389 | 408 |
| #44, 21, 27 \| 1991–1995, 2001–2008 \| Career high 44 G's, 92 PTS in '02–03 | | | | | |
| **Mats Naslund** (LW)—Timra, Sweden | 34 | 8 | 14 | 22 | 4 |
| #26 \| 1994–1995 \| One Cup during career with Habs | | | | | |
| **Peter Nordstrom** (LW)—Munkfors, Sweden | 2 | 0 | 0 | 0 | 0 |
| #56 \| 1998–1999 \| Got homesick and left | | | | | |
| **Michael Nylander** (C)—Stockholm, Sweden | 15 | 1 | 11 | 12 | 14 |
| #92 \| 2003–2004 \| One of many not signed post lock-out | | | | | |
| **Chris Oddleifson** (C)—Brandon, MB | 55 | 10 | 11 | 21 | 25 |
| #22, 28 \| 1972–1974 \| Best years were in Vancouver | | | | | |
| **Paul O'Neil** (C/RW)—Charlestown, MA | 1 | 0 | 0 | 0 | 0 |
| #28 \| 1975–1976 \| Didn't play right field for the Reds | | | | | |
| **Clayton Pachal** (C/LW)—Yorkton, SK | 11 | 0 | 0 | 0 | 26 |
| #6, 28 \| 1976–1978 \| Former 1st round pick | | | | | |
| **Brad Palmer** (LW)—Duncan, BC | 73 | 6 | 11 | 17 | 18 |
| #21 \| 1982–1983 \| 16th overall pick, Minnesota 1980 | | | | | |

| BRUINS REGULAR SEASON STATISTICS | GP | G | A | Pts | PIM |
|---|---|---|---|---|---|
| **Dave Silk** (RW)—Scituate, MA | 64 | 20 | 22 | 42 | 86 |
| #21 \| 1983–1985 \| 1980 USA Olympic Gold | | | | | |
| **Charlie Simmer** (LW)—Terrace Bay, ON | 198 | 98 | 94 | 192 | 136 |
| #23 \| 1984–1987 \| Was on Triple Crown Line in LA | | | | | |
| **Petri Skriko** (LW)—Lappeenranta, Finland | 37 | 6 | 14 | 20 | 15 |
| #18, 29 \| 1990–1992 \| Four 30-goal seasons as Canuck | | | | | |
| **Bryan Smolinski** (C)—Toledo, OH | 136 | 50 | 36 | 86 | 113 |
| #20 \| 1992–1995 \| "Smoke" helped eliminate B's in 2008 | | | | | |
| **Kevin Stevens** (LW)—Brockton, MA | 41 | 10 | 13 | 23 | 49 |
| #25 \| 1995–1996 \| Two Cups in Pitt; hat trick vs. B's in '92 | | | | | |
| **Shayne Stevenson** (RW)—Newmarket, ON | 19 | 0 | 1 | 1 | 28 |
| #49 \| 1990–1992 \| B's 1989 pick; 17th overall | | | | | |
| **Jozef Stumpel** (C)—Nitra, Slovakia | 424 | 75 | 206 | 281 | 80 |
| #48, 16, 22 \| 1991–1997, 2001–2003 \| First Euro to lead B's in scoring | | | | | |
| **Marco Sturm** (LW)—Dingolfing, Germany | 207 | 77 | 66 | 143 | 118 |
| #16 \| 2005–2008 \| One-third of the Joe Thornton trade | | | | | |
| **Tim Sweeney** (LW)—Boston, MA | 91 | 19 | 26 | 45 | 34 |
| #51, 41, 42, 16 \| 1992–1993, 1995–1997 \| Tim, Bob, and Don not related | | | | | |
| **Petr Tenkrat** (RW)—Kladno, Czech Rep. | 64 | 9 | 5 | 14 | 34 |
| #17 \| 2006–2007 \| First goal with B's in his First B's game | | | | | |
| **Joe Thornton** (C)—London, ON | 532 | 169 | 285 | 454 | 617 |
| #6, 19 \| 1997–2005 \| First overall pick in 1997 | | | | | |
| **Mike Walton** (C)—Kirkland Lake, ON | 168 | 60 | 57 | 117 | 92 |
| #11 \| 1971–1973, 1978–1979 \| Orr's buddy nicknamed "Shaky" | | | | | |

| BRUINS REGULAR SEASON STATISTICS | GP | G | A | Pts | PIM |
|---|---|---|---|---|---|
| **Dave Pasin** (RW)—Edmonton, AB | 71 | 18 | 19 | 37 | 50 |
| #37 \| 1985–1986 \| Slow skater; fast shot | | | | | |
| **Barry Pederson** (C)—Big River, SK | 379 | 166 | 251 | 417 | 248 |
| #18, 21, 10, 12 \| 1981–1986, 1991–1992 \| Shipped to Vancouver for Neely | | | | | |
| **Pascal Pelletier** (RW)—Quebec City, QC | 6 | 0 | 0 | 0 | 0 |
| #42 \| 2007–2008 \| AHL Player-of-the-Month, Dec '07 | | | | | |
| **Ray Podloski** (C)—Edmonton, AB | 8 | 0 | 1 | 1 | 17 |
| #43 \| 1988–1989 \| Won Memorial Cup with Neely in Portland | | | | | |
| **Brian Propp** (LW)—Lanigan, SK | 14 | 3 | 9 | 12 | 10 |
| #36 \| 1989–1990 \| Briefly on Neely, Janney line | | | | | |
| **Jean Ratelle** (C)—Lac Ste. Jean, QC | 419 | 155 | 295 | 450 | 84 |
| #10 \| 1975–1981 \| Class act; poor man's Jean Beliveau | | | | | |
| **Marty Reasoner** (C)—Honeoye Falls, NY | 19 | 2 | 6 | 8 | 8 |
| #36 \| 2005–2006 \| Star at BC; 16th overall pick in '96 | | | | | |
| **Nathan Robinson** (C)—Scarborough, ON | 2 | 0 | 0 | 0 | 0 |
| #51 \| 2005–2006 \| Black Canadian last in Germany | | | | | |
| **Randy Robitaille** (C)—Ottawa, ON | 9 | 0 | 2 | 2 | 0 |
| #43, 48, 16 \| 1997–1999 \| MVP of Providence's Calder Cup | | | | | |
| **Brian Rolston** (C/LW)—Flint, MI | 338 | 101 | 135 | 236 | 136 |
| #12 \| 1999–2004 \| Came from Colorado in Bourque deal | | | | | |
| **Jean-Yves Roy** (RW)—Rosemere, QC | 54 | 10 | 15 | 25 | 22 |
| #43 \| 1996–1998 \| All-everything at University of Maine | | | | | |
| **Vladimir Ruzicka** (C)—Most, Czechoslovakia | 166 | 66 | 66 | 132 | 105 |
| #38 \| 1990–1993 \| "Great practice player" | | | | | |
| **Sergei Samsonov** (LW)—Moscow, Russia | 514 | 164 | 212 | 376 | 103 |
| #14 \| 1997–2006 \| Rookie of the Year in IHL and NHL | | | | | |
| **Martin Samuelsson** (RW)—Upplands-Vasby, Sweden | 14 | 0 | 1 | 1 | 2 |
| #43 \| 2002–2004 \| Uppland's best Bruin | | | | | |
| **Andre Savage** (C)—Ottawa, ON | 50 | 8 | 13 | 21 | 10 |
| #54, 28 \| 1998–2001 \| Michigan Tech'er; now in Germany | | | | | |
| **Marc Savard** (C)—Ottawa, ON | 156 | 37 | 137 | 174 | 162 |
| #71, 91 \| 2006–2008 \| Team player? More complete since a B | | | | | |
| **Bob Schmautz** (RW)—Saskatoon, SK | 354 | 134 | 161 | 295 | 444 |
| #11, 17 \| 1973–1980 \| Cherry's beloved lunch-pailer | | | | | |
| **Gregg Sheppard** (C)—North Battleford, SK | 416 | 155 | 220 | 375 | 130 |
| #19 \| 1972–1978 \| Led B's playoff scoring in 1974 | | | | | |

| BRUINS REGULAR SEASON STATISTICS | GP | G | A | Pts | PIM |
|---|---|---|---|---|---|
| **C.J. Young** (RW)—Waban, MA | 15 | 4 | 5 | 9 | 12 |
| #18 \| 1992–1993 \| Belmont Hill 3-sport star; then Harvard | | | | | |
| **Alexei Zhamnov** (C)—Moscow, Russia | 24 | 1 | 9 | 10 | 30 |
| #10 \| 2005–2006 \| Broken ankle ended career | | | | | |
| **Sergei Zholtok** (C)—Riga, Latvia | 25 | 2 | 2 | 4 | 2 |
| #11 \| 1992–1994 \| Died during game in Belarus in 2004 | | | | | |
| **Sergei Zinovjev** (C)—Novokuznetsk, Russia | 10 | 0 | 1 | 1 | 2 |
| #54 \| 2003–2004 \| Achieved stardom in Russia | | | | | |

# CHAPTER

# 14

## ENFORCERS

*above:*

*Darin Kimble played 55 of his 311 NHL games with Boston. Over the years, enforcers have come and gone often, based on their talent level, their ability to fight, and roster chemistry and make-up.*

*left:*

*John Kordic of the Canadiens and Jay Miller square off. Miller's enforcing abilities allowed players like Cam Neely to stay on the ice, rather than spend time in the penalty box fighting for themselves. Miller is 13th all-time in Boston career PIMs.*

To understand hockey is to understand the role of the enforcer. Hockey is a culture of toughness, and the enforcer role is simply one of the elements. Players get hurt, players block shots, players get beat up, players get crushed, thrown, and stymied, and it's accepted as part of the game. Also accepted is fighting. This is not to say everyone would, should, or is expected to fight, but everyone involved in the game, in whatever on-ice capacity, is aware of the fact that fighting is inherent to the environment.

To have those who don't understand or cannot possibly grasp these concepts overseeing the game itself, and ultimately determining its rules, is completely absurd.

The NHL needs to modify the "instigator rule." Presently (spring 2008), a player earns a two-game suspension and loss of wages following three instigator (fight-starting) penalties. During the 2006–07 season, the NHL general managers voted to extend the limit to five instigators before suspension. The NHL Board of Governors overturned it. The instigator rule, as it stands right now, discourages players from sticking up for teammates who are "attacked," cheap-shotted, or roughed up by opponents who have no reason to fear retribution. If player A can cheap-shot player B, then player C, player B's teammate, should be able to retaliate legally, by acting as an enforcer against player A, without fear of secondary penalty or suspension.

Some are concerned that fighting gives hockey a bad name or a bad image. This is an absurd and dangerous notion. Fighting is a popular part of the game, and an effective way to vent frustration and carry out traditional retribution, while allowing the players on the ice to effectively police themselves. By not allowing the players to fight when necessary, frustration fouls, high sticks, cross-checks, and dangerous hits from behind become the alternative retribution. This is what truly hurts the game. Meanwhile, the initial acts of "violence"—high sticks and hits from behind—consistently lead to long-term injuries as they go unchecked. Fines and suspensions aren't enough, and it's only because self-policing is discouraged that these incidents reach the fine-and-suspension stage in the first place.

We naturally see fighting in highlight packages on a nightly basis, a custom as familiar to longtime fans as video of dramatic goals. Conversely, it's only the hits from behind and other dangerous stick fouls that make the national nightly news, and reach a non-hockey or not-yet-hockey audience. Again, when players cross the line and someone is injured and hockey gets tarnished, it's not because of fighting, it's because fighting has been unnaturally curbed. These incidents occur simply because the ability of the players to play hockey, to enforce their own code of ethics, and to police the level of violence on the ice themselves has been greatly compromised by the instigator rule. Raising the suspension threshold from three instigator penalties

*above:*

*Chris Nilan, the Montreal Canadiens all-time leader in penalty minutes, and Terry O'Reilly, the record holder for the Bruins, squared off on countless occasions. From left to right, Chris Nilan, Ray Bourque, Mario Tremblay, Chris Chelios, and Terry O'Reilly.*

to five would be a start towards solving this problem, although eliminating it altogether would be the smarter alternative. Like the designated hitter rule in baseball's American League, the instigator rule's time should have come and gone.

Fighting is a popular part of the game, and an effective way to vent frustration.

This is not to suggest that widespread brawling is attractive. There are other rules and safeguards in place to prevent line brawls, bench-clearing situations, or from additional players (a third man or even more) from joining altercations. The suspensions and fines for events like these are steep, as they should be. However, to prevent a potential fight or two from occurring in a game, a.k.a. fights done for the right reason (such as to diffuse physical tension and discourage cheap-shot violence), compromises the integrity of the game on the ice.

The hypocrisy of "fighting prevents us from growing the sport" is blatantly transparent. In non-traditional markets where hockey has attempted to expand at all professional levels, the fans (just ask them) find the fights and the physical play as one of the allures of attending the games. No one leaves during a fight. No one runs to the concession stand during a fight. Most everyone is on their feet during a fight.

*right:*

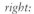

*Brent Hughes played nearly 200 games for the Bruins. Here, he squares off with a young Luke Richardson who, as of 2008, was still active in the League after twenty seasons.*

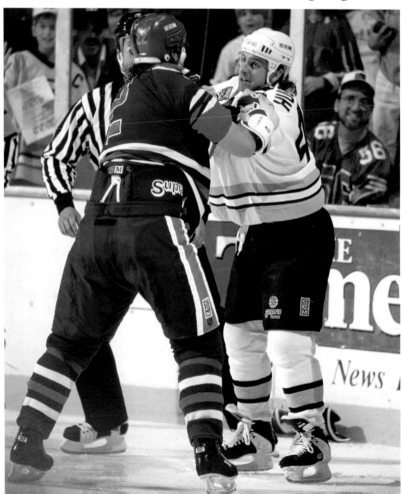

Meanwhile, fighting in hockey is tame compared to the violence and death on race tracks, tame in comparison to the thousands of murders and other acts of brutal violence our children see on TV shows and in the news before they become adults. Should we give the players knives or guns to make it more mainstream? Hockey fighting is honorable: a "mano a mano" duel without weapons. It's an old-fashioned, entertaining, and generally safe way of settling heightened tension, and actually can have the effect of reducing peripheral violence.

Scorers, grinders, and enforcers all understand hockey. This, they have in common. Regardless of their on-ice role, hockey players share an appreciation for the game they all grew up loving. And those very roles can change. Players whose names became synonymous with pugilism didn't necessarily start playing the game with that role in mind. More often than not, fighting and enforcing resulted as the tail end of an evolution.

"A lot of people don't know me. I was more of a Bobby Orr type player," states Jay Miller, earner of 856 Bruins

*below:*

*In an effort to get tougher and harder to play against, the Bruins added free agent Shawn Thornton from Anaheim in 2007-08. En route to 74 season PIMs, Thornton spars with Riley Cote of the Flyers.*

penalty minutes in 216 games. "I'd take the puck at UNH [the University of New Hampshire] and in high school playing left defense, and I would play basically the whole game, and that's what I would do. I would rush the puck and score goals, for the Bay State League in Natick and at UNH. Later, my old coach, Rick Lee, says, 'You ought to do something with your size, instead of fooling around with scoring goals. You can't do it anymore—your speed's gone.'

"I think the scouts knew how I played because I think that's why they drafted me, to create some offense. They didn't draft me to be a tough guy," adds Miller. "I wasn't drafted for that, L.B. [Lyndon Byers] wasn't drafted for that, Bob Probert wasn't; he and others were drafted to be goal scorers and then they molded them into what they needed. That's the same thing that happened to me."

"An enforcer? A disgruntled goal-scorer," P.J. Stock says with a smile. "No, whatever it took to play, to keep me in the

League, whatever I had to do, getting beat up weekly, whatever it was, I'd do it. I found a niche, which was getting beat up, and it paid the bills. I was fortunate my parents were nice enough to bless me with a really thick skull."

Stock, not blessed with size or stature, takes a humble approach to remembering his game. Beat up or beating up, he never backed down from any opponent, even those substantially larger. He'd do whatever necessary, and take whatever abuse might be handed out, to stick up for his team and create an edge.

"The term today is 'energy player,'" Stock adds. "Whatever kept me in there. I was never a fighter growing up, never thought I'd be a fighter. Whatever term you want to use, it kept me in the National Hockey League, and I got to hang out in Boston, New York, Philadelphia, and Montreal for a while."

Stan Jonathan, who won the team's 7th Player Award in 1978, was another Bruin a bit smaller than your average tough guy: a very tough 5-foot-8 inch brawler who always put his teammates first.

"I never did it for myself," Jonathan insists, "I put my teammates first. We all did. That's what I miss the most. We had our hearts in the right place, we were a team, and I'll always be a Boston Bruin.

A Lunch Pail teammate of Jonathan's, John Wensink, nicknamed "Wire," was well known for his haircut and for his tenacious and relentless approach to the game. He literally fought his way into the Bruins lineup starting in 1976–77.

"I'd like to think I could play that regular shift, maybe second or third line," ponders Wensink. "Definitely not first line, but more than just fourth line, but I think I would consider myself an enforcer."

*above:*

*P.J. Stock waving to the crowd at the Garden following a scrap. Undersized as a fighter, Stock garnered great fan support in Boston. Defenseman Calle Johansson of the Capitals looks on.*

Wensink's ultimate moment as a Bruins tough guy was caught on tape. After a brawl with the North Stars, he skated over and challenged Minnesota's entire bench. He stopped a few feet away, and with both hands waved them on, signifying "any takers?" There were none.

"Terry [O'Reilly] and I got into it with a couple of their guys, Jensen was one I think, and then I made my little trip," remembers Wensink. "I hadn't seen the whole thing—all I'd ever seen was the little clip where I stopped in front of the bench—[until] about two years ago [when] a buddy of O'Reilly's in Phoenix, who invited the Bruins alumni out there for a few days, had the whole thing, from the fights, through the stop, until I skated out of the Zamboni doors in the old Garden. That was a weak moment, whatever amount of time that took, the nine seconds or the three seconds. Grapes, he keeps that out in front of people [by showing it on TV], and I think that will be around a long time."

*below:*

*Stan Jonathan pounds a turtling (later coach of the Bruins) Robbie Ftorek of the Quebec Nordiques in 1979-80. Bulldog, fire plug, whatever the preferred term for an undersized fighter, Jonathan fit it. A fiery fan favorite with no quit from 1975 to 1982.*

Then soon-to-be Bruins left wing Al Secord had a different perspective on Wensink's famous moment.

"I guess my first impression [of the Bruins at that time] was when I saw a video of John Wensink challenging the entire Minnesota bench. Do you remember that?" Secord asks. "I think they had a five-man brawl and then Wensink came over to the bench, and he gave them the finger wave and nobody would come over. Then, I think it was the following spring, I was drafted by Boston. You know, Stan Jonathan, Wayne Cashman, and Terry O'Reilly, and I'm thinking, 'This is gonna be one of my toughest training camps of all time. I'm gonna have to fight everybody.' Especially with Don Cherry having and wanting such a tough team. I thought it was going to be nuts and I was going to have to earn my way.

"Actually, when I got to camp in Fitchburg, Massachusetts, the toughest part was rookie camp," Secord clarifies. "We had a couple of exhibition games against the Islanders and the Flyers and we had bench-clearing brawls. We went up to Portland, Maine, on a bus. I had three fights, finally got thrown out after the third one. I had a couple more against the Flyers and I was exhausted after two days. I had a couple goals and five or six fights and I guess Don Cherry was quite impressed.

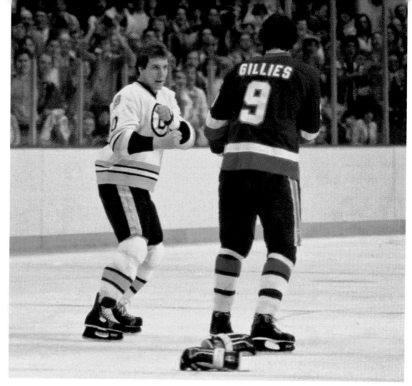

*above:*

*Al "Rocky" Secord drops the mitts with a man considered by many to be one of the toughest fighters of his era, Clark Gillies of the Islanders. The perfect example of a player having to prove his toughness early in his career, Secord left Boston and became a strong goal scorer in Chicago.*

Wensink came over to the bench, and he gave them the finger wave and nobody would come over.

"When I got to the main camp I was expecting to fight Jonathan, Wensink, Cashman, and O'Reilly, but when I got there, it was the quietest training camp I had been to in the last five years," Secord continues. "I had been to juniors, and those were just crazy, and then to rookie camp and then to the main camp. The only thing I remember was Milbury and Cashman hitting each other like cavemen with their sticks right over the head. It was a stick fight. Cashman hit him over the head—I remember Milbury had the Jofa helmet, and Cashman was hitting the Jofa and then it would slide down to his shoulder, and Cashman didn't wear a helmet, so Milbury

*above:*

*Like many a Bruins fan, photographer Steve Babineau loves the fight game. Here, he gets a pose from friend Al Secord, one of his all-time favorite B's.*

*below:*

*During the 1990-91 season, Lyndon Byers goes after Denis Vial during the latter's brief 21 game stint with the New York Rangers. Byers is 9th all-time in Bruins penalty minutes.*

is swinging back, hitting him over the head and bouncing it off his shoulder. The other guys jumped in and stopped it. That was my introduction to the Bruins training camp."

Secord didn't need to fight the veterans to impress Don Cherry. The effort he showed in rookie camp was enough to earn him a spot on the club.

"I remember, after the second rookie game against the Islanders, Cherry had watched my last fight when I finally got thrown out, and he came in the dressing room to specifically talk to me about the fight. I belonged on the team, or I had a real good shot because I was the kind of guy he was looking for," Secord remembers. "He came in saying, 'Next time do this' or 'Do that,' and that was my first introduction to Don Cherry."

A second home during the hockey season for pugilists is the penalty box, which just happens to be Steve Babineau's second home as well. It's a great spot from which to get shots.

"I changed penalty boxes quite a bit from game to game, just to mix things up, change my angles, and depending on if I was looking for shots of a specific player," explains Babs. "I couldn't change during a game because the strobes in the ceiling were hard-wired to a little control box, which I would set up at the beginning of the night in one of the boxes.

"[Gord] Kluzak is killing Ray Neufeld of Hartford during a fight right in front of the penalty box," Babs adds. "He whipped him, just whaled on him. And since it was near the end of the period, the guys were escorted off the ice to their dressing rooms. As Gordie starts away, he skates right in front of me and I yell out, 'Way to go, Gordie!' Instantly I get a backhanded glove punch right in my chest. I forgot I was sitting in the visitor's penalty box, and more importantly, that Whalers enforcer Torrie Robertson was sitting in there with me. 'You're in the wrong box, buddy,' Robertson says. 'Oops, sorry,' I answered," recalls Babineau.

"I shut up and started taking pictures."

An incident that made the Kluzak-Neufeld fight unforgettable for Babs.

Enforcers can remember individual fights with great detail. It's a habit they learn while in the business, because remembering fights means remembering an opponent's tendencies and habits, and to adjust means a chance to win the next time out.

They also remember fights for pure entertainment purposes.

"Wayne Van Dorp, I one-punched him and I got a standing-O," Lyndon Byers recalls proudly. "It was the third period of a Quebec Nordiques game and he was mouthing off. I had fought him in the first period and knuckled him lefty, then in the second period he went to run me and I sticked him in the face, and I caught him for four stitches. So he was royally pissed off at me at the end of the second. It was perfect. Mike Milbury was coach, so 'Dooner' put me out, second shift of the third period, and Van Dorp came out all wound up. I looked at [referee] Paul Stewart and I said, 'Do I have to fight this dummy again? I kill him every time.' We were in a TV time-out, and 'Stewy' looked at Van Dorp and said, 'Do you want to fight 'em again?' and Van Dorp said, 'Yeah, I want to kill 'em,' and Stewy said alright. The linesman dropped the puck right in the middle of a TV time-out and I one-punched him and knocked him out on his butt. The Garden went berserko. It was nuts."

"I think I had a fight with Stephen Peat once," remembers Stock. "No one got hurt. It was a lot of fun, it got a lot of press, and the guys joked about it. It was fun, fun going to the rink after that, couple T-shirts floating around. It was a Saturday or Sunday afternoon. The guys liked it [for its duration and intensity]. We were winning the game. Just a moment that worked out well. It's tough to pick that one moment; there was a bunch of them."

*above:*

*A rare photo of a somewhat calm Chris "Knuckles" Nilan, of course taken while he sat in the penalty box. The proudest NHL moment of the Northeastern product's career: with Boston against Hartford on March 31, 1991, he picked up a record ten different penalties (42 PIMs) in one game.*

"Back when I was in the minors we used to have Dave Brown, myself, John Kordic, and Chris Nilan," recalls Jay Miller. "We were all fighting in the same little division and we'd all learn from each other, and then all of a sudden we all get called up and we're fighting each other again, just in a bigger show. I'd have to say those guys taught me more—you really learned it from experience—they taught me through going through it and gaining experience. Back then if you lost you figured out a way to win. Fortunately, we'd have a chance to fight that person the next night, and maybe eight times a year, and you had a chance to defend your honor and make sure it didn't happen again.

"When I fought Dave Brown I fought him lefty; he couldn't fight rightie," Miller points out. "Your opposite hand, he could never figure it out. By the time he figured it out it was too late. Rick Tocchet fought with both hands. That was scary. Which one do you grab? I learned to do both, more from my early boxing days. Dave Brown, my first fight ever at the Garden, an afternoon game, is obviously always one that I'll remember, but they sent me back down after.

*below:*

*Jim McKenzie of the Hartford Whalers and Cam Neely discuss matters from their respective penalty boxes at the old Garden. Goal scorer Neely, who crosses all player talent categories, would enforce for himself whenever necessary.*

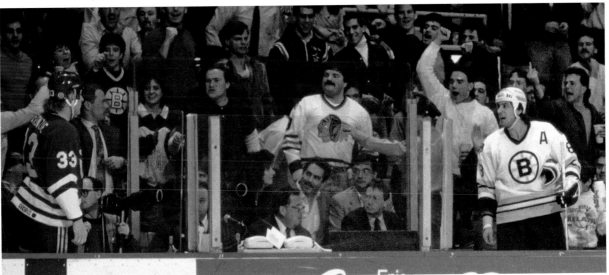

"I would think the Chris Nilan fight was the biggest one, the back-to-back after he butt-ended Rick Middleton," Miller continues. "That would have to be the big one but I had numerous really good ones with the fans. John Kordic, having two Boston kids going at it in the Garden, how much better can you get? They hyped it up more than goal scorers. You look at the old annals of the League, the *Globe* and the *Herald*, they didn't care as much about the goal scorers. They looked at Montreal playing Boston and they interviewed Nilan and myself before they interviewed Ray Bourque and Claude Lemieux. I think that's why we went as far as we did in 1988. I think myself and L.B. really stuck up for our guys and really gave it to them, and I think our guys were more confident. That really helped, it created room. Just think if you could create room now; with a kid like Crosby with some room, he's gonna kill ya."

Fighting, and fighting at the right time and for the right reason, provides a true indication of a team's chemistry and togetherness.

"We'd actually fight in practice. I remember fights in practice throughout the year," says Secord, who came up with the Bruins in 1978–79. "It was like a family, brothers having fights, but that was part of it; but if someone else picked on one of us during a hockey game, that just wasn't going to happen. We stuck up for each other."

"All you have to do is think of John Bucyk, Bobby Orr, Derek Sanderson, Wayne Cashman, Ray Bourque, Cam Neely," adds Byers. "Then to play on successful teams; honestly, that's what I think about—teammates and former guys. Andy Moog, Ray, Cam, Terry O'Reilly, John Wensick: guys that would bleed to death for you. It's that simple. I knew that anybody I played with and wore the Black and Gold, they would bleed for me man, and that's a pretty awesome thing."

"I had been going to the Bruins games all my life, sitting there watching all of the Bruins games," points out Miller. "It was very important to me because that was the Bobby Orr era. I was 12 when they won the Stanley Cup, and I'm sitting there watching the game. Ten years later, I was putting on the same uniform as him. The exciting part about that was, knowing that when I was 12, dreaming about it and it's not even close, people would laugh at you. 'I want to be a Bruin,' I'd say. When I got to college I still didn't know I could play for the Bruins, believe it or not. Coming from Natick and watching all of these Canadians around me playing at UNH, getting drafted, and playing in the League.

*below:*

*John "Wire" Wensink battled everywhere. Not sure if a fight resulted from this encounter with Canadiens Hall-of-Fame defenseman Larry Robinson, working the slot in front of goalie Ken Dryden.*

*above:*

*This Terry O'Reilly-Steve Jensen fight erupted out of a face-off on December 1, 1977. That's Nick Beverley (#26) to the left with Peter McNab. North Star Alex Pirus on the right would soon be pummeled by John Wensink, who after the fight challenged the entire Minnesota bench and received no takers.*

Then I get drafted and I'm thinking there's still no way, but three years later I've got a B's uniform on my back. It was kind of a whirlwind situation where all of a sudden I was there. I always dreamed about it but never thought it was going to happen. Like Bob Sweeney, or Bob Carpenter, or any of the Bruins that grew up around here, you'd be growing up dreaming of it and people would say, 'Yeah, you're good but you're not that good.' That's what it was all about, and then having all of your friends and family watching you."

The dream of playing the game he loved, for the team he loved—it could have been a scorer talking, a playmaker, a grinder, or an enforcer. Dreams come true via hard work regardless of position and status. Just ask Terry O'Reilly, the all-time leader in penalty minutes for the Bruins, who broke into the League in 1972 with very little fanfare, and limited talent.

"Well, it was, at the time, the game was a very physical game," states O'Reilly. "There were very few rules restricting third man in, bench-clearing brawls...the fines were very, I would say, lenient. Suspensions were unheard-of for a fight, so it was a very physical game. If you look at the names of the teams, you know, the Broad Street Bullies, the Big Bad Bruins. For me, the NHL had just expanded, the WHA [World Hockey Association] had just come into being, so the level of professional hockey was somewhat distributed and watered down. It gave me a little extra room to get in there and it was a very physical brand of hockey, and since my skating was weak I could specialize in the other parts of it to buy myself some time. That's basically what I did: I showed a willingness to hit and scrap and all that, while I worked on my skating."

O'Reilly's overall time in Boston practically coincides with that of photographer Steve Babineau. The two arrived at about the same time, and they have skated together and shared common interests. One of those interests is dogs, more specifically, Dachshunds.

"Yep, we've talked about them quite a bit along the way," says O'Reilly. "He's had three or four, we [my family and I] have four now. We both love our Dachshund dogs."

Al Secord is another former Bruin tough guy who's familiar with the life and times of Babineau.

"He was a good guy," Secord states. "I'm really impressed and happy for him that he's had such a long, successful career. I remember he used to skate with us every once in a while, and he was always around. He was part of the fabric."

Babineau would provide Secord with shots of him playing pretty much whenever Secord wanted them, which wasn't often. Players usually think about such collectibles, or about rounding up personal treasures or memories, well after their time has come and gone.

"My kids were sitting around with me and wanting to know, wanting to see some pictures, and we have a couple of grandbabies and they said they wanted to have some of the old stuff, and I said [they] could have it when I'm gone," says Wensink. "They said they wanted stuff like that now and I instantly thought of Steve Babineau. I wasn't sure what I had, but I knew Steve would have it. He's definitely the guy. When I was playing the game, I never thought of collecting stuff, but when its all over, 20, 30 years later you're going, 'Boy, I wish I would have had some stuff.' It's mostly for the grandkids."

Pride, camaraderie, and memories: for the enforcers, maybe even more so than for the grinders, goalies, and playmakers,

*above:*

*2007-08 Bruins rookie Milan Lucic tallied 89 PIMs for the season, here fighting Barret Jackman of the Blues. Lucic is a new version of an old Bruin, qualified as a scorer, a grinder, and an enforcer.*

*below:*

*Mike Milbury is second all-time on the Bruins career penalty minutes list with 1,552.*

it's all about defending and honoring the name on the front of the jersey.

"I truly believe that the guys who came to the rink didn't need anything else other than the fact that they were gonna put that jersey on, to get motivated," states Byers. "That was it. It was pretty simple. Once the boys back in the day laid the groundwork, it was pretty obvious and it was pretty solid."

"[Boston] was really the last pit stop for me in the National Hockey League and it was my favorite, my best, and my most cherished one," points out Stock. "I played with some great players, one who went on to become the MVP of the NHL. Some great leaders, a great team, and it was fun to be a part of it."

"Boston laid a real good groundwork," states Secord, who spent the bulk of his 12 NHL seasons with the Blackhawks. "I would say I had more success in Chicago, but I actually enjoyed more, my years in Boston. It was such a great, tight group of guys. We had a reunion a few years ago in Phoenix and it was the first time since the late '70s or early '80s that we'd all been together in one spot. We had such a nice time out there: we had a little golfing and had a couple of events. We played a charity hockey game. And it was just amazing that after all of those years, we got together—everyone is very fond of one another—and we didn't miss a beat. It was like we were picking up the conversation from yesterday. We all joined in and continued the camaraderie. We had so much in common. We were so close. We were like a bunch of overgrown kids, a band of brothers."

*above:*

*A scrap with the Islanders. Left to right: Goalie Chico Resch, Garry Howatt, Bruin Wayne Cashman, Brad Park, Islanders Wayne Merrick and Bob Bourne. Behind Cashman are goalies Gerry Cheevers of the B's, and Billy Smith of the Isles.*

Enforcers whose careers included or began after 1973-74, the season in which Steve Babineau took his first professional photo at a Bruins game. Defensemen included on this enforcer list were taken off the defensemen list.

| BRUINS REGULAR SEASON STATISTICS | GP | G | A | Pts | PIM |
|---|---|---|---|---|---|
| **Darren Banks** (LW) Toronto, ON<br>#20, 56 \| 1992–1994 \| Sixteen different minor league teams | 20 | 2 | 2 | 4 | 73 |
| **Ken Baumgartner** (LW) Flin Flon, MB<br>#22 \| 1997–1999 \| While playing, business degree at Hofstra | 151 | 1 | 4 | 5 | 318 |
| **Ken Belanger** (LW) Sault Ste. Marie, ON<br>#16 \| 1999–2001 \| Reluctant enforcer—hated fighting | 122 | 5 | 8 | 13 | 317 |
| **Dennis Bonvie** (RW) Antigonish, NS<br>#76, 22 \| 2001–2002 \| AHL career PIM leader | 23 | 1 | 2 | 3 | 84 |
| **Wade Brookbank** (D/LW) Lanigan, SK<br>#28 \| 2006–2007 \| Younger brother Sheldon in NHL | 7 | 1 | 0 | 1 | 15 |
| **Lyndon Byers** (RW) Nipawin, SK<br>#8, 12, 33, 34 \| 1983–1992 \| Scored last goal of 1990 Final | 261 | 24 | 42 | 66 | 959 |
| **Dean Chynoweth** (D) Calgary, AB<br>#47, 28 \| 1995–1998 \| WHL coach and executive | 94 | 2 | 8 | 10 | 259 |
| **Brian Curran** (D) Toronto, ON<br>#34 \| 1983–1986 \| Won Memorial Cup with Neely in Portland | 115 | 3 | 7 | 10 | 407 |

| BRUINS REGULAR SEASON STATISTICS | GP | G | A | Pts | PIM |
|---|---|---|---|---|---|
| **Doug Doull** (LW) Glace Bay, NS<br>#56 \| 2003–2004 \| Once suspended for charging Nedved | 35 | 0 | 1 | 1 | 132 |
| **Aaron Downey** (RW) Shelburne, ON<br>#45 \| 1999–2000 \| Survived horrific stick cut to leg artery | 1 | 0 | 0 | 0 | 0 |
| **Glen Featherstone** (D) Toronto, ON<br>#6 \| 1991–1994 \| Won IHL title with Chicago Wolves in 2000 | 99 | 7 | 13 | 20 | 274 |
| **Bill Huard** (LW) Welland, ON<br>#61 \| 1992–1993 \| Member of first-ever Providence Bruins team | 2 | 0 | 0 | 0 | 0 |
| **Brent Hughes** (LW)—New Westminster, BC<br>#42, 18 \| 1991–1995 \| Finished with Austin Icebats | 191 | 25 | 22 | 47 | 511 |
| **Jamie Huscroft** (D) Creston, BC<br>#28 \| 1993–1995 \| Seven teams; finished with Cap's | 70 | 0 | 7 | 7 | 247 |
| **Stan Jonathan** (LW) Ohsweken, ON<br>#17 \| 1975–1983 \| Bloodied Bouchard, Game 4, '78 Final | 392 | 91 | 107 | 198 | 738 |
| **Darin Kimble** (RW) Lucky Lake, SK<br>#29 \| 1992–1993 \| Seven goals with B's was career/season high | 55 | 7 | 3 | 10 | 177 |

| BRUINS REGULAR SEASON STATISTICS | GP | G | A | Pts | PIM |
|---|---|---|---|---|---|
| **Dan LaCouture** (LW) Hyannis, MA | 55 | 2 | 2 | 4 | 53 |
| #28 | 2005–2006 | Suspended by Ducks; headed to Europe | | | | | |
| **Dan Lacroix** (LW) Montreal, QC | 23 | 1 | 0 | 1 | 38 |
| #40 | 1994–1995 | Islanders' assistant coach | | | | | |
| **Dean Malkoc** (D) Vancouver, BC | 73 | 1 | 0 | 1 | 156 |
| #29, 44 | 1996–1998 | Memorial Cup runner-up with Kamloops | | | | | |
| **Troy Mallette** (LW) Sudbury, ON | 68 | 6 | 8 | 14 | 155 |
| #29 | 1996–1997 | Injuries finished him in Tampa in '97 | | | | | |
| **Nevin Markwart** (LW) Toronto, ON | 299 | 39 | 67 | 106 | 769 |
| #17 | 1983–1988, 1989–1992 | Big heart; tireless sparkplug | | | | | |
| **Alan May** (RW) Swan Hills, AB | 3 | 0 | 0 | 0 | 15 |
| #40 | 1987–1988 | Has blog at alanmayshockeytruth.com | | | | | |
| **Sandy McCarthy** (RW) Toronto, ON | 37 | 3 | 1 | 4 | 28 |
| #10 | 2003–2004 | Juniors with Manny Fernandez in Laval | | | | | |
| **Marty McSorley** (D) Hamilton, ON | 27 | 2 | 3 | 5 | 62 |
| #29 | 1999–2000 | Brashear stick incident ended career | | | | | |
| **Jay Miller** (LW) Wellesley, MA | 216 | 13 | 20 | 33 | 858 |
| #29 | 1985–1989 | With Byers, an intimidating one-two punch | | | | | |
| **Carl Mokosak** (LW) Fort Saskatchewan, AB | 7 | 0 | 0 | 0 | 31 |
| #45 | 1988–1989 | Had 46-goal, 363 PIM Junior season | | | | | |
| **Brantt Myhres** (LW) Edmonton, AB | 1 | 0 | 0 | 0 | 31 |
| #55 | 2002–2003 | Career ended by a Georges Laraque left | | | | | |
| **Andrei Nazarov** (LW) Chelyabinsk, Russia | 110 | 1 | 6 | 7 | 364 |
| #62 | 2000–2002 | Tenth overall pick in 1992—SJ | | | | | |
| **Chris Nilan** (RW) Boston, MA | 80 | 11 | 14 | 25 | 463 |
| #30 | 1990–1992 | As Hab, notorious for Middleton high stick | | | | | |
| **Jeff Odgers** (RW) Spy Hill, SK | 80 | 7 | 8 | 15 | 197 |
| #36 | 1996–1997 | Radio commentator in Atlanta | | | | | |
| **Krzysztof Oliwa** (LW) Tychy, Poland | 33 | 0 | 0 | 0 | 110 |
| #33 | 2002–2003 | "Polish Hammer" won a Cup in NJ | | | | | |

| BRUINS REGULAR SEASON STATISTICS | GP | G | A | Pts | PIM |
|---|---|---|---|---|---|
| **Colton Orr** (RW) Winnipeg, MB | 21 | 0 | 0 | 0 | 27 |
| #75 | 2003–2005 | Dominated fights as rookie, but waived | | | | | |
| **Willie Plett** (RW) Paraguay, South America | 65 | 2 | 3 | 5 | 170 |
| #25 | 1987–1988 | 1977 Calder Trophy winner | | | | | |
| **Marc Potvin** (RW) Ottawa, ON | 33 | 0 | 1 | 1 | 16 |
| #29 | 1994–1996 | Minor league coach; took his own life in '06 | | | | | |
| **Jeremy Reich** (LW) Craik, SK | 90 | 2 | 3 | 5 | 141 |
| #53 | 2006–2008 | Good grit and grind in 2008 playoff round | | | | | |
| **Andre Roy** (LW) Port Chester, NY | 13 | 0 | 2 | 2 | 12 |
| #49 | 1995–1997 | Calder in Providence; Stanley in Tampa | | | | | |
| **Kevin Sawyer** (LW) Christina Lake, BC | 4 | 0 | 0 | 0 | 5 |
| #14, 19 | 1995–1997 | Head injury ended career in '03 | | | | | |
| **Al Secord** (LW) Sudbury, ON | 166 | 39 | 26 | 65 | 337 |
| #20 | 1978–1981 | Had 54-goal season with Blackhawks in '82–'83 | | | | | |
| **Bruce Shoebottom** (D) Windsor, ON | 35 | 1 | 4 | 5 | 53 |
| #40, 45 | 1987–1991 | Appreciative fans threw shoes on ice | | | | | |
| **Louis Sleigher** (RW) Nouvelle, QC | 83 | 16 | 21 | 37 | 65 |
| #25 | 1984–1986 | Not true heavy; finished career with B's | | | | | |
| **Al Stewart** (LW) Fort St. John, BC | 4 | 0 | 0 | 0 | 17 |
| #31 | 1991–1992 | Three seasons as Maine Mariner | | | | | |
| **P.J. Stock** (C) Montreal, QC | 130 | 1 | 12 | 13 | 282 |
| #42 | 2001–2004 | His "ass-kicker" T-shirts became popular | | | | | |
| **Shawn Thornton** (LW) Oshawa, ON | 58 | 4 | 3 | 7 | 74 |
| #? | 2007–2008 | Won Stanley Cup with Anaheim in '07 | | | | | |
| **John Wensink** (LW) Cornwall, ON | 248 | 57 | 55 | 102 | 429 |
| #18 | 1976–1980 | "Wire" challenged the North Stars' bench | | | | | |

CHAPTER

# 15

## GRINDERS

*above:*

*Derek "Turk" Sanderson was another Bruin who left after Boston's second Cup and headed for the money of the WHA, where he played only eight games for the Philadelphia Blazers. He returned to the Bruins in February of 1973 and wore #17, his old #16 since taken by Fred O'Donnell. This is a shot from his second game back.*

*left:*

*Don Marcotte and Gregg Sheppard, taken at Madison Square Garden in New York. Marcotte earned renown as a penalty killer and as a shadow, a left winger who covered the opponent's most volatile scorer. Sheppard was a third line center with some scoring punch, whose career bridged the end of the Big Bad Bruins through to the start of Cherry's Lunch Pail Gang.*

Those Bruins forwards who are not "scorers" or "enforcers" are "grinders," because a gritty, grinding style of play is the fundamental characteristic of what it means to be a Bruin. It's what these fans and the organization look for and want. We could have called these other forwards "skaters," or simply "forwards," but "grinders" seemed the appropriate way to go. One will notice from the compilation below, that those who didn't have much desire to grind or battle, will have very few numbers in the "games played" category.

Meanwhile, a beautiful thing about the Bruins over the last 35 years is that so many of the great players fit into so many physical categories. Cam Neely may be the ultimate example. He's a grinder, a scorer, and an enforcer. To different degrees in each of the categories, Terry O'Reilly would be another example of a guy who had all three labels covered.

Steve Babineau saw Taz's career from start to finish.

"If a guy was between Terry and the puck, he wasn't going around them," Babineau points out, "he was going through him. Going into the corner, he didn't have the stickhandling of, say, a Neely, but he had the 'feet' handling capabilities like no other. Even when his stick was in an awkward position, he'd still come out of the corner with the puck in his skates and he'd make a play. I used to watch him work on his footwork at practice. He'd literally bring the puck out with his feet."

The typical solid grinder fights on occasion, scores on occasion, but mostly shift disturbs, digs, mucks in the corner, and works hard everywhere. Some listed as grinders do one or

*left:*

*P.J. Axelsson celebrating a goal with Ray Bourque against Toronto goalie Curtis Joseph. Axelsson through 2007-08 was the most recent, longest tenured Bruin, having started his career in the Hub in 1997. A smart two-way forward, "Axey" is a penalty killing phenom.*

two of these things well, while some do them all well. Most would make pretty good penalty killers.

Swede P.J. Axelsson, a Bruin since 1997, will go down as one of Boston's best ever penalty killers.

"You play for the sign on your jersey," Axelsson states. "You play for the organization, you play for the guys in the room. The longer you are in one place, you like the sign [emblem] a lot more."

It's just what you'd expect to hear from a talented grinder, and what you'd hope to hear from a Bruin.

While Axelsson tallies a point in about every three of his games, Don Marcotte scored about every other game, in a career that began four decades ago and encompassed 15 years, from the late '60s to the early '80s. Each will go down as one of the most effective two-way players in team history.

> I was a pretty good goal scorer, but if I wasn't going to score all the time, I had to come back and help, so I was more a good two-way player.

"I came up with the Bruins. I was signed when I was 16 years old," Marcotte remembers. "I was a pretty good goal scorer, but if I wasn't going to score all the time, I had to come back and help, so I was more a good two-way player. That's

*The shadow being shadowed. Whenever Wayne Gretzky was on the ice, Steve Kasper was on the ice following him. Here, the roles reverse as Kasper breaks out of his zone. Kasper played 564 games with the Bruins.*

*Norwood native Tom Songin played 43 games for Boston. His uncle Butch Songin played quarterback for the Boston Patriots.*

what kept me in the League all of those years—I could score a bit, but I'd help the defense, kill penalties, and play against all of the stars from the other teams, which was good.

"I played with mostly all the new kids coming up," Marcotte continues. "My first year when I came up I played with [Derek] Sanderson and [Ed] Westfall, and then [Gregg] Sheppard came in and I played with him for a year—that was probably my best year ever—then I lost him right away and I played with Andre Savard who came up the next year after that. All the new kids coming up...I ended up playing with them because I was a good two-way player, so I could cover up for them."

Norwood, Massachusetts, native Tom Songin began his 43-game NHL/Bruins career in 1978. A productive offensive player at Boston College, and literally a point-a-game man at the American Hockey League level, Songin's role changed in Boston. The last step to the NHL is the steepest, and on endless occasions, based on talent, role, ice time, and opportunity, players will find their AHL and NHL numbers differing dramatically. Scorers become grinders hoping to score.

"My first goal was on assists from Wayne Cashman and Jean Ratelle," recalls Songin. "That was after I went out

to the Pacific Hockey League to play. There was the Long Beach Sharks [then Rockets], San Diego Mariners, Phoenix Roadrunners, and San Francisco Shamrocks. I made it, and I had good numbers. At the end of the season I got a call; Johnny Carlton, a Bruins scout, invited me to camp. I played in all of the exhibition games that year, but was sent down as the last cut, and spent the season in Rochester."

Songin received a call-up and spent the last 17 games with Boston.

"It was a privilege, a big honor, and I was very happy and lucky," Songin adds. "My family was happy. It was a thrill and a half. I don't know what to say. It's a little odd because it really wasn't a dream come true; when I was a kid I thought I'd be a baseball player."

Bob Sweeney entered Boston College almost a decade after Songin. He too was a prolific scorer there, and a one-time Beanpot MVP. His NHL career represented balance, with points, penalty minutes, and perseverance. He played for 10 seasons, with his first six in Boston.

"Any kid growing up in the Boston area, if you had a chance to play for your hometown team, that was your dream come true," states Sweeney. "A few of us, including myself, had that opportunity. Bobby Carpenter was a teammate, Johnny Carter, Andy Brickley. Mike Milbury was our coach. It was a unique situation during my era. We had four or five guys from the Boston area and it was a successful era for the Bruins. It was a special time for us. We never got to the finish line so to speak, to capture the Cup, but we had a good run for about six years there and we're proud of that."

Those four players, Axelsson, Marcotte, Songin, and Sweeney, represent a good portion of the four different decades Steve Babineau covered the Boston Bruins.

For reference and memories, the players listed below all did a lot of mucking, grinding, and battling for the Bruins, without distinctively thrusting themselves into the scorer or enforcer categories.

*left:*

*Bob "Swoop" Sweeney was a college scorer and former Beanpot MVP at Boston College whose role changed after turning professional. The tall forward became a battling grinder with Boston, here being held by Jamie Macoun of the Calgary Flames.*

*below:*

*Wayne Cashman, one of the great cornermen in hockey history, a grinder who could work the walls, attempts to score on Gary "The Cobra" Simmons of the California Seals during the 1975-76 season. A former captain, "Cash" played more than a thousand games for Boston.*

1. *Peter Douris*   2. *Robert "Butch" Goring*   3. *Landon Wilson*   4. *Rob Dimaio*   5. *Dave Poulin*

6. *Hank Nowak*    7. *Andre Savard*    8. *Martin Lapointe*    9. *Luc Dufour*    10. *Dave Forbes*

*left:*

*The Crowder brothers played tenacious hockey for the Bruins during the eighties, with Keith's (right) career spanning the entire decade. Older brother Bruce, who played 390 less games than his sibling in Boston, went on to coach Northeastern University.*

Forwards whose careers included or began after 1973–74, the season in which Steve Babineau took his first professional photo at a Bruins game.

| BRUINS REGULAR SEASON STATISTICS | GP | G | A | Pts | PIM |
|---|---|---|---|---|---|
| Earl Anderson (RW)—Roseau, MN | 64 | 12 | 16 | 28 | 10 |
| #16, 27, 28 \| 1975–1977 \| Traded for Walt McKechnie in '75 | | | | | |
| Scott Arniel (LW)—Kingston, ON | 29 | 5 | 3 | 8 | 20 |
| #29 \| 1991–1992 \| Coaches the Manitoba Moose in the AHL | | | | | |
| Brent Ashton (LW)—Saskatoon, SK | 87 | 19 | 24 | 43 | 58 |
| #18 \| 1991–1993 \| Nine different NHL teams in 14 seasons | | | | | |
| Per Johan Axelsson (LW)—Kungalv, Sweden | 722 | 97 | 160 | 257 | 260 |
| #57, 11 \| 1997–2008 \| Longest current time with B's | | | | | |
| Dave Barr (RW)—Toronto, ON | 12 | 1 | 1 | 2 | 7 |
| #17, 27, 32 \| 1981–1983 \| Great junior player in Lethbridge | | | | | |
| Randy Burridge (LW)—Fort Erie, ON | 359 | 108 | 115 | 223 | 275 |
| #37, 12 \| 1985–1991 \| Twice won Bruins 7th Player Award | | | | | |
| Wayne Cashman (LW)—Kingston, ON | 1027 | 277 | 516 | 793 | 1041 |
| #12 \| 1964–1965, 1967–1983 \| Bruins Captain; best corner-man ever | | | | | |
| Carl Corazzini (C)—Framingham, MA | 12 | 2 | 0 | 2 | 0 |
| #52 \| 2003–2004 \| Speed to burn his best attribute | | | | | |
| Lou Crawford (LW)—Belleville, ON | 26 | 2 | 1 | 3 | 29 |
| #37, 39 \| 1989–1990, 1991–1992 \| Coach Marc Crawford's brother | | | | | |
| Bruce Crowder (RW)—Essex, ON | 217 | 43 | 44 | 87 | 133 |
| #32 \| 1981–1984 \| Outscored younger brother in '82 playoffs | | | | | |
| Keith Crowder (RW)—Windsor, ON | 607 | 219 | 258 | 477 | 1261 |
| #18 \| 1980–1989 \| Rode shotgun with Linseman and Simmer | | | | | |
| Rob Dimaio (RW)—Calgary, AB | 272 | 35 | 62 | 97 | 301 |
| #19 \| 1996–2000 \| "The Pocket Tocket" played bigger than size | | | | | |
| Brian Dobbin (RW)—Petrolia, ON | 7 | 1 | 0 | 1 | 22 |
| #51 \| 1991–1992 \| Star with London Knights of OHL | | | | | |

| BRUINS REGULAR SEASON STATISTICS | GP | G | A | Pts | PIM |
|---|---|---|---|---|---|
| Clark Donatelli (LW)—Providence, RI | 10 | 0 | 1 | 1 | 22 |
| #50 \| 1991–1992 \| 62 pts in 43 GP for BU in '85–86 | | | | | |
| Dave Donnelly (C)—Edmonton, AB | 62 | 9 | 12 | 21 | 65 |
| #29 \| 1983–1986 \| Part of Bellows/Kluzak draft day deal | | | | | |
| Shean Donovan (RW)—Timmins, ON | 76 | 6 | 11 | 17 | 56 |
| #22 \| 2006–2007 \| Speed to burn; not a finisher | | | | | |
| Peter Douris (RW)—Toronto, ON | 148 | 24 | 25 | 49 | 38 |
| #16 \| 1989–1993 \| Member of Boston's last Cup Final team | | | | | |
| P.C. Drouin (LW)—St. Lambert, QC | 3 | 0 | 0 | 0 | 0 |
| #40 \| 1996–1997 \| Cup of coffee during B's worst season | | | | | |
| Luc Dufour (LW)—Chicoutimi, QC | 114 | 20 | 15 | 35 | 154 |
| #29 \| 1982–1984 \| 35th overall pick in 1981 | | | | | |
| Mikko Eloranta (LW)—Turku, Finland | 118 | 18 | 23 | 41 | 76 |
| #22 \| 1999–2002 \| Striking resemblance to PJ Axelsson | | | | | |

| BRUINS REGULAR SEASON STATISTICS | GP | G | A | Pts | PIM |
|---|---|---|---|---|---|
| **Matti Hagman** (C)—Helsinki, Finland | 90 | 15 | 18 | 33 | 2 |
| #28 \| 1976–1978 \| First Finn born and trained to make NHL | | | | | |
| **Taylor Hall** (LW)—Regina, SK | 7 | 0 | 0 | 0 | 4 |
| #23 \| 1987–1988 \| Average 2 pts a game final year of junior in Regina | | | | | |
| **Jay Henderson** (LW)—Edmonton, AB | 33 | 1 | 3 | 4 | 37 |
| #38, 51 \| 1998–2001 \| Last player taken in '97 draft | | | | | |
| **Matt Herr** (C)—Hackensack, NJ | 3 | 0 | 0 | 0 | 0 |
| #63 \| 2002–2003 \| Big scorer at Hotchkiss Academy in CT | | | | | |
| **Kenneth D. Hodge** (C/RW)—Windsor, ON | 112 | 36 | 40 | 76 | 30 |
| #10 \| 1990–1992 \| Could be listed as scorer; Ken's son | | | | | |
| **Jeff Hoggan** (LW)—Hope, BC | 46 | 0 | 2 | 2 | 33 |
| #32 \| 2006–2008 \| College hockey with Nebraska-Omaha Mavericks | | | | | |
| **Benoit Hogue** (LW)—Repentigny, QC | 17 | 4 | 4 | 8 | 9 |
| #33 \| 2001–2002 \| Eight teams; won a Cup with Dallas | | | | | |
| **Ron Hoover** (C)—Oakville, ON | 17 | 4 | 0 | 4 | 31 |
| #39, 44 \| 1989–1991 \| Drafted by Whalers out of Western Michigan | | | | | |

| BRUINS REGULAR SEASON STATISTICS | GP | G | A | Pts | PIM |
|---|---|---|---|---|---|
| **John Emmons** (C)—San Jose, CA | 22 | 0 | 2 | 2 | 16 |
| #23 \| 2001–2002 \| Very rare Bruin from California | | | | | |
| **Peter Ferraro** (RW)—Port Jefferson, NY | 51 | 6 | 9 | 15 | 44 |
| #42 \| 1998–2000 \| He and brother Chris played at University of Maine | | | | | |
| **Tom Fitzgerald** (RW)—Billerica, MA | 71 | 4 | 6 | 10 | 40 |
| #12 \| 2005–2006 \| Player Development Director for Pittsburgh | | | | | |
| **Dave Forbes** (LW)—Montreal, QC | 284 | 53 | 52 | 105 | 220 |
| #14 \| 1973–1977 \| Career marred by Boucha stick incident | | | | | |
| **Doug Gibson** (C)—Peterborough, ON | 52 | 7 | 18 | 25 | 0 |
| #22, 27 \| 1973–1974, 1975–1976 \| Finished career in Austria | | | | | |
| **Mike Gillis** (LW)—Sudbury, ON | 125 | 17 | 24 | 41 | 104 |
| #14, 22, 34, 33 \| 1980–1984 \| Nicknamed Dobie after TV show | | | | | |
| **Matt Glennon** (LW)—Hull, MA | 3 | 0 | 0 | 0 | 2 |
| #13, 39 \| 1991–1992 \| Starred at Archbishop Williams High School | | | | | |
| **Robert "Butch" Goring** (C)—St. Boniface, MB | 39 | 13 | 21 | 34 | 6 |
| #22 \| 1984–1985 \| Came after Cups with NYI | | | | | |
| **Bob Gould** (C/RW)—Petrolia, ON | 77 | 8 | 17 | 25 | 92 |
| #18 \| 1989–1990 \| Checking center on last Cup Final team | | | | | |
| **Rod Graham** (LW)—London, ON | 14 | 2 | 1 | 3 | 7 |
| #28 \| 1974–1975 \| Later coached Kingston of the OHL | | | | | |
| **Travis Green** (C)—Castlegar, BC | 146 | 21 | 17 | 38 | 146 |
| #39 \| 2003–2006 \| Face-off specialist; best known as Leaf | | | | | |
| **Michal Grosek** (LW)—Vyskov, Czech Rep. | 96 | 5 | 20 | 25 | 104 |
| #22 \| 2002–2004 \| European winger idolized Neely | | | | | |
| **Bob Gryp** (LW)—Chatham, ON | 1 | 0 | 0 | 0 | 0 |
| #28 \| 1973–1974 \| Scored 38 goals with '72–73 Boston Braves | | | | | |
| **Paul Guay** (RW)—Providence, RI | 5 | 0 | 2 | 2 | 0 |
| #37, 45 \| 1988–1989 \| Starred at Mount St. Charles Academy | | | | | |
| **Ben Guite** (C)—Montreal, QC | 1 | 0 | 0 | 0 | 0 |
| #50 \| 2005–2006 \| Dad Pierre played in WHA | | | | | |

| BRUINS REGULAR SEASON STATISTICS | GP | G | A | Pts | PIM |
|---|---|---|---|---|---|
| **Ryan Hughes** (C)—Montreal, QC | 3 | 0 | 0 | 0 | 0 |
| #47 \| 1995–1996 \| 22nd overall pick for Quebec in 1990 | | | | | |
| **Joe Hulbig** (LW)—Norwood, MA | 31 | 2 | 2 | 4 | 12 |
| #48 \| 1999–2001 \| Suffered head injury vs. Ottawa in Nov. 2000 | | | | | |
| **Dave Hynes** (LW)—Cambridge, MA | 22 | 4 | 0 | 4 | 2 |
| #27 \| 1973–1975 \| Two time 50-point scorer at Harvard | | | | | |
| **Brad Isbister** (LW)—Edmonton, AB | 55 | 6 | 17 | 23 | 46 |
| #21 \| 2005–2006 \| Izzy or isn't he; failed to replace Knuble | | | | | |
| **Greg Johnston** (RW)—Barrie, ON | 183 | 26 | 28 | 54 | 119 |
| #29, 39 \| 1983–1990 \| Eight straight seasons split NHL/minors | | | | | |
| **Steve Kasper** (C)—Montreal, QC | 564 | 135 | 220 | 355 | 450 |
| #11 \| 1980–1989 \| Fine career overshadowed by coaching | | | | | |
| **Jarmo Kekalainen** (LW)—Tampere, Finland | 27 | 4 | 3 | 7 | 14 |
| #29 \| 1989–1991 \| Became big shot hockey exec | | | | | |
| **Fred Knipscheer** (C)—Fort Wayne, IN | 27 | 6 | 3 | 9 | 16 |
| #43, 48 \| 1993–1995 \| Series-winning goal vs. Habs in '94 | | | | | |

| BRUINS REGULAR SEASON STATISTICS | GP | G | A | Pts | PIM |
|---|---|---|---|---|---|
| **Doug Kostynski** (C)—Castlegar, BC<br>#25, 34 | 1983–1985 | Finished career in Finland | 15 | 3 | 1 | 4 | 4 |
| **Antti Laaksonen** (LW)—Tammela, Finland<br>#57 | 1998–2000 | Won Calder Cup with Providence | 38 | 7 | 5 | 12 | 4 |
| **Steve Langdon** (LW)—Toronto, ON<br>#26 | 1974–1976, 1977–1978 | Called up to play four playoff games in '76 | 7 | 0 | 1 | 1 | 2 |

| | GP | G | A | Pts | PIM |
|---|---|---|---|---|---|
| **Josh Langfeld** (LW)—Fridley, MN<br>#23 | 2005–2006 | National champion for Michigan; GWG vs. BC in '98 | 18 | 0 | 1 | 1 | 10 |
| **Martin Lapointe** (LW)—Ville St. Pierre, QC<br>#20 | 2001–2004 | Five-million-dollar-a-year free agent | 205 | 40 | 43 | 83 | 255 |
| **Guy Larose** (C)—Hull, QC (4 playoff games)<br>#41 | 1994–1995 | Son of Montreal multi-Cup winner Claude Larose | 0 | 0 | 0 | 0 | 0 |
| **Jeff Lazaro** (LW)—Waltham, MA<br>#14 | 1990–1992 | Wasn't black, but endured racial slurs | 76 | 8 | 19 | 27 | 98 |
| **Pat Leahy** (RW)—Boston, MA<br>#55, 83 | 2003–2006 | Specialized in shot blocking; broke hand | 49 | 4 | 4 | 8 | 19 |
| **Richie Leduc** (C)—Perrot, QC<br>#18 | 1972–1974 | Five playoff games, 9 PIM, in 1974 | 33 | 4 | 4 | 8 | 14 |
| **Moe Lemay** (LW)—Saskatoon, SK<br>#36, 37 | 1987–1989 | Helped beat Habs in 1988 playoffs | 14 | 0 | 0 | 0 | 23 |
| **Milan Lucic** (LW)—Vancouver, BC<br>#17 | 2007–2008 | Won Memorial Cup with Vancouver Giants | 77 | 8 | 19 | 27 | 87 |
| **Craig MacDonald** (C)—Antigonish, NS<br>#33 | 2003–2004 | Harvard man; NHL journeyman | 18 | 0 | 3 | 3 | 8 |
| **Craig MacTavish** (C)—London, ON<br>#32, 27, 14 | 1979–1984 | Last NHLer to go without a helmet | 217 | 44 | 66 | 110 | 74 |
| **Don Marcotte** (LW)—Asbestos, QC<br>#21, 29 | 1965–1966, 1968–1982 | Guy Lafleur's shadow; lunch-pailer | 868 | 230 | 254 | 484 | 317 |

| BRUINS REGULAR SEASON STATISTICS | GP | G | A | Pts | PIM |
|---|---|---|---|---|---|
| **Marquis Mathieu** (C)—Hartford, CT<br>#61 | 1998–2001 | Pest center for Providence Calder Cup | 16 | 0 | 2 | 2 | 14 |
| **Trent McCleary** (RW)—Swift Current, SK<br>#25 | 1996–1997 | Edgy and inexpensive acquisition | 59 | 3 | 5 | 8 | 33 |
| **Marty McInnis** (RW)—Hingham, MA<br>#10 | 2001–2003 | Former BC star; 13-year NHL career | 96 | 11 | 13 | 24 | 46 |
| **Walt McKechnie** (C)—London, ON<br>#18 | 1974–1975 | Played Sarnia Junior B with Phil Esposito | 53 | 3 | 3 | 6 | 8 |
| **Scott McLellan** (RW)—Toronto, ON<br>#33 | 1982–1983 | Career ended after two years in minors | 2 | 0 | 0 | 0 | 0 |
| **Glen Metropolit** (C)—Toronto, ON<br>#13 | 2007–2008 | Made team on camp try-out; made an impact | 82 | 11 | 22 | 33 | 36 |
| **Mike Millar** (RW)—St. Catharines, ON<br>#42 | 1989–1990 | Later played 10 seasons in Germany | 15 | 1 | 4 | 5 | 0 |
| **Bob Miller** (C)—Medford, MA<br>#14, 32 | 1977–1981 | UNH and 1976 U.S. Olympic Team | 263 | 55 | 82 | 137 | 13 |
| **Jon Morris** (C)—Lowell, MA<br>#29 | 1993–1994 | Went from Bruins to Italy | 4 | 0 | 0 | 0 | 0 |
| **Mark Mowers** (C)—Decatur, GA<br>#18 | 2006–2007 | Gymnast wife trained with Bela Karolyi | 78 | 5 | 12 | 17 | 26 |
| **Ray Neufeld** (RW)—St. Boniface, MB<br>#19 | 1988–1990 | Whaler during team's first NHL season | 15 | 1 | 3 | 4 | 28 |
| **Eric Nickulas** (RW)—Hyannis, MA<br>#72, 21, 47 | 1998–2001, 2005–2006 | Tabor Academy and UNH | 45 | 7 | 10 | 17 | 24 |
| **Kirk Nielsen** (RW)—Grand Rapids, MN<br>#60 | 1997–1998 | Four years at Harvard; two with P-Bruins | 6 | 0 | 0 | 0 | 0 |
| **Kraig Nienhuis** (LW)—Sarnia, ON<br>#38 | 1985–1988 | Won national championship with RPI in '85 | 87 | 20 | 16 | 36 | 39 |
| **Jim Nill** (RW)—Hanna, AB<br>#8 | 1983–1985 | Distinguished assistant GM with Red Wings | 76 | 4 | 11 | 15 | 143 |
| **Petteri Nokelainen** (RW)—Imatra, Finland<br>#56 | 2007–2008 | 16th overall pick in 2004, NYI | 57 | 7 | 3 | 10 | 19 |
| **Hank Nowak** (LW)—Oshawa, ON<br>#18 | 1974–1977 | Boston last NHL stop; playoff goal in '75 | 111 | 18 | 15 | 33 | 81 |
| **Fred O'Donnell** (RW)—Kingston, ON<br>#16 | 1972–1974 | Went to Canucks for Bobby Schmautz | 115 | 15 | 11 | 26 | 98 |
| **Billy O'Dwyer** (C)—Boston, MA<br>#10 | 1987–1990 | A "Southie," Don Bosko High School, Boston College | 102 | 13 | 21 | 93 | |
| **Samuel Pahlsson** (C)—Ornskoldsvik, Sweden<br>#27 | 2000–2001 | Won a Cup with Anaheim | 17 | 1 | 1 | 2 | 6 |
| **Grigori Panteleev** (LW)—Gastello, USSR<br>#13 | 1992–1995 | Played 2006 Olympics with Latvia | 50 | 8 | 6 | 14 | 12 |
| **Davis Payne** (LW)—Port Albernie, BC<br>#44, 17 | 1995–1997 | Long-time minor league head coach | 22 | 0 | 1 | 1 | 14 |

| BRUINS REGULAR SEASON STATISTICS | GP | G | A | Pts | PIM |
|---|---|---|---|---|---|
| **Scott Pellerin** (C/LW)—Shediac, NB | 35 | 1 | 5 | 6 | 6 |
| #33 \| 2001–2002 \| Scored MN Wild's first ever exhibition goal | | | | | |
| **Dave Poulin** (C)—Timmins, ON | 165 | 34 | 68 | 102 | 117 |
| #19 \| 1989–1993 \| Hero vs. Whalers in Game 4 of 1990 playoffs | | | | | |
| **Wayne Primeau** (C)—Scarborough, ON | 101 | 13 | 16 | 29 | 115 |
| #20 \| 2005–2007 \| One-third of the trade for Joe Thornton | | | | | |
| **Davis Payne** (LW)—Port Albernie, BC | 22 | 0 | 1 | 1 | 14 |
| #44, 17 \| 1995–1997 \| Long-time minor league head coach | | | | | |
| **Scott Pellerin** (C/LW)—Shediac, NB | 35 | 1 | 5 | 6 | 6 |
| #33 \| 2001–2002 \| Scored MN Wild's first ever exhibition goal | | | | | |
| **Dave Poulin** (C)—Timmins, ON | 165 | 34 | 68 | 102 | 117 |
| #19 \| 1989–1993 \| Hero vs. Whalers in Game 4 of 1990 playoffs | | | | | |
| **Wayne Primeau** (C)—Scarborough, ON | 101 | 13 | 16 | 29 | 115 |
| #20 \| 2005–2007 \| One-third of the trade for Joe Thornton | | | | | |
| **Sean Pronger** (C)—Dryden, ON | 11 | 0 | 1 | 1 | 13 |
| #46 \| 1999–2000 \| Older brother of Chris | | | | | |
| **Joel Prpic** (C)—Sudbury, ON | 15 | 0 | 3 | 3 | 2 |
| #39 \| 1997–1998, 1999–2000 \| 6-foot-7; played at St. Lawrence | | | | | |
| **Jake Rathwell** (RW)—Temiscamingue, QC | 1 | 0 | 0 | 0 | 0 |
| #16 \| 1974–1975 \| Was once a Buckaroo and a Sword | | | | | |
| **Dave Reid** (LW)—Toronto, ON | 387 | 89 | 92 | 181 | 115 |
| #34, 31, 36, 17 \| 1983–1988, 1991–1996 \| NHL Network commentator | | | | | |
| **Doug Roberts** (RW)—Detroit, MI | 55 | 5 | 8 | 13 | 9 |
| #28 \| 1971–1974 \| Name not on Cup, but on team for '72 win | | | | | |
| **Kent Ruhnke** (RW)—Toronto, ON | 2 | 0 | 1 | 1 | 0 |
| #29 \| 1975–1976 \| Signed to a five-game tryout agreement | | | | | |
| **Derek Sanderson** (C)—Niagara Falls, ON | 389 | 135 | 159 | 294 | 686 |
| #23, 27, 17, 16 \| 1965–1974 \| The legendary Turk | | | | | |
| **Craig Sarner** (RW)—St. Paul, MN | 7 | 0 | 0 | 0 | 0 |
| #? \| 1974–1975 \| On 1972 USA silver medal Olympic team | | | | | |
| **Andre Savard** (C)—Temiscamingue, QC | 228 | 52 | 62 | 114 | 144 |
| #11 \| 1973–1976 \| Sixth overall pick in 1973 draft | | | | | |
| **Dave Scatchard** (C)—Hinton, AB | 16 | 4 | 6 | 10 | 28 |
| #38 \| 2005–2006 \| Was Joe Thornton's first fight; both rookies | | | | | |
| **Peter Schaefer** (LW)—Regina, SK | 63 | 9 | 17 | 26 | 18 |
| #72 \| 2007–2008 \| One of the weirdest stick blades in hockey | | | | | |
| **Sean Shanahan** (C/RW)—Toronto, ON | 6 | 0 | 0 | 0 | 7 |
| #7 \| 1977–1978 \| One of two to wear number 7 between Espo and Ray | | | | | |
| **Barry Smith** (C)—Surrey, BC | 19 | 1 | 0 | 1 | 2 |
| #28 \| 1975–1976 \| 1975 Memorial Cup MVP for New Westminster | | | | | |
| **Vladimir Sobotka** (C)—Trebic, Czech Rep. | 48 | 1 | 6 | 7 | 24 |
| #60 \| 2007–2008 \| Played with Czech Republic—World Junior | | | | | |
| **Tom Songin** (RW)—Norwood, MA | 43 | 5 | 5 | 10 | 22 |
| #19, 28 \| 1978–1981 \| On Fullerton Wall, Northwood School | | | | | |

| BRUINS REGULAR SEASON STATISTICS | GP | G | A | Pts | PIM |
|---|---|---|---|---|---|
| **Yan Stastny** (C)—Quebec City, QC | 38 | 1 | 5 | 6 | 29 |
| #43 \| 2005–2007 \| Son of Peter, brother of Paul | | | | | |
| **Mike Stevens** (LW)—Kitchener, ON | 7 | 0 | 1 | 1 | 9 |
| #36 \| 1987–1988 \| Brother Scott a Hall-of-Fame inductee | | | | | |
| **Cam Stewart** (LW)—Kitchener, ON | 83 | 3 | 7 | 10 | 72 |
| #26, 16 \| 1993–1997 \| Panthers to Wild in expansion draft | | | | | |
| **Mike Sullivan** (C)—Marshfield, MA | 77 | 5 | 13 | 18 | 34 |
| #42 \| 1997–1998 \| Head coached Bruins to 2004 Division title | | | | | |
| **Ron Sutter** (C)—Viking, AB | 18 | 5 | 7 | 12 | 24 |
| #10 \| 1995–1996 \| A twin; one of six brothers to play in NHL | | | | | |
| **Bob Sweeney** (C/RW)—Concord, MA | 382 | 81 | 112 | 193 | 504 |
| #42, 20 \| 1986–1992 \| Bruins Foundation charity director | | | | | |
| **Chris Taylor** (C)—Stratford, ON | 37 | 3 | 5 | 8 | 12 |
| #50, 38 \| 1998–1999 \| 16 pro seasons; still going in Germany | | | | | |
| **Tim Taylor** (C)—Stratford, ON | 128 | 24 | 18 | 42 | 112 |
| #26 \| 1997–1999 \| Hip replacement ended career in Tampa | | | | | |
| **Dave Thomlinson** (LW)—Edmonton, AB | 12 | 0 | 1 | 1 | 17 |
| #41 \| 1991–1992 \| 43rd overall pick by Toronto in '85 | | | | | |
| **Nate Thompson** (C)—Anchorage, AK | 4 | 0 | 0 | 0 | 0 |
| #51 \| 2006–2007 \| Providence 'C' was 2003 6th rounder | | | | | |
| **Rick Tocchet** (RW)—Scarborough, ON | 67 | 32 | 22 | 54 | 131 |
| #22 \| 1996–1997 \| '97, went to DC in blockbuster | | | | | |
| **Graeme Townshend** (RW)—Kingston, Jamaica | 22 | 2 | 5 | 7 | 19 |
| #48 \| 1989–1991 \| Coached Greensboro in ECHL | | | | | |
| **Tony Tuzzolino** (C)—Buffalo, NY | 2 | 0 | 0 | 0 | 0 |
| #46 \| 2001–2002 \| Michigan State grad; plays in Italy | | | | | |
| **Kris Vernarsky** (C)—Detroit, MI | 17 | 1 | 0 | 0 | 2 |
| #76 \| 2002–2004 \| Last played near hometown in Port Huron | | | | | |
| **Jim Vesey** (C/RW)—Boston, MA | 4 | 0 | 0 | 0 | 0 |
| #54 \| 1991–1992 \| Attended Christopher Columbus High School | | | | | |
| **Ben Walter** (C)—Beaconsfield, QC | 10 | 0 | 0 | 0 | 4 |
| #72, 56 \| 2005–2007 \| Dad Ryan played 15 years in NHL | | | | | |
| **Wes Walz** (C)—Calgary, AB | 73 | 9 | 12 | 21 | 44 |
| #37, 13 \| 1989–1991 \| 11 seasons in NHL, four in Swiss League | | | | | |
| **Dixon Ward** (RW)—Leduc, AB | 63 | 5 | 13 | 18 | 65 |
| #29 \| 2000–2001 \| Almost a goal a game at University of North Dakota | | | | | |
| **Landon Wilson** (RW)—St. Louis, MO | 130 | 12 | 21 | 33 | 91 |
| #27 \| 1996–2000 \| Bruins traded 1st round pick for him | | | | | |
| **Chris Winnes** (RW)—Ridgefield,CT | 29 | 1 | 4 | 5 | 6 |
| #40 \| 1990–1993 \| Northwood School and UNH | | | | | |
| **Rob Zamuner** (LW)—Oakville, ON | 178 | 26 | 24 | 50 | 58 |
| #17 \| 2001–2004 \| Surprise pick; '98 Olympic Team Canada | | | | | |
| **Jeff Zehr** (LW)—Woodstock, ON | 4 | 0 | 0 | 0 | 2 |
| #54 \| 1999–2000 \| Chris Simon gave him "body bag" threat | | | | | |

Grinders

# Scrapbook

It's hard to believe that 35 years have gone by since I shot my first game back in the 1973–74 season. I'm closing in on 1,700 total games and should have reached that number by the time this book is published. I've driven many miles around our great Northeast region and across Canadian provinces. I've seen so many players come through the Bruins organization (350 or so). I have so many memories of the Garden, NHL players, and friends I've met along the way. And what's great for me with this book is that I have captured all this through my camera, which will allow me to keep those memories forever. I really have bled Black and Gold for 35 years, just like all the die-hard Bruins fans. However, my closeness with the organization and its players makes me feel like I've bled a little more than most.

Starting out as a young fan working freelance as a photographer for the *Hockey News* for three years, which at the time paid very little but got me into games for nothing, I was living the dream of every Bruins fan. Plus, I had the best seat in the house. However, I quickly found out that my passion as a Bruins fan changed and would be recognized when Bruins management took notice of my work. It started to look like I really knew what I was doing.

I got married in June of 1973 just before I started covering games for the first time. I really feel my wife, Anita, just thought at the time I had figured out a

*The first hockey magazine Babineau ever bought, March 1964.*

*left to right: Charlie Simmer, Brian Babineau on the crossbar, Keith Babineau on Bourque's knee, Ray Bourque, Chris Babineau. "My three sons"—1985.*

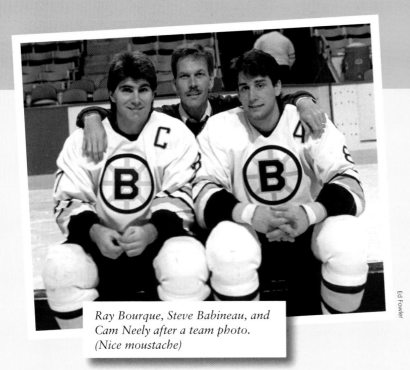

*Ray Bourque, Steve Babineau, and Cam Neely after a team photo. (Nice moustache)*

Ed Fowler

way to go to games without paying for a ticket. Thank God I married a Canadian girl; I think I had a little more rope to pursue this career. After all, she had attended all those Boston Braves and New England Whalers games when I had season tickets during the '72–'73 season.

After we got married and I started to convert our apartment bathroom into a darkroom three days a week to supply material to *The Hockey News*, *Hockey Digest*, and various local publications,

*Thank God I married a Canadian girl; I think I had a little more rope to pursue this career.*

*Bobby Orr and Chris Babineau prior to Orr's Hall-of-Fame induction in Toronto.*

my rope was getting shorter. Fortunately, not much later, I found myself in 1977 as team color photographer for a storied Original Six franchise. Plus, I was now shooting mostly color film, which I could not develop at the apartment, so my rope got extended even further. Meanwhile, other opportunities opened up with national publications, the Topps card company, and various other clients. When that money started to arrive, it understandably made Anita happy!

During the first 20-year span of my photography business, I also held a full-time job with Dennison and G.C.C. Technologies, working as a distribution, manufacturing, and inventory control manager. The experience I gained working in these companies, I feel, helped me later when I established my own business, in how to deal with scheduling, budgets, relationships, and other responsibilities. I was able to manage my regular job and shoot 50 to 60 hockey games a year, to be away from home so much, to have four kids, and to be successful with the photography because of Anita's understanding and her appreciation of my passion for the game.

In 1964, when I was 13 years old, I asked my mother for 50 cents to buy a copy of *Hockey Illustrated*. Little did I realize that that book would set me on a path into sports photography. Up until then there was very little written about hockey in *Sports Illustrated* or

*Brian Babineau took this picture of dad Steve setting up Sergei Samsonov, Ray Bourque, and Joe Thornton for a shot at center ice.*

*In 1964, when I was 13 years old, I asked my mother for 50 cents to buy a copy of Hockey Illustrated. Little did I realize that that book would set me on a path into sports photography.*

*Sport Magazine*, yet here was a magazine dedicated to the game of hockey, loaded with black-and-white pictures. It was the issue with a color action cover of Chicago Blackhawk goalie Glenn Hall and defenseman Elmer "Moose" Vasko skating into the camera, and it changed it all for me. How that photographer (Harold Barkley) stopped the action and made a great color image was something that I had never seen before. I bought every issue of that magazine from then on and had to convince my mother to let me buy three copies of each issue a few years later. That's when they put full-color pinups in the centerfold section, and I wanted to put the pictures on my bedroom wall while keeping one issue intact. Barkley, a photographer in Toronto, dominated with

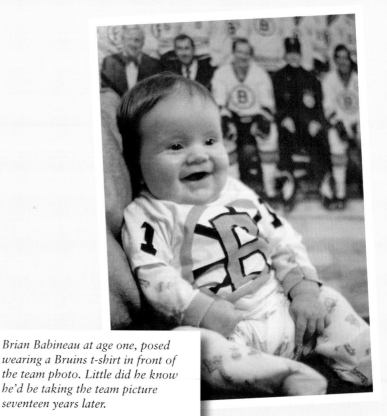

*Brian Babineau at age one, posed wearing a Bruins t-shirt in front of the team photo. Little did he know he'd be taking the team picture seventeen years later.*

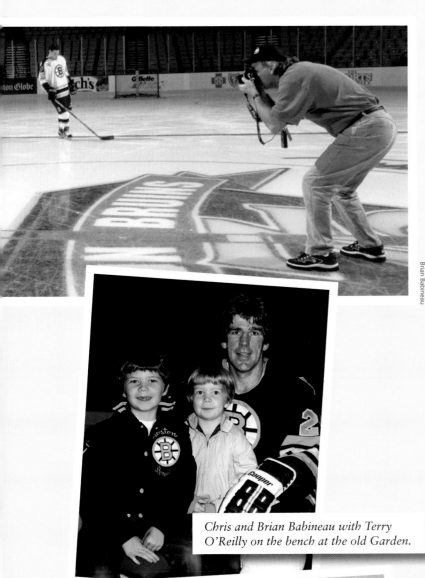

Brian Babineau

*Chris and Brian Babineau with Terry O'Reilly on the bench at the old Garden.*

*Don Cherry holding one-year-old Chris Babineau at Steve Babineau's apartment during a meeting to review photography.*

his color work on all the great players: Howe, Mahovlich, Delvecchio, Ullman, Mikita, Sawchuk, Beliveau, Richard, etc. The only disappointing thing was they never ran Bruins players; maybe Bucyk once. My bedroom was plastered with these pinups. Barkley's work definitely had an impact on my direction in life. I consider him a pioneer in hockey photography, being one of the first to use strobe photography in game situations. Just recently, I also found out that he was more of a glamour, all-around photographer, and also that he was disabled. I wish I had met him. It was a thrill for me years later when my work started to appear in the same magazine. I wonder if my son Brian looks at my work the same way I look at Barkley's.

Good luck happens to all of us sometime in life and having my first camera stolen by someone who broke into our house in 1972 turned out to be a blessing in disguise. The insurance claim allowed me to buy a better camera with adaptable lenses. This allowed me to get closer to the action from wherever I was sitting, oftentimes in obstructed-view seats in those early days.

A chance phone call to *Hockey News* editor Charlie Halpin asking him why they didn't have any pictures of the W.H.A. players, and his response—"Kid, we just don't have any"—opened the door. He asked me if I'd like to shoot for him until he could get me a season credential. My first thoughts were that my mom was going to kill me for making this phone call to Montreal, and what was I going to do with my Whalers season tickets that I bought for me and Anita (if I wasn't shooting)! I'm grateful to Charlie for taking that call and giving me the break that I needed to shoot professional hockey, even if it was the other league at the time. I was shooting on a credential for the biggest hockey publisher in the world and it was just a matter of time before I was shooting the "big show" and the Bruins for *The Hockey News*. A year later that experience began.

I shot for the Bruins for two seasons and supplied all of their color photography for brochures, posters, yearbooks, and programs, using available light photography, which I had figured out how to use to get good results. That's when I figured I had to step up to the next level and get a new camera that worked with strobe lighting that could be mounted in the catwalk at the Garden. I had the camera covered finance-wise, but the strobes were a minimum $6,000 investment. I sat down one night with Paul Mooney, president of the Bruins and the Garden, and explained the advantage of the high-quality images produced using these strobes. It would enhance their yearbook, press guide, program covers, and merchandise posters and prints. Taking better pictures using this equipment would mean more revenue for the team. So I asked Mr. Mooney to buy the strobes and in return I would give the team three years' worth of yearbook pictures and any updated blowups needed for the Boards and Blades Club. I figured this was a no-brainer for the building and the team. His response was, "Kid, you buy the strobes, I'll have them installed for you and let you use the electricity for nothing."

I figured that my career had reached a roadblock. I explained my dilemma to my parents, and despite the fact they had no clue what I was talking about, they loaned me the $6,000 for the strobes. That decision, along with a new

244

Brian Babineau

*Babs and P.J. Stock. Brian took this from a ladder on the ice.*

Biff Spitnick

*Babs and Phil Esposito displaying the limited-edition print of his jersey retirement night when Ray Bourque handed over number 7.*

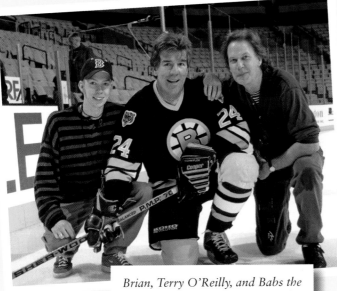

*Brian, Terry O'Reilly, and Babs the first year the Fleet Center opened. O'Reilly was playing in the NHL alumni All-Star game the next day.*

Diane Sobolewski

*Keith and Brian in 1988 at the Garden, and twenty years later in the same pose at the TD Banknorth Garden: Keith an assistant equipment manager and Brian a team photographer.*

camera, opened up doors with new clients within just one season. I recouped my investment by signing contracts to supply images of NHL players to various licensees of the League. I thank Mr. Mooney for putting the ball in my court on decision making, and for giving me the freedom with the team and building to use my strobes with no restrictions.

It didn't dawn on me until I was hired by Tehabi Books as a photo editor for a book that was being written by Clark Booth, *The Boston Bruins: Celebrating 75 Years*, that I had captured one-third of the history of this storied franchise with my work. It really hit home that all the time and effort that I had put in meant something. I researched Booth's story lines, scrambled through all of my pictures, and also did research at the Hockey Hall of Fame and Boston Public Library to find additional photography, which in some cases did not exist. It then sunk in that while my work covered the Bruins, it was far more than that. The library of images I had compiled on the game over 35 years was a significant body of work. It made me feel as though all of the effort was justified on a lot of levels.

I was so lucky to be accepted by all the players, coaches, and staff of the organization. It made my job easier to have their confidence and support on ideas. I think they knew I was going to accomplish the end result in the most efficient way. To have so many players simply call me Babs from decade to decade made me feel like I was part of the team. Veteran players telling rookies and new Bruins to go see Babs for pictures became a tradition passed from Cheevers to Cashman to O'Reilly to Park to Bourque to Thornton to Murray to Chara.

A fringe benefit to my hockey-shooting career has been a little taste of the rock-and-roll world. I've always loved Neil Young's music, ever since first seeing him way back in 1970 at what is now the Wang Center. I ended up going to see him a number of times (concert details a little hazy), and I started taking photos of his concerts. The man is a legend, and his music, his change in styles, has opened my ears to rock, folk, country, blues, or whatever he was playing. I also related to Neil because of other similarities—being a tall drink of water, I myself 6-foot-3; I was thin, about 155 pounds soaking wet back in the day; I sang in the church choir; and people say I look just like him. I've since gone on to respond that I'm his stunt double.

In 1988 I asked Bill Brett, sports photographer with the *Boston Globe*, if he could pull some strings and get me a pass to shoot Neil at Great Woods in Mansfield, Massachusetts. He was then playing blues with a new band and performing for two nights. Mission accomplished: I got to shoot both shows. The kicker was that I met Neil prior to the second show at his hotel with 10-year-old Brian in tow. I introduced myself as the Bruins photographer and he quickly responded as if I knew his dad, Scott. His late father was a Hall of Fame sports writer in Canada. The connection was made. I've since amassed an archive of more than 10,000 images of Neil in concert, and I've provided him photos for a number of purposes, including his Bridge School charity, for which our photo and poster efforts have helped raise more than $150,000.

Many hockey players love Neil, especially the older ones and the Canadian ones, so I've swapped quite a few concert

Brian Babineau

*Babs, daughter Jamie Babineau and Neil Young on the steps of his studio in Mountainview, California, 1992.*

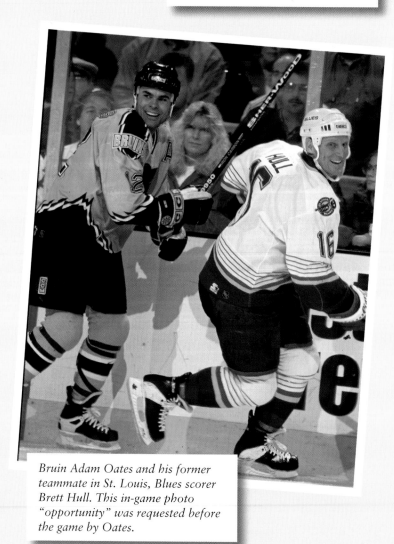

*Bruin Adam Oates and his former teammate in St. Louis, Blues scorer Brett Hull. This in-game photo "opportunity" was requested before the game by Oates.*

Babs talks hockey with Neil Young's father Scott, prior to a charity concert in Mountainview. The late Scott Young was a Hockey Hall-of-Fame honored sports writer.

Brian Babineau

photos for cool hockey stuff. Al Iafrate gave me an All-Star jersey once, Joe Juneau hit me up for some recordings and photos, and Juneau and others have made donations to The Bridge School.

The best was Adam Oates. He approached me a few days before Christmas one year, asking me if I could get him one of Neil's guitars signed for his buddy Brett Hull. My first response was, "Are you crazy? Neil's not going to give up a guitar like you give up hockey sticks." I went home that night and wondered how I could find a compromise. I took a chance and called Neil's ranch in California and spoke to his wife, Peggi. She said giving up a guitar was indeed unlikely, but explained that one of his favorites was a D45 Martin acoustic. So I asked her if I was able to find a similar guitar and send it to the ranch, would Neil sign it for Brett Hull? Absolutely! So I went guitar hunting to a classic guitar store in Cambridge, [MA] and to my amazement they had a beat-up D45 Martin guitar that still sounded great. "Oatsie" sent me a check for the guitar, I couriered the guitar to California, Neil signed it, and Oatsie gave it to "Hullie" for Christmas. That was a pretty damn good gift if you ask me, and I'm glad I could help out with something so cool.

Rob Simpson is a Neil fan as well; I found that out even before he agreed

Neil Young. Steve Babineau has provided countless concert photos for the rock star's music paraphernalia and for his Bridge School charity.

to write (and edit) this book for me with his publisher. But it was eight months or so after our writing agreement that Neil came rolling into town, late in 2007. Every night of the concert tour seemed to conflict with Bruins games, which Rob helped commentate on television. One night, though, he was able to run (literally) over after a home game and catch most of the show at the Orpheum. Post-concert, after a patient wait, Rob was able to meet Neil and talk hockey with him for five or 10 minutes. Despite Rob's love for the man's music, it was 18 years between Neil shows for Simpson (his first was in Melbourne, Australia, in 1989). I'm very happy I was able to hook him up.

As you'll often find with hockey people, and often times learn from hockey

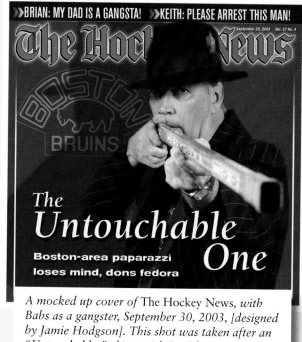

BRIAN: MY DAD IS A GANGSTA! ▸▸KEITH: PLEASE ARREST THIS MAN!

The Hockey News

September 30, 2003    Vol. 57 No. 4

BOSTON BRUINS

The
*Untouchable*
One

**Boston-area paparazzi
loses mind, dons fedora**

Brian Babineau

*A mocked up cover of* The Hockey News, *with Babs as a gangster, September 30, 2003, [designed by Jamie Hodgson]. This shot was taken after an "Untouchables" shoot with Joe Thornton, who turned out to be not-so-untouchable.*

*To have so many players simply call me Babs
from decade to decade made me feel like
I was part of the team.*

people: it's family first. The same goes for me. The fact that I have been lucky enough to have two of my sons, Brian and Keith, attend games and work over the last 15 years with me has been very special. Keith was eight years old when he started filling water bottles on the players' bench, then moving to visiting team locker room attendant for 13 years, and finally, at age 25 in 2007, being added as full-time assistant equipment manager for the Bruins. To take last year's 2007–08 team photo was special for me, knowing he was in the picture.

Brian was 15 years old when he took his first picture, and for 16 years he's been assisting me in expanding our responsibilities as team photographers for the Boston Bruins, Boston Celtics, Boston

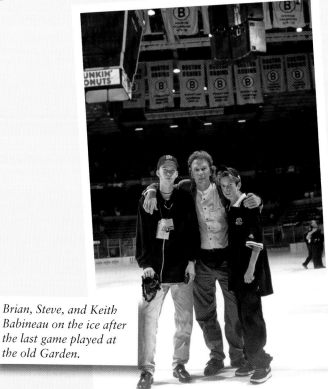

*Brian, Steve, and Keith Babineau on the ice after the last game played at the old Garden.*

Armen James

Lauren Roache

*Brian, Jamie, and Babs worked together behind the scenes at practically every Bruins game the last few seasons.*

Red Sox, Manchester Monarchs, and the Boston Garden. Brian went to school to bring the ever-changing technology in today's photography, such as digital images and photo editing, to the table, enabling us to expand our photography capabilities beyond being game action shooters. His computer graphics work and ideas have brought some creative promotional concepts to the table for the Bruins and the Garden. I'm sure that in the early stages of his photography I taught him a few things, but he has taught the old man a lot more in the new age of photography. I would have been overwhelmed had I tried to handle it all myself. Brian will carry the torch with the Bruins hopefully for another 35 years and keep the Babs name rolling for a few more decades.

My dad always told me to leave something behind. Four great kids—Chris, Brian, Keith, and Jamie—this book, and a few hundred thousand or so photographs on the game of hockey... I think he's smiling!

Brian Babineau

*Ray Bourque, Milt Schmidt, and Bobby Orr standing behind Steve Babineau at the 2007 alumni golf tournament.*

Index